DENNIS BENSON'S

CREATIVE BIBLE STUDIES

ROMANS—REVELATION

By Dennis C. Benson

Group Books

Loveland, CO

DEDICATION

To Dennis and Delores Benson—mentors, friends
and parents—with appreciation and affection.

DENNIS BENSON'S CREATIVE BIBLE STUDIES: ROMANS—REVELATION

Copyright © 1988 by Dennis C. Benson

Sixth Printing, 1994

Credits

Edited by Cindy S. Hansen
Designed by Jean Bruns
Cover Design by RoseAnne Buerge
Illustrations by Kay Marquardt

Scripture quotations are from the Holy Bible, New International Version.
Copyright © 1973, 1978, 1984 International Bible Society. Used by permission of
Zondervan Bible Publishers.

Library of Congress Cataloging-in-Publication Data

Benson, Dennis C.
  Dennis Benson's creative bible studies.

  Contents: [v. 1. without special title] — [v. 2.]
Romans-Revelation.
  1. Bible.   N.T.—Textbooks.   I. Creative Bible studies.
BS2408.B37 1985   225'.07   85.71044
ISBN 0931-52901-8 (soft: v.1)

ISBN 0931-52952-2   Dennis Benson's Creative Bible Studies: Romans-Revelation

Printed in the United States of America

CONTENTS

INTRODUCTION

The 17-year-old nervously twists her hands. Her gaze is fixed on the floor. The TV lights cast strange shadows on her freshly washed hair. Her body freezes as the interviewer asks about her life on the streets.

"Me and my husband, Richard, and our baby lost everything. We were living in our car and eating in the soup kitchen." She weeps softly as she talks about how she wasn't able to feed her baby.

"A few people from some special program talked to us and brought us to this wonderful apartment." She surveys the room. "We came into this room and it was so beautiful. There was food in the kitchen and a real bathtub. You wouldn't believe how special we felt when we saw the freshly cut flowers. We meet for Bible study and prayer each morning. Everybody encourages me and tells me God will help me as I look for a job. My husband and me both have jobs now. We'll get our own place soon. You can tell these people really love Jesus."

The people who run this special program in Dallas are living out Jesus' words: "I was a stranger and you invited me in" (Matthew 25:35b), and James' words: "Suppose a brother or sister is without clothes and daily food. If one of you says to him, 'Go, I wish you well; keep warm and well fed,' but does nothing about his physical needs, what good is it?" (James 2:15-16). These people are experiencing the passages in the deepest and most meaningful way. There is no better way to study the Bible than to live out its message.

Dennis Benson's Creative Bible Studies: Romans—Revelation offers Bible studies that help young people experience the scripture and live out their faith. The creative studies cover every passage from Romans through Revelation.

The first volume of *Dennis Benson's Creative Bible Studies* offers hundreds of creative studies for the Gospels and Acts. Both volumes are published by Group Books. Both volumes combined give you and your students a complete look at the entire New Testament.

Each Bible study consists of the following elements:

● **Focus:** This is the thrust for each study. Each study focuses on teenagers' needs, concerns and spiritual growth.

●**Insight:** This element consists of brief thoughts about each passage to help "set the scene" for the session. Some of the comments in the "Insight" will seem like a paraphrase of the passage. Yet please note that we are making the comments as a launching pad for the creative Bible study. At other points, you will notice more direct academic opinions. These opinions are offered to help clarify the passages.

●**Preparation:** This is a listing of materials and other needs for the study. The "Preparation" offers tips on how to prepare by using the resources around you. The following hints will help you prepare each study:

a. Involve young people in preparing the studies. When the study calls for videotaping commercials or soap operas, have the young people videotape; when it calls for gathering props, let the young people gather them; when it calls for inviting a guest speaker, let the teenagers decide who to ask and make the call. Involving young people in preparation gives them ownership of the study and develops their leadership skills.

b. Most materials can be found in your home or church. Other items can be purchased at a low cost or borrowed.

c. The studies in this book are designed for one-hour class sessions unless otherwise stated.

d. A chalkboard and chalk may be substituted for newsprint and markers.

e. Students will need Bibles for each study. Bring a variety of translations so students can compare the similarities and differences of the texts.

f. Ask yourself these questions about each study: "What is the message of the passage? What is the context? What is the writer's purpose? What is the scene?" Try to imagine the setting and characters by viewing the biblical text from the perspectives of several people. For example, an apostle, a new believer or a child.

●**Bible Study:** This is a step-by-step outline to lead your students through the scripture. The studies help young people use their senses to experience the passages. Your prayers and personal Bible study are vital to your success as an authentic Bible teacher. And your problems, fears and anxieties are also important in your call to faithfulness as a teacher. Bring everything you are and can be to this wondrous encounter with the creative Word of God.

Some of the activities include physical exertion such as running, walking, hiking, aerobics and relays. When preparing for the activities, plan for safety. Encourage young people to warm up prior to exercising; remind group members to keep safety first in their minds for all activities.

●**Action:** This element offers an idea to help young people live what they learn in each study. Ideas range from cultivating personal spiritual growth to reaching out to others. At the beginning of each study, allow time for students to discuss their experiences as they lived the Word.

TEN QUALITIES OF THE STUDIES

In both volumes, 10 qualities of the studies help you teach the Bible creatively and authentically.

1. *Historical:* The context, content and history of the passages are taken seriously. Consult your favorite commentary, Bible dictionary or other academic resource to help you understand each text. When I wrote the studies, I consulted a wide range of resources as I read the passages; then I considered the students' needs and brought the two together. Two particularly helpful resources were *Peake's Commentary on the Bible* (Nelson) and *The Oxford Annotated Bible* (Oxford University Press).

The clues to creative teaching and communication are always found in the passages themselves. That is why it's important to supplement your preparation with personal Bible study about historical aspects of the passages and how the passages relate to people's needs today.

2. *Spiritual:* The Holy Spirit is the guiding force in these studies. Through the Spirit's influence we have perspective and are creative, authentic and courageous. The Spirit shows us the fullness of God's Word. The Spirit allows us to be all that we can be—creative children of God.

3. *Incarnational:* Christ was sent by God. He was made man. It is therefore our task to make the written Word flesh among our students. This is done by the Spirit's power, not by clever gimmicks.

To help students live their faith, each Bible study results in action. To experience God's Word is to be compelled to respond. Since Christ lives in us, we are different in practical and observable ways.

4. *Inductive:* Methods and teachings are drawn from the texts themselves. Every text has been probed, prayed about, and played with in order to let the methodology for teaching it escape. Our whole task is to let the students crawl into the passages and draw out messages for their lives.

The teaching style for these studies is unique. Young people become students of the passage rather than students of the leader. As the leader, you are called to trust that God will work through your students. They are not empty vessels in which to pour your wisdom. You are transformed from an ''answer person'' to a teacher who enables others to know the Bible intimately.

5. *Wholistic:* This book focuses on both education and action. A believer's relationship to the gospel should always include worship, study, fellowship and service. Many other Bible studies focus on study and forget the other aspects. These studies touch each area. God in Christ speaks to the whole person.

6. *Experiential:* These studies look at the important role our senses play in learning and spiritual growth. Senses are gifts from God. Our existence depends on the senses. We would fall, drown, be burned or run over if our senses didn't warn us of danger. We also learn about every essence of life through our senses.

We are called to use every means to draw people to Christ's saving message. God came to us through Christ's physical humanity and forgave us through Christ's suffering, death and Resurrection.

7. *Confessional:* These Bible studies are based on my confessional roots as a person of faith. My faith added a unique viewpoint to the studies. Your personal faith will add a unique viewpoint for your students. Your students' faith will add unique viewpoints for you.

Each one of us has a different confessional perspective. We're a diverse community working together to know God's Word for our lives.

8. *Provisional:* Both volumes combined give you creative Bible studies on every passage in the New Testament. However, these studies only provide an outline or guide to the real Bible study you will fashion for your students. Each youth group has its own students, history and setting. All youth groups are different, because people are different. Adapt and modify the studies to meet your needs.

God has called you to consider these vital aspects of teaching. You are the person who makes this encounter with the gospel an authentic experience for your own group.

9. *Risky:* People will be changed as a result of this close encounter with God's Word. People's lives will be challenged. Behavior and lifestyles will be seen in the light of the Good News. Group members will affirm their faith again and again.

Students will discover that the gospel compels believers to share the message with others. We are called to pass on what we know. We are called to be servants.

10. *Bible-based:* The studies are based on the texts themselves. I suggest you get as close to the passage as possible by reading different translations. The New Testament was written originally in Greek. Every English translation is an attempt to express the Greek thought in our own language. It is important to get as close to the original proclamation as possible if we are to make our lives a translation of the gospel.

EVALUATION

After you have completed your unique and exciting Bible study, informally evaluate the experience by asking these questions:

- How did it go?
- Did the "fun" detract from the message? Explain.
- Was I prepared? If not, how can I be better prepared for the next study?
- Was I meeting the needs of the youth? Or did I end up lecturing, dominating or controlling them? Explain.
- Did I listen to the young people? Explain.

These questions can't be answered easily, but it's important that you try. Evaluation is most helpful in the context of a support system. Find a person (within or without your church) and develop a regular time of sharing and evaluation. Such a person must be a trusted friend you can cry with in despair or failure as well as laugh with in joy and success.

Guide the students in evaluating the studies. It is not helpful to encourage bare positive or negative comments. Your task is not to get approval or criticism. You want the participants to sift through how God has touched them. In the course of exploring their experiences with God's Word, you will discover clues for growth and improvement in your teachings and methods.

In the process of evaluation, if you feel that the study was a "failure," refrain from blaming the students, yourself or this book. Remember to focus on the good that happens in every Bible study. God can take any situation and use it for God's glory. Are we called to be successful? No. We're called to be faithful in our teaching of God's Word.

A HOST OF WITNESSES

This volume came into being with the help of four special people. Gary Cecil provided creative aid in my work with Romans. Fred Dickerson helped with 1 and 2 Corinthians. He worked hard in feeding me scholarly and creative insights from these fantastic texts. E. Jane Mall and Mardie MacDonald were particularly helpful at key moments of my work. Their brilliant ability to find creative communication clues in any text continues to stun me. These extraordinary people came to my aid when I was under a great pressure of time. My special appreciation of these four people can never be forgotten.

I also would like to express my appreciation to the many of you who have stopped me at workshops, written letters and called about your special use of the creative Bible studies in the first volume. I thank God that I have been able to participate with you in the most glorious ministry of the church: teaching the Word of God. If you have suggestions, ideas or other responses, feel free to contact me at 4516 Philadelphia, Dayton, Ohio, 45406.

May God continue to bless us as we risk to bring our young people into a living relationship with Christ.

—*Dennis C. Benson*

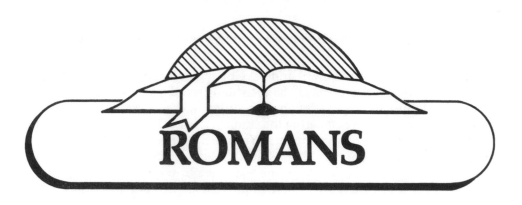

ROMANS

INTRODUCTION TO ROMANS

"Would you please send me everything you know about radio and television? Oh, I need it by next week for my term paper."

Students frequently request instant research from me. I guess I should be flattered that they turn to me. I always want to help them; however, I often struggle trying to include 20 years of experience in a quick, brief letter.

In this Epistle, Paul is trying to include as much as he can about his ministry and faith. He is about to visit the Roman church for the first time. Perhaps this concern and sense of urgency make Romans helpful to us. Many people think this Epistle is Paul's most important work. Bits and pieces from this book pepper most Christians' theology. There is something universal about its message. Some scholars think the texture of Romans is richer theologically than Paul's other Epistles because he may have spent more time working on it.

This is Paul's longest letter. In it, he develops some of his most important themes such as sin and justification by faith, forgiveness and peace, and the relationship between Jews and Gentiles. Romans offers hope and many comforting promises to Christians who struggle with their day-to-day lives. "For I am convinced that neither death nor life, neither angels nor demons, neither the present nor the future, nor any powers, neither height nor depth, nor anything else in all creation, will be able to separate us from the love of God that is in Christ Jesus our Lord" (Romans 8:38-39).

ROMANS 1:1-15 • PAUL, A SERVANT OF JESUS CHRIST

FOCUS
Serving Christ.

PREPARATION
Purchase a long piece of rope at a hardware store. Be sure it is long enough to loop around each group member's right wrist and link the group members in a straight line.

Gather a blindfold for each person, one pair of scissors, bread, water, butter, jelly, knives, spoons, presweetened Kool-Aid and a Bible.

Work out a route from your usual meeting room to a "slave barracks" (such as a basement or furnace room). Place the food in the slave barracks for snacks at the close of the meeting.

INSIGHT
Paul offers a standard greeting to the church at Rome—including his identification, the name of the addressee and the blessing. He describes himself as a servant of Jesus Christ and an apostle who is called to bring the name of Christ to all nations.

Paul then offers thanksgiving for the witness of their faith. The people in Rome are in his prayers always. He yearns to see them so they can be mutually strengthened by each other. Paul's duty is to preach to all people, regardless of race or culture.

In this study, group members will participate in a trust walk and experience servanthood.

BIBLE STUDY
1. Ask group members to sit in a circle, then blindfold them. Read Romans 1:1-15 and encourage them to listen carefully to the words.

2. Loop the rope around each person's right wrist so that group members are tied in a line facing the same direction.

3. Ask the students to imagine they are slaves or servants. They can't decide anything for themselves. Their bodies, minds and spirits are subject to the wishes of another.

4. Order them to stand. Lead them on a trust walk. Follow your prepared path from the meeting room to the slave barracks.

5. Ask students to sit on the floor. Have them imagine they are slaves for the rest of their lives. Ask:
- How do you feel about being a slave?
- What aspect of your freedom do you miss the most?

6. Say that Paul begins his letter to the Romans by identifying himself as a servant of Christ. Ask:
- What does Paul mean by being a servant of Christ?
- How is being bound to Christ similar to being an earthly slave? different?

● How would you feel bound as a slave to God?

● What would you lose? gain?

7. Go around to each person and remove his or her blindfold. Cut the rope so that each person still has a loop tied around his or her wrist. Say that Christ also commands us to serve one another and to do it with love (Galatians 5:13). Bring out the bread and water and let the participants serve each other.

Say: "Christ wants us to be servants to him and to others, but this is not drudgery. It's a joy, because through serving you show others the nature of Christ." Add a splash of joy to the refreshments by passing around butter and jelly for the bread and presweetened Kool-Aid for the water.

8. Close with a prayer of thanksgiving about the joy of being Christ's servant.

ACTION

Ask the students to wear their rope bracelets during the week as reminders of their servanthood to Christ. Ask them each to do one special act of servanthood for a family member. For example, pick up groceries at the store, help a brother or sister with homework or clean the house. At the next meeting, talk about their acts of servanthood.

ROMANS 1:16-32 • REFUSING TO ACKNOWLEDGE THE TRUTH

FOCUS
Sin.

PREPARATION
Gather small items such as a safety pin, washer, bolt, spool of thread, chipped button and marble. Place them in a box. Each person will need a pencil, Bible and a copy of the "Sin Inventory" handout.

INSIGHT
Paul is not ashamed of the gospel. God has the power to rescue people who are drowning spiritually. Salvation is for everyone who believes.

In this passage, Paul says that God's wrath is delivered upon the ungodly who suppress and attack the truth. These sinners follow and worship idols in the shape of humans, birds, animals and reptiles. They give their bodies to sexual perversions. They are responsible because they know plainly what God has said, yet they refuse to follow God. By their own free will they encourage others to be evil.

In this study, group members will complete a "Sin Inventory" handout and discuss the sin in the world and in their lives.

SIN INVENTORY

Instructions: Write an example of each sin. An example of wickedness could be murder or robbery.

Sin   **Example**

   1. Wickedness

   2. Evil

   3. Desire for others' possessions

   4. Jealousy

   5. Murder

   6. Dissension

   7. Deceit

   8. Malice

   9. Gossip

  10. Pride

  11. Boastfulness

  12. Disobedience to parents

  13. Immorality

  14. Faithlessness

  15. Meanness

BIBLE STUDY

1. Gather everyone in a circle, then say: "During this study, we'll talk about sin in the world and in our lives. Paul talks about sin in Romans 1:16-32." Go around the circle and let each young person read a verse of the passage.

2. Give each person a "Sin Inventory" handout and a pencil. Ask participants to write an example for each sin. An example of wickedness could be murder, robbery or a current news story.

3. Ask the young people to underline five of the most obvious sins they notice in their daily world. Discuss their choices. Ask:

● Why do some sins seem more obvious than others?
● Which ones do you personally suffer from the most?
● Why are people so cruel?
● How are the sins committed today like the sins mentioned in the passage?
● What does Paul say about humanity's sinfulness?

4. Have students circle three sins that they find most tempting. Discuss:

● Why are these sins difficult to avoid?
● How can we overcome sin with Christ's help?

5. Ask each person to repeat a personalized version of Romans 6:14. For example: "Sin will not conquer me. I live under God's grace." Then close with a prayer, thanking God for the freedom Jesus gives us from sin.

ACTION

Pass around the box of odds and ends. Ask students to select something that reminds them of one sin they want to overcome with Christ's help. For example, a safety pin could symbolize biting gossip or a chipped button could symbolize a broken friendship. Ask young people to carry the items during the next week as reminders to work on these areas. For example, a person could try to mend a broken friendship by asking his or her friend for forgiveness.

ROMANS 2:1-29 • JEWS AND GENTILES

FOCUS
Judging others.

INSIGHT
Paul addresses both Jews and Gentiles. There is no excuse for their behavior. When they judge others they judge themselves. They are

PREPARATION

Gather wanted posters from the post office and a pencil for each person. You also will need a Bible and a worn-out, tattered coat. (If you can't find a wanted poster, create one of your own.)

guilty of the very sins they accuse others of committing. They can't simply assume that God's kindness will free them from responsibility. God loves and forgives in order that we should repent. Those who honor and glorify God will gain eternal life. Jews and Christians are equally responsible for doing good works. God shows no partiality.

In this study, group members will look at "wanted" posters and discuss being judgmental.

BIBLE STUDY

1. Gather in pairs or trios. Give each person in the small groups a pencil and a wanted poster. Have members look at the posters while you read Romans 2:1-29.

2. Ask each group to list on the posters the sins these people must have committed to be wanted by authorities.

3. Share the lists of sins. Ask: "Would the people described in these posters be welcomed in our church? Why or why not?"

4. Ask one person to put on the tattered coat and role play an outcast. Ask the rest of the young people to role play the congregation on a Sunday morning. Encourage students to portray how church members would react if a ragged-looking outcast came to a worship service.

5. Allow a few minutes for the role play, then discuss:
● How would church members react to an outcast?
● How would the outcast feel?
● What does the passage say about judging others?
● How should we react to outcasts?
● Do we have the right to judge others? Why or why not?

6. Gather in small groups again. Ask students to list sins they've committed that relate to those the wanted people have been accused of. For example, hating someone or desiring another person's possessions. Have young people share these lists. Then ask:
● How are the two lists similar? different?
● Are there "big" sins and "little" sins? Explain.

7. Place all the wanted posters in the center of the room. Gather around them and join hands. Pray for forgiveness of sins; ask God for help in not judging others.

ACTION

Encourage young people to take their wanted posters home with them and tape them to their mirrors. Ask them to pray every morning for strength to be faithful and non-judgmental of others.

ROMANS 3:1-31 • TRUE RIGHTEOUSNESS

FOCUS
Undeserved love.

PREPARATION
Tell the group members to come to the meeting hungry. (You also could plan this study for one of the meals during a retreat.)

Gather rice, pizza, dessert, eating utensils, napkins, plates, tables, chairs, 3x5 cards, pencils, one freshly pressed choir robe, one Timex watch, posterboard, a marker and a Bible. Write the following rules on the posterboard:

●You must wear a freshly pressed, long choir robe at all meals.

●You must wear a Timex watch upside down on your left wrist at all meals.

●You must keep your right shoe laced and your left shoe unlaced at all meals.

Read the study so you'll know the sequence of activities. Prepare the food. Put on the robe, wear the watch upside down, and untie your left shoelace.

INSIGHT
Paul draws upon his own heritage as he addresses the advantage of being Jewish, the value of circumcision, and the relationship between law and faith.

Paul says God is not the God of the Jews only; God is Lord of all. We all have sinned and fall short of the glory of God. We can be saved only through God's freely given love. Christ has taken our place through his blood.

Circumcision is an outward sign of faith; it can't assure salvation. Although we are not justified by outward signs of faith or other works, we can't simply relax and say that our sinfulness and failure to follow God are opportunities for God's forgiveness. Our sin will be judged as sin.

The law helps us realize we are responsible for our actions. The gospel helps us know we are saved by God's grace (Romans 3:23-24).

In this study, group members will participate in an unusual meal and talk about law, grace and forgiveness.

BIBLE STUDY

1. As group members arrive, greet them in your unique apparel. If they ask why you are dressed that way, simply say: "I am your teacher. Soon, all will be made known to you."

Invite them to sit down at the tables. Say: "We have been invited to participate in a meal. I hope you all are hungry. The catch is that each of us will be rewarded according to how well we follow certain rules."

2. Show the posterboard and read aloud the rules. After reading each rule, look happy because you have perfectly followed that rule (nobody else has). Allow a few moments for groans, then say: "Oh well. It looks like I have followed all of these rules and you haven't. We each will be rewarded according to our actions."

3. Serve everyone a spoonful of rice. You eat pizza or some other mouthwatering delight.

4. After a few minutes of noisy objections, quiet everyone. Read Romans 3:1-31, then ask:

• How was this experience similar to Paul's message in this passage?

• If we are saved by how well we keep rules, how many will receive their reward? Explain.

5. Bring out pizza and dessert for everyone. As you serve it say, "All good things come from God through Christ."

6. Read Romans 3:23-24. Ask:

• How did it feel to receive a reward even though you hadn't followed the rules?

• How can you balance responsibility to do good works and reliance on God's grace?

• How can you accept God's freely given, undeserved love?

7. Close with a prayer thanking God for the food and for the free gift of love.

ACTION

Ask the students to do something during the next week specifically in response to what God has done for them. Give each person a 3x5 card and a pencil. Have students each write on their card the name of one person (family member, friend, new person at school). Tell the young people to act toward that person in an undeserved, unearned, loving way each day. For example, help a friend with homework, bake a cake for dessert, or call a new person at school and invite him or her to a party.

ROMANS 4:1-25 • ABRAHAM, JUSTIFIED BY FAITH

FOCUS

Greatness.

PREPARATION

Gather paper, pencils, tape, a packet of seeds and a Bible. On separate sheets of paper, write one "spiritual giant" such as Abraham, Paul, Peter and

INSIGHT

Paul talks about Abraham, who was justified by faith. Justification by faith means that by faith we receive God's blessing and forgiveness, not by the works we do. Justification by faith means that God's promise was not for Abraham alone, but for all who believe in Christ, who was raised from the dead.

In this study, group members will draw their spiritual family trees and discuss how their faith has grown.

Mary. Copy two "Spiritual Family Tree" handouts for each person.

BIBLE STUDY

1. As students enter, tape a "spiritual giant" sheet of paper to each of their backs. Allow five to 10 minutes for young people to guess the name on their paper. They can ask each other only yes or no questions. For example: "Am I male?" "Am I mentioned in the Old Testament?"

2. After several people have guessed correctly, have the group members remove their papers and gather in a circle.

3. Give each person a pencil. Ask the students to list 10 people who are their heroes and heroines. These mentors can come from any field or period in history. Give the students a chance to discuss these important influences in their lives. Ask:
- Why have you chosen these heroes and heroines?
- What characteristics do you admire most?
- How are you most like these people? least?

4. Read Romans 4:1-25. Have the students compare their heroes and heroines with Abraham, who was faithful even when there was no reason for him to be.

5. Open the packet of seeds and take one out. Say: "Every characteristic of the seed has been preserved in its genetic code. The seed's future makeup is outlined in it now.

"Similarly, our future makeup was outlined before we were born. Psalm 139:13 says, 'For you created my inmost being; you knit me together in my mother's womb.' As the years go by, our family members, friends, mentors, and all our heros and heroines help us grow."

6. Give each student one copy of the "Spiritual Family Tree" handout. Ask students to name the people who have made it possible for them to have faith today. These can be grandparents, parents, ministers, Sunday school teachers or people they have never met or known personally.

7. Discuss their spiritual roots. Ask:
- Why have you chosen these people?
- What characteristics do you admire most?
- How are you most like these people? least?

8. Compare their heroes and heroines with their list of spiritual mentors. Ask:
- Do you need to adjust your list of contemporary models? Why or why not?
- If spiritual ancestors have done so much for us, what is our responsibility? What is our role in carrying on this genetic code of faith? (For example, "We try to model our lives according to their teachings.")

9. Ask everyone to join hands for a closing one-word prayer. Begin the prayer by saying: "Heavenly Father, thank you for the gift of our faith heritage. Hear us as we name our mentors of the faith." Go in a clockwise direction, allowing time for each person to name a mentor.

ACTION

Give each person another "Spiritual Family Tree" handout. Encourage the students to discuss this study with their parents. Their parents can fill in their own spiritual history and talk about it with their teenagers.

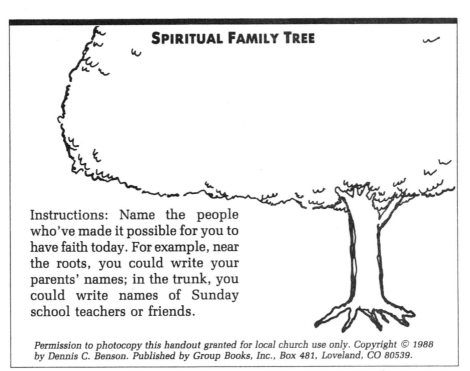

SPIRITUAL FAMILY TREE

Instructions: Name the people who've made it possible for you to have faith today. For example, near the roots, you could write your parents' names; in the trunk, you could write names of Sunday school teachers or friends.

ROMANS 5:1-21 • *SAVED THROUGH CHRIST*

FOCUS

Living in God's presence.

PREPARATION

On separate slips of paper, write the key words in this passage: love, peace,

INSIGHT

Some people consider this to be the most important chapter in the Book of Romans and one of Paul's most significant writings.

Since we have been justified by faith, we have peace with God. Through Christ's intercession we are ushered into the presence of God's glory. This means we can actually rejoice

grace, suffering, hope, patience, character, rejoice, boast, glory of God, disobedience, eternal life. Place the slips of paper in a box and place the box in the front of the meeting room. Gather pencils, 3x5 cards and several Bibles.

in our sufferings. Suffering produces endurance, endurance produces character, and character produces hope. Hope will not let us down because God pours love into our hearts by the Holy Spirit.

While we were still in sin's grip, Christ died for us. It's hard to imagine people giving up their lives even for a righteous person. Yet Christ died for us while we were still sinners.

In this study, group members will perform charades and learn key words in the passage.

BIBLE STUDY

1. As the young people arrive, ask them to take a slip of paper from the box. Have them greet each other using the word. A greeting using the word "hope" could be: "Hi. I hope you'll have a good time during this meeting." A greeting using the word "suffering" could be: "I'm glad you're here. I'd be suffering if you weren't." Ask students to keep their slips of paper and sit down.

2. Form groups of two or three people. Divide Romans 5:1-21 into as many parts as there are small groups. Assign one part to each group and ask each small group to read aloud its assigned verses.

3. Have the small groups share their understandings of the words they pulled out of the box. What did Paul mean when he used those words in the passage?

Ask each of the small groups to choose one word and create a charade to portray its meaning. A charade for the word "love" could be: One person portrays Christ. One at a time, sad people come to him, he hugs them, they happily go on their way.

4. Gather the small groups. Let them guess each other's charades.

5. Remind the students that Paul uses these and other words to reveal that Jesus is our mediator and link to God. Say: "God loves us so much. God sent Christ to die for our sins. Because of Christ, we are always in God's presence. God is with us and never deserts us." Ask:

●How do you feel knowing God is always with you?

● Are there times in your life you'd be proud to have God by your side? Explain.

● Are there times you'd feel ashamed if God were by your side? Explain.

●What makes it difficult to remember you're in God's presence when you're at school? home? work?

●How does this reality change the way you act and live in your daily life?

6. Close by gathering in a prayer circle. Ask students to offer one-sentence prayers using the words on their slips of paper. For example, the person who chose "eternal life" could say, "Thank you, God, for the gift of eternal life through your Son."

ACTION

Ask young people to write messages on separate 3x5 cards such as "God gives us eternal life," "God's grace is enough" or "Christ died for our sins." Arrange to have the students be the ushers at worship next Sunday. Ask them to distribute the cards to the worshipers.

ROMANS 6:1-23 • NOT UNDER THE LAW

FOCUS

Freedom from sin.

PREPARATION

Plan a slave sale. Ask students to offer their services for one weekend for projects such as doing church maintenance, helping elderly members grocery shop or washing windows. Publicize the sale several weeks in advance.

Follow the sale with a discussion. Gather paper, pencils and a Bible.

INSIGHT

Apparently Paul was asked if one should continue in sin so that God's grace may be freely encouraged. Paul rejects such an idea. All of us who are baptized are united with Christ and his life, death and Resurrection.

Grace certainly requires a response of dedication. We are now slaves to righteousness, not to sin. The price of sin is death; however, the free gift of God is eternal life in Christ.

In this study, group members will participate in a "slave sale."

BIBLE STUDY

1. Conduct the slave sale after a Sunday morning worship service. Let participants find a partner, then auction the "slave teams." Congregation members purchase the services by donating money. The slave teams are contracted for a weekend to do various services and projects at the church and in the community.

2. After the service is completed, gather the young people for a discussion.

3. Read Romans 6:1-23. Ask:

● How did your slavery experiences relate to this passage?

● Were there moments when you really felt like slaves? Explain.

4. Give each person a sheet of paper and a pencil. Ask the members to draw a line down the middle of the page. Have them label one side "Slave to Sin" and the other side "Slave to Righteousness."

Have the young people discuss what it means to be a slave to sin. Ask: "Does being a slave to sin mean that sin and bad things rule your life? Why or why not?" Ask them to list 10 wages (or results) of sin under the first column. Examples could be unhappiness, anger and alienation from others.

Now ask students what it means to be a slave to righteousness. Ask: "Does being a slave to righteousness mean that Christ rules your life? Why or why not?" Have them list the wages (or results) of righteousness under the second column. Examples could be happiness and contentment.

Discuss the answers. Say: "Some wages may be immediate, others may be long-term. Some wages may be positive, some negative. For example, being a slave to righteousness may mean gaining the gift of eternal life but suffering in the present life." Ask:

● How do you feel about the two lists?

● Why does Paul encourage his listeners to be slaves to Christ?

5. Tell the young people that once we were slaves to sin, but Christ came and freed us; he is our Savior.

Form a slave chain by gathering in a circle and having students link arms. Pray: "God, we're chained to sin and to the world. Forgive us."

Have the students drop their links, then pray, "Thanks for the freedom from sin and the freedom to do your will."

ACTION

Talk about how you will use the money raised in the slave sale. Donate the money to a favorite charity, shelter, service or mission organization. Discuss donating services to the same organization at a later date.

ROMANS 7:1-25 • *SIN AND THE LAW*

FOCUS
Expected behavior.

PREPARATION
Purchase lollipops or thin candies that easily melt in your mouth yet are tempting to bite into. Gather paper, pencils, Bibles, 3x5 cards, various kinds of fruit, a knife, spoons and bowls.

INSIGHT
Paul wants readers of this letter to understand that believers are freed from sin. He uses an analogy to present the message.

A law is only binding during a person's life. For instance, a married woman is bound by law to her husband during his life. However, if he dies, she is free under the law. Likewise, we have died to the law through Christ. We can now live for him.

Paul says that the law is not evil. The law increases our awareness of what sin is. Sin makes us do what we do not want to do.

In this study, group members will experience a tempting treat and discuss expected behavior and Christ's forgiveness.

BIBLE STUDY

1. Gather young people in a circle, then say: "Paul tells how the law helps us know what sin is. Paul struggles with sin. He knows what he's not supposed to do, but in his humanness he does it anyway." Go around the circle, letting each person read one verse of Romans 7:1-25.

2. Give everyone a thin piece of candy or lollipop. Allow members to put the sweets in their mouths, but tell them it's a *law* that they must not bite into them. They are to savor them as long as possible without chewing.

3. After several minutes ask:
● Was this easy or hard to do? Explain.
● What made this simple act so tempting?
● Was it difficult to keep from biting into the piece of candy? Why or why not?
● How is this like Paul's description of his struggle with sin and temptation?

4. Pass around an apple and ask each person to say how it symbolizes temptation. For example, it could be a reminder of the Garden of Eden. Ask young people to describe a time when they found themselves doing something they didn't want to do. Ask them to focus on the feelings and not the particular sin if it is embarrassing.

5. Gather the students in twos or threes, then distribute paper and pencils.

25

6. Have the small groups make a list of the laws under which they live. What are the rules or expected behavioral norms in their world? For example, teenagers must attend school.

7. Gather the class and discuss the rules:

● How can you deal with the failure to live up to the demands of the law?

● How does Christ's death and Resurrection affect this problem in your life?

● What does forgiveness mean?

8. Prepare a salad by slicing the apple and other fruit. Give everyone a bowl of fruit salad. Pray before you eat, "God, thanks for freedom from sin through Christ."

ACTION

Give the students each a 3x5 card. On one side of the card, have them write one rule they have difficulty following. On the other side of the card, have them write their own version of Romans 7:24-25. For example: "Who will help me through tough, tempting times in life? I thank God for the gift of Jesus—my help, my Savior." Ask young people to tape their cards to their mirrors as daily reminders that God's love and forgiveness are never ending—even when we fail to follow rules.

ROMANS 8:1-39 • CHILDREN OF GOD

FOCUS

Our adoption.

PREPARATION

Gather paper, pencils, a Bible and recorded sounds of nature or serene music. Invite a lawyer to come to the last part of this study to discuss adoption agreements. Meet in a carpeted room.

INSIGHT

We are children of God. We have been adopted and are now God's heirs. This means we must suffer with Christ if we are to be glorified with him. Paul states the marvelous way by which God grants salvation to those who believe. God works through the Spirit for our benefit. If God is for us, who can be against us? If God justifies, who can condemn us?

Paul states that nothing can ever separate us from God's love—not tribulation, distress, persecution, famine, nakedness, peril, death, life, angels, principalities, things present, things to come, powers, height, depth nor anything in the created order.

In this study, group members will participate in a guided meditation, listen to a lawyer and discuss adoption agreements.

BIBLE STUDY

1. Play recorded sounds of nature or serene music. Ask participants to lay on the carpet in a comfortable position. Turn the lights low. Read Romans 8:1-39.

2. Say: "Romans 8:1-39 tells us the Spirit makes us children of God. I'm going to lead you on an imaginary journey. During this time, you'll meet the Spirit and feel Christ's presence. This imaginary journey is called a 'guided meditation.' It's a way for you to slow down and think about God's presence in your busy life. I'll speak slowly during this journey. Close your eyes and use your imagination.

"Close your eyes and relax. We are going to search deep within us for the Spirit of God. Let God enter into you. God's presence casts out all fear and worry. The Spirit is coming into your toes. The Spirit is rushing through your limbs and body. You feel a slight tingle. You feel the Spirit move through your body. Follow its movement within you . . . Now the Spirit is racing up your neck . . . Feel the change in the temperature of your face as it reaches the top of your head.

"You are now bathed in God's Spirit. Light replaces the darkness you have experienced. Look down the corridors of your mind. See those spots of darkness . . . See the fear, shame and confusion that have dwelt there for a long time. The Spirit's light is overpowering the shadows. The fears can be seen clearly. Look back in your imagination . . . There is a long hall leading to the place that bothers you most . . . You are getting closer and closer . . . You stop . . . You actually can smell that lump of spiritual garbage that has locked you into sin . . . How do you feel about looking at that stumbling block? How do you feel about the sin that keeps you from being absorbed by the Spirit?

"Stop . . . Look back from where you have come . . . There is someone looking at you! It is a man . . . He is far away . . . But he is moving closer . . . Look at the stranger . . . He seems friendly . . . He looks familiar . . . It's Jesus! Look into his face . . . See his eyes . . . He is smiling . . . He is walking with you toward the darkness at the end of the hall . . . Feel Jesus' hand around your shoulder . . . The assurance is so good . . . You are about to face the sin that has bothered you so much . . . You feel you must tell Jesus about it . . . In your imagination, tell Jesus about it . . . (Long pause) . . . Jesus is listening to you. He understands fully all the fear, shame and anger . . . How will you respond? Watch his face carefully . . . He is smiling . . . He hugs you . . . Feel his acceptance, his love, his tenderness . . . Ask him what you must do about this piece of your life. He is telling you . . . Listen carefully to what he is saying to you . . . (Pause)

"Look down the hall toward the darkness. It is gone! Only the light of the Spirit fills you . . . Walk away from your past and back into this room . . . Hear again the reality of this room and feel the presence of others around you . . . You are here with me and the others now . . . In just a minute you will open your eyes . . . Open them.''

3. Ask the participants to describe their feelings after experiencing this journey:

- What were the most moving moments for you?
- What did Jesus tell you to do?
- What does it mean to have the Spirit live in you?
- How does this make you a child of God?
- What does it mean to be a child of God?

4. Say: ''Paul tells us that if we are led by the Spirit, we are children of God. God adopts us.'' Allow a few moments for young people to define adoption. For example, adoption is to legally take in a person as a member of your family.

5. Introduce the guest lawyer. Ask him or her to explain an adoption agreement. Distribute paper and pencils. Ask the students to write an adoption agreement concerning themselves and God. Have them search Romans 8 for phrases to support the aspects they want to include. For example: We are God's children. It is agreed that God is for us, so nobody can be against us. It is agreed that neither life nor death nor any troubles will separate this parent from his children. I am protected from what I fear and worry about.

6. Give the students a chance to discuss their agreements. Compare their agreements to the legal adoption agreement. How are they similar? different?

7. Ask the students to describe times they feel most threatened or worried about their security and lives. Ask:

- How does being a child of God offer you security in worrisome times?
- How does your adoption as a child of God ease the fear of everyday tough times?

8. Close the study by experiencing a group hug. Place the lawyer in the center of the circle. Ask everyone to take several steps toward the center and squeeze. Have everyone yell, ''Thanks, God, for adopting us.''

ACTION

Print the adoption agreements in your church newsletter or Sunday bulletin. Ask several students to present their insights to a church school class.

ROMANS 9:1-33 • GOD IS THE POTTER

FOCUS
God's will.

PREPARATION
Gather several recent newspapers, modeling clay, newsprint, a marker and a Bible.

INSIGHT

Paul anguishes over the fact that his kinsmen, the Jews, have not accepted Christ. They have all the foundational resources for this step: covenants, law, worship and prophets. Not all who are descended from Abraham are children of Abraham. Descendants are not of the flesh, but of the promise. Paul uses Old Testament passages to show that kinship with God is based on promise not blood.

God created humanity. The Creator forgives whomever the Creator wants to forgive. Just as the potter has the right to make something beautiful out of the clay.

In this study, group members will prepare symbols from clay.

BIBLE STUDY

1. Pass out a page from a recent newspaper to each person.

2. Ask participants to find stories about people from various backgrounds who give witness to the glory of God in unexpected ways. These could be stories about doctors, Christians, non-Christians or people who rescue flood victims.

3. Write these people's names on a piece of newsprint.

4. Give the students each a large clump of modeling clay and assign them each a person from the news. Invite them to imagine they are God's potters. Ask them to form a vessel that represents their assigned person. For example, a student could form a bowl from the clay to symbolize a person who offered food and water during a drought.

5. While potters are forming their symbols, read Romans 9:1-33. Focus on verses 20-24.

6. Ask students to share their sculptures and describe how God could use such a person for good. Ask:

• Can God work through non-Christians as well as Christians?

• How did it feel to be shaping the form of one of God's servants? Is

there power in this task? Explain.
- How do you know God is the "molder" of your life?
- Do you have freedom if God decides all things? Explain.

7. Invite the students to combine all their pieces into a unified vessel.

8. Gather around the vessel and join hands. Offer thanks to God for molding our lives to do God's will.

ACTION

Place the clay creation in the church narthex or in the main Sunday school meeting room. Place a sign by it that says, "God is the potter; we are the clay."

ROMANS 10:1-21 • GOD'S WORD

FOCUS

Listening and understanding.

PREPARATION

Invite your pastor to attend this study. Ask him or her to share his or her perspective about preaching. Bring a three- to five-minute taped (audio or video) portion of a recent sermon. Gather writing materials, several tape players, cassette tapes, microphones and Bibles.

INSIGHT

Paul notes that the Jews can be saved. They are not beyond God's grace; they simply don't understand Christ. They are close to believing. If they confess with their lips that Jesus is Lord and believe in their hearts that he has been raised from the dead, they will be saved. Confession and belief are keys to justification and salvation. This avenue to Christ is the same for Jews and Gentiles.

Why haven't people responded to the gospel? Why haven't they believed? Paul uses several Old Testament texts to prove that unbelievers are simply disobedient and won't listen.

In this study, group members will talk with the minister about worship and prepare three-minute sermons about the text.

BIBLE STUDY

1. Usher the students into the sanctuary. Say: "Welcome to our church. Let's prepare our hearts for worship." Allow a few minutes of silence, then play the taped portion of a recent sermon.

2. Say: "Preparing our hearts for worship and listening to God's Word set the scene for our study. We'll have a chance to talk with our minister about our worship services, how a sermon is prepared, and how we can receive God's Word.''

Introduce your guest and ask him or her to describe how he or she prepares a sermon. Ask:

- How do you prepare for a sermon?
- Who speaks to us during a sermon?
- How should we receive what is being said?
- How can we open ourselves to listen better? (For example, we can open ourselves to receive God's Word by praying before each worship service.)

3. Read Romans 10:1-21. Say: ''Paul tells us that faith comes from what is heard; what is heard comes through preaching. Apparently the Israelites heard the gospel but wouldn't listen.

''You will be divided into small groups. Each group will prepare a three-minute sermon, then record it on tape. All of us will have a chance to hear the message.''

Form small groups of twos or threes. Give each small group writing materials, a cassette tape player, cassette tape and microphone.

4. Tell the students to prepare a three-minute sermon on verses 14-17 of this chapter: ''How, then, can they call on the one they have not believed in? And how can they believe in the one of whom they have not heard? And how can they hear without someone preaching to them? And how can they preach unless they are sent? As it is written, 'How beautiful are the feet of those who bring good news.'

''But not all the Israelites accepted the good news. For Isaiah says, 'Lord, who has believed our message?' Consequently, faith comes from hearing the message, and the message is heard through the word of Christ.''

Encourage the minister to offer suggestions and ideas to the small groups.

5. Once all groups have finished, ask everyone to sit in the pews or chairs. Pray that God will open the students' ears and hearts to hear the Word. Ask one person from each small group to enter the pulpit and play the three-minute sermon.

6. After all groups have presented their sermons, discuss how the sermons affected the students:

- What did you learn from the sermons?
- How does God speak to us through sermons?
- How did you prepare yourself to hear God's Word?
- What does it mean to listen to God's Word?
- What does it mean to understand God's message?

7. Close by forming a circle around the worship area. Ask young people to thank the minister for some aspect of his or her ministry. For example, they could thank him or her for coming to this study, for his or her sermons or for listening when a friend was needed.

ACTION
Plan a worship service for a nursing home. Play the taped sermons for the residents. Read some scriptures, lead prayers and sing hymns.

ROMANS 11:1-36 • WE ARE THE BRANCHES

FOCUS
God's family.

PREPARATION
Bring a potted tree to the class, or meet at a nursery. Ask a nursery employee to describe the process of grafting. You also will need a Bible, a branch, construction paper leaves, yarn, paper, markers and tape.

INSIGHT
Paul reminds his readers that he is a Jew. God has not deserted believers. As long as there is a remnant, there is hope. Those who don't respond to God's Word are blinded to the truth. Paul hopes that his ministry to the Gentiles will move the Jewish people to act.

Paul uses the image of a branch being grafted to a tree. The Gentiles can't take credit for being part of the tree at the expense of the Jews. "If some of the branches have been broken off, and you, though a wild olive shoot, have been grafted in among the others and now share in the nourishing sap from the olive root, do not boast over those branches" (Romans 11:17-18a). God is the gardener who does the grafting. God can break off or graft all branches to the tree—whether the branches are Jews or Gentiles.

In this study, group members will compare a real tree to the passage.

BIBLE STUDY
1. Gather in a circle around the potted tree. Read Romans 11:1-36.

2. Ask the guest to explain the basics about trees and the process of grafting. Gather the students closer to the tree; encourage them to touch the branches, bark and connection points on the tree.

3. Compare the tree to the passage. Ask:
● What does grafting mean? (To add a tree shoot to the trunk of another—allowing it to become a permanent part.)
● What does Paul mean about Gentiles being grafted into the faith?
● Who can God "graft" into the faith? Is the faith reserved for a select few? Explain.
● How does this tree symbolize your faith? Is your faith new? old? growing? stagnant? green?

4. Pass around a branch, and let each student describe how it represents something about his or her faith. For example: "I've been so busy that my faith has been put on hold for a while. But I'll start growing. I'll graft myself to a daily time of prayer and nourish my faith."

5. Give the students each a marker and a construction paper leaf. Have each person write his or her name on the leaf. Tape the leaves along a long piece of yarn so it looks like a branch. At one end, tape a sign that says, "God's Family."

Ask the students to hold on to the branch. Close by praying: "Thanks for being our source, our root, our foundation of faith. Thanks for grafting us into the family of God. Amen."

ACTION

Divide the students into small groups. Ask them to prepare a five-minute devotion based on this study. Give each small group construction paper leaves, yarn, tape and markers. Invite the students to go to various Sunday school classes and present the devotion. Have them tape each class' "branch" to the classroom wall.

ROMANS 12:1-13 • *CHRISTIAN QUALITIES*

FOCUS

Using our gifts.

PREPARATION

Obtain one large cardboard box for each pair of students. Most grocery stores offer boxes free of charge. Since the participants will be writing on them, you may want to slit the boxes on one side and turn them inside out. By doing this, you'll have no printing on the outside.

Each pair will need a construction paper square, and a marker or crayon. You will need a Bible and the

INSIGHT

Paul urges his readers to submit their bodies as living sacrifices to God. The believer must not conform to the world, but be transformed by the renewing of his or her mind. A believer's goal is to grasp God's will—what is good, acceptable and perfect.

All believers are one body in Christ, yet all have different gifts. We need to use our gifts, whether they are prophesying, serving, teaching, encouraging, contributing, aiding or giving money.

Paul tells of Christian virtues such as holding on to love, outshining each other in demonstrating honor, never failing in zeal, rejoicing in hope, being patient in tribulation, praying constantly, giving to saints in need and practicing hospitality.

In this study, group members will discover

following Christian contributions written on slips of paper. Write two of each since participants will be finding their partners by matching slips of paper. Prepare one extra in case an odd number of young people come (you'll then form pairs and one trio).

- Speaking God's message.
- Serving others.
- Teaching the faith.
- Inspiring others.
- Helping others with their physical needs.
- Helping others with their emotional needs.
- Showing kindness to others.

ways to develop their gifts and contribute to the Christian community.

BIBLE STUDY

1. As students enter, distribute the slips of paper. Tell them the slips of paper contain Christian contributions. Ask them to find another person who has the same Christian contribution.

2. Ask the pairs to sit. Read Romans 12:1-13. Say: "Paul presents how the faith community responds to Christ in its life together. Each person contributes in a unique way." Ask the pairs to read their slips of paper aloud one at a time.

3. Give each pair a box and a marker or crayon. Ask young people to list on their box 10 ways a person can contribute to the Christian community using the aspect listed on their slip. For example, a pair who had "Serving others" could list:

- Volunteer to read scripture for a worship service.
- Offer to help teach Sunday school.
- Drive an elderly congregation member to a doctor's appointment.
- Drive an elderly congregation member to a church service.

4. After several minutes, gather the group and let each pair share its list.

5. Ask the students to arrange their boxes to represent how these parts work in the church. For example, they could place the boxes in a pyramid shape to symbolize our oneness in Christ and that all Christians support each other and affirm their gifts.

6. Distribute the construction paper squares to the young people. Ask them to complete this sentence: "My contribution is . . ." Ask them to think of a contribution they'd like to make and write it on their square. A person may want to practice servanthood and volunteer to help teach vacation Bible school.

7. Sit around the box structure. Close with a prayer focusing on each of the Christian contributions. Let young people pray silently for the contributions they'd like to make.

ACTION

Ask students to act upon their contributions this week. A person may call the Sunday school superintendent and volunteer to teach. Ask students to report their progress at the next study. Place the box sculpture in an area where congregation members can see it.

ROMANS 12:14-21 • PRAY FOR THOSE WHO PERSECUTE

FOCUS
Loving our enemies.

PREPARATION
Gather a copy of the *Good News Bible* for each person. Look through the book and find a line drawing for each student. Note the page numbers. You also will need butcher paper, markers, tape, paper and pencils.

INSIGHT
Paul explains the Christian's relationship with those outside the community of faith. Believers should pray for those who persecute them, be happy with those who are happy, cry with those who are crying, and live in love with one another. There is no reason to be boastful or arrogant. The community of faith is not a place for revenge. If an enemy is hungry or thirsty, we should take care of him or her. We must overwhelm evil with kindness.

In this study, group members will use the *Good News Bible: The Bible in Today's English Version* to learn about loving those who hurt us.

BIBLE STUDY

1. Greet the group members and introduce the study by saying: "We're going to learn about loving people who hurt us. It's easy to love those who love us, but Christians are called to love all people—even the unlovable."

2. Give each person a copy of the *Good News Bible,* a paper and pencil. Assign each person a page with a line drawing on it. (Romans 6:6 depicts people laying heavy loads of sin at the foot of the cross; Romans 16:16 depicts two people embracing.)

3. Ask young people to meditate on the cartoon as you read Romans 12:14-21. Say, "As you look at the cartoon and listen to the passage, remember the thoughts and feelings that first enter your mind."

4. Read the passage, then ask:
- Does the cartoon speak to you in a special way? Explain.
- Can you see yourself in the cartoon? Why or why not?
- Does it remind you of something that has happened to you or is

happening to you now? If so, what?

5. Ask the students each to write on their paper a one-sentence caption about the passage and cartoon. For example, a person assigned to a drawing that shows two people embracing each other could write "Love even your enemies."

6. Allow time for group members to discuss their captions. Ask:
● What is the most difficult part of living, according to this passage?
● Why is it hard to love our enemies?

7. Tape all captions on a long piece of butcher paper. Title it "Love Your Enemies." Ask young people to use the markers and decorate the paper to symbolize the passage. Tape it to the meeting room wall.

8. Gather everyone in a semicircle in front of the butcher paper mural. Have young people use their caption as part of the closing prayer. A person with the caption "Love even your enemies" could pray, "God, help us love all people, no matter how hard they are to like."

ACTION

Ask group members to choose one person they have trouble even liking. Have them do or say one nice thing to the person this week. It may be as simple as saying hello to that person in the school hallway.

ROMANS 13:1-14 • CHRISTIANS AND THE GOVERNMENT

FOCUS
Controversial topics.

PREPARATION
Write "0," "50," and "100," each on a different piece of construction paper. Place a chair in the middle of the meeting room. Tape the "0" to one wall, the "50" to the chair, and the "100" to the opposite wall. Gather refreshments, a Bible

INSIGHT
Verses 1-7 have presented a struggle for many people over the ages. Do these verses mean we should go along with an oppressive government? Or is Paul simply sending a message to the Roman authorities?

Paul is speaking to people in a state that is often hostile to the Christian community. Overall, Paul still has confidence in the government, and he encourages Christians to be subject to the authorities, to pay taxes and to honor those to whom honor is due.

In this study, group members will grapple with controversial topics.

and several newspapers.

A good resource for this study is *Controversial Topics for Youth Groups*, by Edward N. McNulty (Group Books).

BIBLE STUDY

1. Explain that you have set up the room as a continuum. Tell the group members you are going to ask several questions and they have to go to the spot on the continuum that represents each answer. Ask:

● How has your day been so far? (0 = bad; 100 = great)

● How many of you have read the newspaper today? (0 = haven't read it; 100 = have read it front page to back page)

● How do you feel about being at this study? (0 = excited; 100 = extremely excited)

2. Form small groups by gathering group members according to their last answer. Ask the small groups to sit down while you read Romans 13:1-14.

3. Recap Paul's message in verses 1-7 by saying: "Christians in Paul's day were confused about how much they should go along with the government. Paul tells them to respect authority. Much confusion and anger have emerged over this question today. The battle of church and state is as real today as it was in Paul's day. In this study, you're going to get a chance to voice your thoughts about how much Christians should go along with issues facing our government today."

4. Give each of the small groups a newspaper. Have them find one controversial topic and prepare a description to present to the class. It could be a story about abortion, AIDS, alcohol abuse or divorce.

5. Have each group present its controversial topic. For example, a small group could describe a story of a church sheltering illegal aliens. After the group presents its story, ask the question: "Should the church be involved and concerned with rights of illegal aliens?" Have those who totally disagree go to the "0"; those who totally agree go to the "100"; those with varying opinions go to the corresponding spot between the two extremes.

6. When group members have found a place on the imaginary line, have them sit down and talk with the people near them. They are to discuss why they took this position and think of several reasons why they feel they are right.

7. After a few minutes, ask students to move to the *opposite* position on the continuum. If they were at "100" they would now go to "0." After they change positions, ask them to think of several reasons why they could hold the opposite view to the one they just defended.

8. Repeat this process for each group's controversial topic.

9. Discuss the experience as a large group. Ask:

●How did you feel defending both positions?

●Were you ever alone on an opinion? If so, how did you feel?

●Did you gain something by seeing both sides of the issue? Why or why not?

●Should Christians try to see both sides of an issue? Why or why not?

●How does your experience relate to the passage? Was Paul trying to see both sides of an issue? Explain.

10. Tell the students the importance of Christians being aware of current topics and being personally interested in them. Also explain that Christians are to be part of the world, not secluded from the world.

11. Close by asking one final continuum question: "How hungry are you for refreshments?" (0 = not hungry; 100 = starved) Say a prayer then serve the goodies!

ACTION

Ask young people to read the newspaper this week. Have them each choose one issue, think about their opinion, then discuss it with their parents or a close friend. Ask them to think about how others feel opposite from them. How should Christians deal with people of differing opinions? How should they deal with their chosen topic?

ROMANS 14:1-23 • HELPING OTHERS BELIEVE

FOCUS
Stumbling blocks.

PREPARATION
Place one chair for each group member in a circle. In the center of the circle, place many obstacles such as an empty box, chair and block of wood. Gather one blindfold for each person, newsprint, a Bible and a marker.

INSIGHT
Paul encourages his readers not to dispute issues such as dietary matters or sacred days. We have no right to judge others' actions. God will judge us all.

Nothing is unclean in itself. However, if we do something that may be misunderstood as unclean, we should act differently. We should never place stumbling blocks in a person's way. The kingdom of God does not deal in right or wrong foods; it is grounded in righteousness, peace and joy in the Spirit.

In this study, group members will participate in an obstacle course and discuss stumbling blocks to Christianity.

BIBLE STUDY

1. Place blindfolds on the students as they come into the room. Lead them each to a chair and seat them.

2. Read Romans 14:1-23. Encourage young people to picture the situation Paul is describing. Ask them to imagine stumbling blocks such as what to eat, what not to eat, when to worship and when not to worship.

3. Tell the students that there are many obstacles in the center of the circle. They have to find their way through the obstacles to the opposite side. Once they find their way, they must sit down in another chair. Allow several minutes for this activity. Encourage the students to be careful and move slowly.

4. When all have finished, pair the young people. Ask one partner in each pair to remain blindfolded and the other to take off his or her blindfold. Now allow a few minutes for the seeing partner to lead the other around the obstacles to the other side.

5. Allow all young people to remove their blindfolds. Ask:
- What was difficult when all of you were blindfolded?
- What obstacles were tough to overcome?
- What difference was there when your partner led you?
- What do we do today that might place obstacles in the way of potential believers? What might mislead others? (For example, drinking or smoking at a party, cussing or skipping church.)
- What aspects about your own behavior might cause another to stumble?

6. Let the young people choose one obstacle from the center of the circle and compare it to an obstacle in real life. For example: An empty box could represent an outside appearance of Christianity and an inside emptiness. A cold, metal chair might represent a cool reception of a new class member. Write the obstacles on a piece of newsprint.

7. Close by praying for help in overcoming these obstacles. Reread Romans 14:13: "Therefore let us stop passing judgment on one another. Instead, make up your mind not to put any stumbling block or obstacle in your brother's way."

ACTION

Make an obstacle course for the elementary-age Sunday school children. Pair a teenager with an elementary-age person. Let the teenagers blindfold the young people and lead them through the obstacle course. Ask each teenager to tell the story of Romans 14:1-23 and discuss it with his or her young partner.

ROMANS 15:1-33 • BEARING BURDENS

FOCUS
Responsibility.

PREPARATION
Gather a Bible, newsprint, markers, construction paper, glue, scissors, aluminum foil, and telephone wire or copper wire. Prepare three sculpturing stations: one with wire; one with aluminum foil; and one with construction paper, glue and scissors.

INSIGHT
Paul underscores the need for the strong in the faith to support the weak. We are not to please ourselves; we are responsible to help others. We should follow Christ's example and bring the body together.

In this study, group members will sculpt symbols of worries or burdens, then choose a way to help needy people in the community.

BIBLE STUDY
1. Introduce the theme of responsibility and bearing one another's burdens by having a relay race. Divide into two groups. Choose two light people to be "burdens." Each relay team member carries the burden to a certain point, returns to the line and transfers the burden to the next person. The first team done wins.

2. Ask everyone to sit down, then read Romans 15:1-33. Remind the students that Paul has written a letter that challenges, criticizes and teaches his readers. One thing he emphasizes is that believers must bear the burdens of the weak.

3. Ask young people to think of the burdens, worries or cares of needy people. For example, lack of food, lack of clothing or lack of money. List these on newsprint.

4. Explain that you have prepared three sculpturing stations. One station includes wire; one includes aluminum foil; and one includes construction paper, scissors and glue. Let the young people go to a station of their choice and form a burden or worry of a needy person. For example, a person could cut and glue construction paper coat and pants to represent the need for clothing.

5. After students finish their sculptures, have them describe the need.

6. Gather in a circle and close with a prayer. Have each person pray one sentence about his or her sculpture then place it in the center. For example, "God, please be with people who are in need of warmth and clothing."

Action

Choose one or two needs and develop a plan of action for bearing the burden. For example, choose to host a clothing drive or a food drive for needy people in your community.

ROMANS 16:1-27 • WITH A HOLY KISS

Focus

Appreciation.

Preparation

Gather an instant-print camera, film, butcher paper, tape, markers, Hershey's Kisses, writing materials and a Bible. Tape the butcher paper to the wall. Obtain a list of all the members of the church. You may want to ask the minister or church secretary

Insight

The last chapter of Romans contains personal greetings and notes from Paul. He commends Phoebe, a deaconess, to the readers. They are to provide her with whatever she needs in her ministry. Paul also asks that they greet Prisca (Priscilla) and Aquila, who risked their lives for his life.

Paul asks his readers to avoid people who create dissensions and difficulties. These people do not serve Christ, but their own appetites.

Paul concludes his letter with a benediction.

In this study, group members will write notes of appreciation to congregation members.

about some of the members who are not well-known.

This activity can be done with congregations with as many as 150 members. However, if your church is larger and you feel the task is overwhelming, write notes of appreciation to church leaders and teachers.

BIBLE STUDY

1. As students enter, take instant-print pictures of them. Have students tape the pictures to the butcher paper on the wall.

2. Read Romans 16:1-27. Remind the students that Paul is focusing on the importance of real people who are part of the church's ministry. People bring ministry to life.

3. Distribute writing materials, then divide students in pairs. Ask them to imagine that the apostle was including them in his ministry team. Have them write what Paul would say about their partner's contribution to the work of spreading the gospel. For example: "Judy brought two friends to church in the last month. One of them wants to become a member of the church."

4. Share the contributions.

5. Tell the young people they are now going to write notes of appreciation to congregation members for their contributions. Form groups of four by having each pair team up with another pair. Divide the list of congregation members and give the names to the teams. Ask the young people to write a quick, one-sentence description or note of thanks to each person. For example, "Roger Smith, thanks for your warm smile and handshake as you greet people on Sunday mornings." Check with the groups from time to time to see how they're doing.

6. Ask the students to read some of their notes.

7. Work as a whole group to edit the notes into a smoothly flowing epistle to your church. You can even add a personal note at the beginning and end in the apostle's style. For example, "The youth group members, called to be apostles, greet you in the name of Jesus Christ, our Lord." Read the finished epistle.

8. Give the young people a chance to affirm each other. Distribute markers and let students decorate the butcher paper. Ask them to write thank-you notes by each picture.

9. Give each group member enough Hershey's Kisses so he or she can give one to each youth group member. Allow time for each person to "greet one another with a Hershey's Kiss" (Romans 16:16a) and tell one thing he or she appreciates about each person.

ACTION

Read the letter to the congregation during a Sunday morning worship service. The response will be electrifying. Most people don't really feel they are part of the ministry.

1 CORINTHIANS

Amy and Jill came tumbling around the corner of the garage. Our 5- and 2-year-old daughters had been waiting anxiously for their special present. Their delighted cries made their mother and me feel wonderful. They loved the idea of getting their own swing set for the back yard. However, their joy quickly vanished as they saw their father struggling with a huge box of screws, bolts, nuts and pipes. The only ingredient lacking was a comprehensive set of instructions. The scene steadily deteriorated as I worked for 10 hours on the swing set. The girls finally got to swing—the next day.

Paul is writing from Ephesus to a special church community. He is speaking to a young congregation. He covers a comprehensive set of instructions to maintain a faith community in the midst of confusion. Paul wants to give as much information as possible to help them avoid the confusion that comes with a lack of knowledge. The writer talks about Jesus' Resurrection, the Last Supper, speaking in tongues, prophecy and other gifts of the Spirit.

Paul walks with the Corinthians in low moments of dispute, immorality and division. Their struggles and Paul's wisdom apply to us today. First Corinthians is a vital book for all Christians.

1 CORINTHIANS 1:1-31 • ONE IN CHRIST

FOCUS
Varying beliefs.

PREPARATION
Bring a Bible. Prepare the following questionnaire to poll the young people about their beliefs and views. Make copies, because the young people will use the same questionnaire to poll others. Use the sample and add questions of your own.

INSIGHT
Paul opens this letter with a style of greeting common to the people at that time. Then he quickly jumps from affirming the Corinthians to expressing concern for the dissension among them. Paul is concerned that the Corinthian church has fractured into ideological camps. They have chosen different teachers to follow. He asks how they can pursue such divisions when Christ is one.

Paul claims he did not come to baptize or give theological lectures; he was sent by God to preach the gospel. Paul contrasts wisdom and foolishness. The cross is seen as folly to non-believers; however, for believers it represents God's power.

Paul explains that God takes the lowly, lifts them up and makes them special. People can't boast of their progress. All believers must attribute every good thing to Christ.

In this study, group members will voice their beliefs and values.

BIBLE STUDY

1. Loosen up the students by playing a quick crowdbreaker called "Shake a Hand." Students listen to descriptions and shake people's hands who match them. Use these ideas and add your own:

Shake a person's hand who:
- is wearing a watch.
- is wearing white tennis shoes.
- is wearing a sweater.
- has pierced ears.
- has brown hair.
- has a great smile.

2. Gather young people in a circle and read 1 Corinthians 1:1-31. Say: "Paul tries to calm the arguments among the Corinthians. They were dividing according to differing beliefs. Paul asks them not to divide themselves, because Christ is not divided."

3. Tell the participants they'll have a few minutes to answer some questions about their beliefs. You'll read a statement. All who agree will stand; all who disagree will remain sitting. You'll allow several minutes for discussion after each point.

4. Read the "I Believe . . ." statements one at a time.

I BELIEVE . . .
QUESTIONNAIRE

1. War is against God's will.

2. Sex before marriage is wrong.

3. (Your denomination) is saved, but other churches will be punished.

4. Christians should never drink alcohol.

5. Christians should defend themselves against communists.

6. God forgives us only after we have stopped doing something wrong.

7. Divorce is a sin.

8. Only conservative Christians are saved.

9. Liberals are the most faithful servants of Christ.

10. (Popular TV preacher) is the only one preaching the gospel today.

Permission to photocopy this handout granted for local church use only. Copyright © 1988 by Dennis C. Benson. Published by Group Books, Inc., Box 481, Loveland, CO 80539.

---

5. After the questionnaire is complete and all participants have voiced their opinions, ask:
- Why do Christians have so many differing viewpoints?
- Is it okay to have differing viewpoints? Why or why not?
- What was Paul's warning to the Corinthians?
- How does the passage apply to our lives?

6. Say: "People always will experience and believe things differently from others. That's because people are not clones of each other. They have minds of their own. Paul simply warns us not to become so divided in our opinions that we lose sight of Christ. We all are one through him."

7. Close the study by asking everyone to stand as far away from each other as possible. Pray, "Lord, sometimes it seems like our beliefs are so different—we feel separated from each other."

Ask students to walk to the middle of the room and form a circle with their arms around one another's shoulders. Pray: "Thanks for your Son who erases all differences and brings us together. Amen."

ACTION

Distribute copies of the questionnaire. Ask students each to poll their family and friends. Compile the results at your next meeting. You also can print the questionnaire in the church bulletin or newsletter to gain a clearer understanding of congregation members' viewpoints.

1 CORINTHIANS 2:1—3:3 • INFANTS IN CHRIST

FOCUS
Growing in faith.

PREPARATION
Gather several Bibles, a children's music album (such as a Muppets' album), a record player and a ball.

INSIGHT
Paul reminds the Corinthians that he did not come to them speaking wise and persuasive words. He simply proclaimed Christ. Paul argues against the world's wisdom and reasoning; only God gives true wisdom and insight.

In this study, group members will play childhood games and discuss growing in the faith.

BIBLE STUDY
1. Play children's music as the youth group members enter the room.

2. Lead children's games such as "London Bridge Is Falling Down," "Ring Around the Rosie" and "Mother, May I?"

3. Gather the participants, then ask four volunteers to read the passages. Use these groupings: 2:1-5; 2:6-10; 2:11-16; and 3:1-3.

4. Say: "Paul tells his readers that he did not use difficult words and complicated wisdom when preaching the gospel. He simply preached Christ's crucifixion.

"People apparently criticized Paul for his simple teachings. So he defends himself by comparing spiritual growth to physical growth. Little babies are fed milk then gradually fed solid food. It's the same with new Christians. Paul addresses them as 'infants in Christ.'"

5. Play a couple of other children's games such as "Hide and Seek" or "Keep Away." Then say: "Child psychologists claim that children learn games like these from other children, not from adults. They seem to know the rules without actually learning them." Ask:

● How does this simple knowledge-sharing compare with the secret and hidden wisdom Paul talks about in 1 Corinthians 2:7?

● How does God give you wisdom and the ability to believe?

● Do you "know" some things without actually learning them? Explain. (For example, knowing your parents love you.)

● How did you learn the games you played? Who actually taught them to you? Do you remember?

● Do you have to be a certain age before you hear and understand the wisdom of God? Why or why not?

6. Say: "Just as little children seem to know certain rules such as sharing and following the leader, Christians are given knowledge by God's Spirit. No matter what our age, we receive wisdom from God. From a little child's insights during a children's sermon, to a senior citizen's insights about life—God gives everybody wisdom and knowledge.''

7. Gather everyone in a circle and let group members share some of their knowledge about God. Bounce a ball from one person to another. Have each person who catches it complete the sentence: "God is . . ." Answers could be: "God is love," "God is a brilliant sunset on a winter night" or "God loves us no matter how old we are." Bounce the ball to everyone, letting each person complete the sentence.

ACTION

Ask group members to talk to several people of varying ages (a brother or sister, a friend, a parent, an aunt or uncle, a grandparent or elderly neighbor). Have group members ask each person to complete the sentence: "God is . . ." and bring their answers back. Compare answers. Discuss whether or not the wisdom of God increases with age.

1 CORINTHIANS 3:1-23 • A FIRM FOUNDATION

FOCUS

Christian basics.

PREPARATION

Get a copy of *The Three Little Pigs.* This can be found at your local library, from a parent or in the children's department at your church. Ask the students to bring pillows. You also will need a Bible, thank-you notes, stamps and pencils. (This study works especially well as a late-night devotion at a lock-in or an evening Bible study at a retreat.)

INSIGHT

Paul says the Corinthians' dissension demonstrates their lack of maturity as believers. He uses the metaphor of working a garden. It takes many steps of preparation and care to plant a crop, but only God ensures the growth.

Paul switches from the imagery of growing to that of building. Proclaiming Christ is like an experienced builder who builds the foundation then adds gold, silver and precious materials.

Paul must be hurt by the apparent division of opinion in comparisons between other spiritual teachers and himself. Sinful pride is displayed in the Corinthians' critical comparison of Apollos and Paul. Every spiritual attribute has been given to us by God. Nobody can boast.

In this study, group members will go back to their childhood, talk about when they first learned the basics of the faith, and hear and create a story.

BIBLE STUDY

1. Gather students in a circle and have them get comfortable—have them take off their shoes and fluff their pillows. Read *The Three Little Pigs.* Ask the participants if they remember this story from their childhood. Allow time for describing memories.

2. Give the young people a few minutes to stand, stretch to the ceiling, touch their toes, take a deep breath and yawn. Ask them to get comfortable again, and read 1 Corinthians 3:1-23 storybook style. For example, "Once upon a time, Paul (who was an apostle) wrote a letter to a church . . .''

3. After you finish reading the passage, say: "Paul says Christian faith grows and develops just as people grow and develop. Babies are fed milk. As they grow older, they progress to solid food. First a builder must build a foundation, then he can add to it. Otherwise, nothing firm supports the growth.'' Ask:

- How is this like the story of the three little pigs?
- Which pig took time to build a firm foundation?
- What was the outcome?

4. Ask the students to think of a person who helped build a foundation of faith for them. Ask: "Who taught you the Christian basics? Was your teacher a parent? grandparent? Sunday school teacher? minister?'' Let everyone describe the person and the basics that were taught.

5. Close the session by paraphrasing the passage. Let everyone add a sentence. For example:

Person 1: "Once upon a time Paul preached to some people at a church.''

Person 2: "The people at the church were arguing.''

Person 3: "The arguing was causing division.''

Person 4: "They were new Christians and had to be reminded that they needed a firm foundation of the Christian basics.''

Continue in this manner until everyone has added a sentence to the paraphrase. Then say, "The moral of the story is . . .'' Let the group shout out a moral such as "Build on a firm foundation!''

ACTION

Distribute thank-you notes, stamps and pencils. Ask the group members to write a note of appreciation to the person who helped lay a foundation of Christian basics for them. Mail the thank-you notes.

1 CORINTHIANS 4:1-21 • *SCOLDING BELOVED CHILDREN*

FOCUS
Criticism.

PREPARATION
Gather Bibles, relay supplies, newsprint, a marker and two chairs.

INSIGHT
Paul tells his readers that he's not trying to shame them. He's scolding them as beloved children. Though they have countless guides in Christ, they have few fathers. They are to imitate Paul. He became their father in Christ through the gospel.

In this study, group members will talk about an embarrassing moment when they were scolded as a child.

BIBLE STUDY

1. Run some relays to get group members warmed up and laughing. Try wheelbarrow races, bouncing a ball to a line and back, and running forward and backward.

2. Divide into small groups. Ask the young people to read the passage within their small groups.

3. Ask the members in the small groups to each share an incident from their childhood when they did something bad and were publicly punished. For example: A person could describe a time in fifth-grade when he misspelled a word on a test. The teacher told the whole class about his mistake and had him look up the word in the dictionary in front of them. Another person could tell of a time she ran into the street after a ball—her dad yelled at her in front of her friends and made her go inside the house.

4. As a large group, share some of the situations. Write them on newsprint.

5. Set two chairs in the center of the circle. Ask a volunteer to role play the childhood situation in which he or she was scolded and embarrassed. The student will sit in one chair and be the scolder. The other chair will remain empty as if the child were in it. For example, the person shakes a finger and says: "John, you misspelled 'beautiful.' You were the only one to misspell it. Go look it up in the dictionary. We'll wait for you to tell us the correct way to spell it."

6. Ask other students to role play other ways the situation could've been handled. For example, the teacher takes John aside and says: "John, you misspelled 'beautiful' on your test. Let's go to the dictionary and look it up together."

7. Let all who wish, role play their situations and other ways they could've been handled.

8. Tell the group members that Paul was scolding the Corinthians for choosing favorites and for the dissension among them. Ask a volunteer to role play Paul scolding the Corinthians. The volunteer may want to read verses 8-13 readers-theater style. Then ask:

● Was there another way Paul could have reprimanded the Corinthians? Explain.

● Is a stern scolding sometimes necessary to set people on the correct path, or is a quiet conversation the best way? Explain.

● How should criticism be given? (Allow time for group members to discuss answers such as privately, calmly and criticizing out of love not out of hurt.)

9. As a group, pray for easing of bad memories and embarrassing times. Ask for the gift of maturity that permits loving criticism and correction.

10. Gather in pairs for a time of affirmation. Have the young people find an item in the room that represents an appreciated quality in their partner. For example, a ball to represent a bouncy personality; a red coat to represent enthusiasm; a bottle of lotion to represent a soothing, listening ear. Let the pairs exchange their items and explain the appreciated quality.

ACTION

Ask the students to talk to their parents about the embarrassing situation they shared in the Bible study. Their story may have happened within the family, at school or in the church. The students may be surprised to discover their parents never knew about the situation.

Have the students encourage their parents to tell about a painful, embarrassing situation they remember from their childhood. Sharing feelings about the situations will help parents and teenagers grow closer together.

---

1 CORINTHIANS 5:1-13 • CHURCH DISCIPLINE

FOCUS

Loving concern or judging?

PREPARATION

Gather a Bible, a marker, a gavel, slips of paper,

INSIGHT

Paul responds to the stories he has heard about immorality among the Christians. A man is living with his stepmother in sin. These people are arrogant when they should be mourning for the sin within the church body.

The apostle refers to another letter in which he wrote that they should not associate with

writing materials, several Bible dictionaries and newsprint. Write the sins listed in the "Insight" section each on a slip of paper so that every student will have one. Tape the slips each to the bottom of a chair. Set the chairs in a circle.

people who are guilty of immorality, greed, idolatry, slander, alcohol abuse or swindling.

In this study, group members will write descriptions of "sinners" and discuss whether or not we have the right to confront fellow Christians.

BIBLE STUDY

1. Ask everyone to sit on a chair. Read the following directions and have the young people move accordingly:

● All those who read the Bible today, move two chairs to the right.

● All those who are wearing blue, move four chairs to the left.

● All those who like their steak cooked medium, move one chair to the left.

Add statements of your own. Let young people move according to their answers. Eventually participants will pile three and four (or more) on a chair. Keep going until a young person makes it back to his or her original chair.

2. Introduce the study by saying: "In 1 Corinthians 5:1-13, Paul criticizes people within the church for living in sin. He says it's the church's responsibility to judge its members—not those in the world. God will judge those in the world."

3. Read 1 Corinthians 5:1-13. Ask students to look at the bottom of their chair and remove the slip of paper.

4. Divide into small groups and give each group a Bible dictionary. Distribute writing materials. Ask each student to write a description of a person who is consumed by a particular sin. Encourage students to write modern-day descriptions and give their sinner a first name. For example: "Mary loves money. She earned $100 last weekend and spent it all on herself—she gave nothing to the offering."

5. After group members have finished writing their descriptions, tell them they are gathered as a ruling body that has the responsibility to judge those who have sinned within the church.

One at a time, let students play the role of the sinner. The rest of the group members are judges who question the sinner and decide whether he or she should be thrown out of the church. After each judgment, pound the gavel and say: "So ruled. Next case."

Let everyone portray a sinner. Then ask:

● How did you feel as an accused sinner?

● How did you feel as a judge?

● How do you feel about the responsibility of judging others in the church?

51

●How do some people abuse this responsibility? (Discuss hypocritical attitudes such as shunning divorced members or unwed mothers.)

●How do you balance being judgmental and lovingly confronting a fellow Christian about a sin?

6. Develop a list of principles to follow when confronting a fellow Christian. For example, "Confront out of concern for the person, not to hurt him or her." Write the principles on newsprint.

7. Say: "Although Christians should be concerned with fellow Christians' sins, we also need to remember that nobody is without sin. We must examine our motive when confronting a fellow Christian. If our motive is to get even or feel better than him or her, we are not confronting out of love."

8. Gather in a circle and allow a few moments of silence for students to meditate on some of their sins. Pass the gavel from person to person and have each one say, "God, forgive my sins." After everyone has held the gavel, say: "God has forgiven each one of you your sins through Christ. Amen."

ACTION

Ask students to each choose a congregation member to pray for this week. The person could be going through a divorce, or experiencing alcohol or drug addiction. At the end of the week have young people think of one way to help that person. For example, offer to babysit or supply a hot meal.

---

1 CORINTHIANS 6:1-11 • INJUSTICE

FOCUS
Forgiveness.

PREPARATION
Set up the room as a theater. The front is the stage; chairs are in rows. Bring a Bible, popcorn, pop, writing materials, songbooks and 3x5 cards. Ask several young people to prepare the two skits.

INSIGHT
Paul advises his readers to stay away from secular judges when there is a dispute among them. Christians will participate in the final judgment; they should avoid being judged by people in the world.

Just having a lawsuit between two believers is failure. Why can't a believer live with injustice from another Christian? Paul is amazed that Christians are cheating and defrauding other Christians.

In this study, group members will rewrite the ending to two skits and discuss forgiveness.

BIBLE STUDY

1. Ask the young people to sit in the chairs. Lead them in preshow singing with songs such as "I'm Gonna Sing" and "Hallelu" from *Songs* (Songs and Creations).

2. Read 1 Corinthians 6:1-11. Say, "This passage sets our stage for the first skit." Introduce the actors in the first skit.

● *Skit 1:* Jimmy was small—the shortest kid in the class. He spent the first two months in the new school as one bully's punching bag. One day the big kid knocked him down and ripped the sweater his mother had made before her death. Jimmy couldn't take it anymore. He turned on the bully and let out a violent scream. His head struck the bully's stomach. The bully fell back with a surprised groan. Jimmy's fists struck the bigger boy's face. Jimmy felt a great weight lifting as he pounded on his enemy.

3. After the skit, ask all viewers to remember the details for later discussion. Then introduce the second skit and actors.

● *Skit 2:* Mary looked up from her papers. The man standing in front of her desk was ill at ease. Her heart pounded as she tried to control herself.

"Edward Dooley," he said.

This was the man who fired her father 10 years ago. She remembered the pain and despair as her father tried to explain his job loss to the family. Mary could still feel the shame that radiated from him. She had been speechless and unable to comfort him. That night he took his life.

"Edward Dooley. What can I do for you?"

"I'm applying for the position in sales. The man in personnel told me you were doing the hiring. I really need employment. I haven't been lucky recently."

The anger and hatred boiled within her. The time had come for revenge.

She scanned his résumé and asked several questions.

"Things look good to me. I will let you know within the next few days."
The man smiled and relief shown in his eyes.

"You don't know what this means to me. Thank you, miss."

The old man left her office. Mary stared at the door for a full 10 minutes.
She then took the man's application and wrote across the top: "Rejected.
Drinking problem. Recommend that he not be considered for any position."

4. After the skit, allow an intermission. Serve popcorn and soft drinks.

5. Call students back and divide into two groups. Assign one group
the first skit; assign the other group the second skit. Distribute writing
materials and ask the two groups to write a different ending for their
assigned skit. The endings need to correspond with Paul's message in the
passage. Paul talks about our forgiveness in Christ. We are justified in his
name. Another ending for the second skit could be: "The old man left her
office. Mary prayed for a full 10 minutes, asking God to help her forgive.
She then took the man's application and wrote across the top: 'Accepted.
Recommend that he be hired for the position.' "

6. Let group members act out the new endings. Discuss:
- How were the endings different?
- Why does revenge feel good at times?
- How does it feel to forgive someone?
- What is Paul's message about revenge and forgiveness?

7. Distribute a 3x5 card to each person. On one side have young people
complete this sentence: "I need to forgive . . ." On the other side have
young people complete this sentence: "I need forgiveness from . . ." Pray
silently for the forgiveness requests.

8. Finish eating the popcorn and then clean the "theater."

ACTION

Ask the students to act on what they wrote on their 3x5 cards. Have them
forgive a person and ask forgiveness from another.

1 CORINTHIANS 6:12-20 • THE TEMPLE OF THE HOLY SPIRIT

FOCUS
Physical fitness.

PREPARATION
Go to the library and
check out lively music and

INSIGHT
Paul tells the Corinthians the body is meant
for the Lord. Christ was bodily raised from the
dead; he also will raise believers. Our bodies
are part of Christ—temples of the Holy Spirit.
We do not belong to ourselves, Christ has purchased us. We must glorify God in our bodies.

a "Chicken Fat" exercise record. Rent an exercise video and bring the necessary equipment. Ask young people to wear sweat suits or comfortable clothing. Gather a Bible, pears, peaches, celery, raisins, fruit, juice, paper plates and napkins.

In this study, group members will perform aerobics and discuss physical fitness.

BIBLE STUDY

1. Warm up the young people by having them march in place to music. While they are marching in place, read 1 Corinthians 6:12-20. Explain Paul's emphasis on the body being the temple of God. We must keep the temple in good condition.

2. Exercise to the video, to the lively music and to "Chicken Fat." After the aerobic workout and cool down, discuss:

● What do we do to hurt our bodies?

● Since our bodies are temples of God, what are our specific responsibilities? (Encourage young people to provide practical ideas such as dieting, exercising and eating nutritiously.)

● Is there a balance between making ourselves look great so that we keep with the world's standards and caring for our bodies to please God? If so, how do we maintain that balance?

3. Close the study with healthy refreshments. Make "Beautiful Body Salads." Everyone makes a body out of a pear half (torso), peach half (head), celery sticks (legs and arms) and raisins (eyes). Eat the creations!

ACTION

Request to lead the Sunday school opening. Have group members lead the children in exercises. After the exercises, participants can have fruit and juice and discuss the importance of nutrition since our bodies are temples of God.

1 CORINTHIANS 7:1-40 • GUIDELINES FOR MARRIAGE

FOCUS

Dating and marriage.

PREPARATION

Invite a happily married couple to your Bible study. Prepare them to talk about

INSIGHT

Paul gives some guidelines for marriage. He believes that the wife doesn't rule over her body, but her husband does. In the same sense, the husband doesn't rule over his body, but his wife does. Paul believes that the end of the world will be in their lifetime, so he recommends single people remain single.

55

their dating and marriage experiences. Have them discuss the tempting situations dating sometimes brings and why sex is best when kept for marriage. They can address questions such as:

● How did your parents tell you the facts of life?

● Did you learn more facts from parents? school? friends? church?

● Was the information correct or misleading? Explain.

Ask them to tell a story from their lives that relates to this passage. For example, they could describe an argument when the wife wanted to cut her hair and her husband wanted it to grow. The husband used 1 Corinthians 7:4 to support his view.

If you can't get a married couple to come to your study, interview a couple and record it on a cassette tape or videotape. Bring a Bible and a bag of string licorice.

In this study, group members will meet with a married couple and discuss dating and marriage.

BIBLE STUDY

1. Introduce the guests and gather everyone in a circle. Get to know each other better by asking the participants each to say their name and something good that happened to them the previous week.

2. Read the passage, then ask the guests to share a story that relates to some part of the passage. Ask them to describe the ups and downs of dating and marriage. Have them tell how they learned the facts of life. Encourage the young people to ask questions.

3. Allow time for students and guests to discuss the most difficult aspects of Paul's teaching on sexuality. Ask:

● Why would Paul teach these things to the Corinthians?

● Why would he tell them it's best to remain single?

● How did the belief that the end was near affect the teachings?

● What are some difficulties concerning your own sexuality?

● What aspects of dating are frustrating?

● Is it difficult to refrain from sex until marriage? Why or why not?

● How does the Christian faith help during tempting times?

● How did you learn the facts of life? Did you learn from parents? teachers? friends? brothers? sisters? church? Were the things you learned misleading? helpful? vague?

● What suggestions would you give little brothers and sisters concerning sex and dating?

4. Conduct a dedication of the marriage vows for the married couple. Let the married couple reread their parts of the marriage service and let the group members read the parts of the pastor and congregation.

5. Give each person some string licorice, and gather in a circle. Say that an old phrase referring to getting married is "to tie the knot." Ask participants to tie the ends of their licorice to form a large circle. Have them stand inside the circle and hold on to the licorice. Say that this symbolizes

God's never-ending circle of love for us.

Pray: "God, whether we are single, whether we marry or are married, despite who we are or what we do, help us to know you love us and care for us. Your love encircles us our whole lives. Thanks for your Son. Amen."

6. Serve fresh licorice for refreshments.

ACTION

Ask group members to interview church members about their dating and marriage experiences. Record the interviews on a cassette tape. Have each interviewee complete two statements: "If I could give one dating guideline, it would be . . ." and "If I could give one marriage guideline, it would be . . ." Play the recorded interviews at the next session.

1 CORINTHIANS 8:1-13 • *CAUSING OTHERS TO STUMBLE*

FOCUS
Peer pressure.

PREPARATION
Bring a blindfold, a Bible, 3x5 cards, pencils, chairs and obstacles (such as boxes) to the session.

INSIGHT
Paul speaks about eating food offered to idols. Of course, he knows that since idols represent nothing, eating such food would do nothing to the Christian. However, there is the question of what others would think. The weak might think that if a Christian eats food offered to an idol, the Christian is endorsing idol worship.

We have a responsibility to those who might stumble. If eating this food would cause another to fall, we shouldn't eat it.

In this study, group members will play games that illustrate peer pressure.

BIBLE STUDY

1. Introduce the study by saying: "Paul tells us not to cause others to stumble. Today, many things we do can cause others to stumble. We may pressure friends to lie to their parents or cheat on a test; others may pressure us to do the same.

"This study is on peer pressure. To begin, let's play some games that illustrate this pressure."

2. Divide into two groups. Time groups to see who can pile on top of each other and form a pyramid the fastest. Then run piggyback races (make sure lighter group members do the riding).

3. Discuss the concept of negative peer influence. Paul seemed aware that such an influence was active in the church at Corinth. Read 1 Corinthians 8:1-13. Ask:

● How are you influenced by others without realizing it?

● What kinds of acts are you pressured to do by your friends or acquaintances? (For example, tell dirty jokes, drink, smoke or go to a movie on a Saturday night without your parents' consent.)

● Why do people do things to please their friends?

4. Say: "Peer pressure is not always bad. Christians in Paul's time could cause others to fall away from Christ, yet they could also bring them to the faith." Have the students share positive influences from others. Ask:

● How have others influenced you positively?

● What are positive ways you have influenced others? (Discuss ways such as encouraging a brother or sister to study for a test or asking a friend to come to youth group.)

5. Encourage group members to keep positively influencing each other. Say that they can avoid negative peer pressure by praying and listening to God. God speaks in a gentle whisper (1 Kings 19:12). Illustrate this point by playing a game called "The Pressure's On."

Ask a volunteer to go with you into another room; have the rest of the group stay in the regular meeting room. Blindfold the volunteer and say: "When you are called into the meeting room, your goal is to find your way through a maze. I'll be the gentle whisper of God's voice. Trust me to lead you." Have the volunteer wait until you give the signal to come into the room with the others.

In the meeting room, quickly set up a maze of chairs and obstacles. Tell the group members that your voice represents the gentle whisper of God. When the volunteer comes into the room, you'll give him or her the right directions to find his or her way through the maze. The others are to shout wrong advice and try to get the volunteer to go off track.

Ask the volunteer to come in, and begin playing the game. Afterward, talk about the experience. This is an amazing way to illustrate negative peer pressure and the need to listen to God—trusting that God will guide you through life.

ACTION

Give young people each a 3x5 card and a pencil. Say: "This card represents a stumbling block in your life. Think of something you do (or don't do) that could be a stumbling block to another. (For example, skipping church or having a bad attitude on Monday mornings.) Write down one stumbling block you want to delete from your life. Practice removing it this week."

1 CORINTHIANS 9:1—10:33 • THE GOOD RACE OF FAITH

FOCUS
Faith.

PREPARATION
Plan to meet at a running track at a local high school. Ask group members to wear comfortable clothes and proper running shoes. During this study, group members will be running around the track. Encourage those who are not used to running to walk and not overdo it. Bring a Bible, cups, and Gatorade or juice.

INSIGHT
Paul turns to his personal reputation. He defends his true apostleship through his claim that he saw Christ and through his work with the Corinthians. They are a sign of his apostleship.

Later in the passage he urges his readers to run the good race of faith. To be a spiritual athlete one must be disciplined. A physical athlete receives only a momentary reward while the Christian is given an imperishable reward.

Paul recaps the story of our spiritual parents' deliverance out of Egypt. They were rescued but failed to be faithful. God was not pleased with them. This is a warning to us. We also have been blessed but are tempted to fall away like the ancients.

God is faithful and will not let us be tempted beyond strength to resist. No matter what we do, all must be done for God's glory. Paul reminds his readers that he relates to all people only so they might experience the glory of God and be saved.

In this study, group members will walk or jog around a track and discuss the good race of faith.

BIBLE STUDY
1. Meet at the track and lead participants through some stretching exercises. Stretch the entire body—including calves, thighs, ankles and arms.

2. Say that on the signal they are to run or walk once around the track then meet for a brief discussion. They'll do this four times. By the end of the study they will have run or walked one mile.

3. Yell, "Go." After the athletes go around the track once, gather them for a brief portion of the lesson. Read 1 Corinthians 9:24-27. Emphasize that we are all runners in a race. A race in real life produces only one winner. In the race of faith, all Christians win eternal life. Allow time for the athletes to discuss their feelings about being in the race of faith. Ask:
●What makes being a Christian difficult? easy?
●How can you maintain energy to run the race of faith during your

59

entire life?

4. Let the athletes run or walk their second lap. Then gather for another portion of the lesson. Read 1 Corinthians 10:13. This passage says that God is faithful and won't let us be tempted beyond our strength. Ask the runners and walkers to think of a time they were tempted. Ask:

● How did God help you through?

● Do you ever feel like giving up the race of faith? If so, how does God help you during those down times?

5. Allow time for young people to share. Then say, "You may be tempted to quit running or walking, but I know you have the strength to continue." Have participants complete their third lap, then gather and read 1 Corinthians 10:24. Ask:

● What does it mean to seek the good of others rather than the good of yourself?

● How do you feel when others receive a reward and you don't? (For example, running a race and coming in last; trying out for band and not making it; trying out for a part in a play and not getting it.)

● How can you take that instance and be thankful for the good that happened to someone else?

6. Encourage group members to run or walk their last lap. Gather them and read 1 Corinthians 10:31. Say, "Paul tells his readers that no matter what they eat, drink or do—everything should be done to glorify God." Ask:

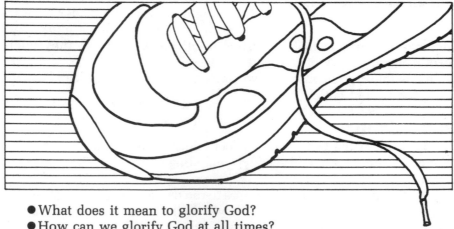

● What does it mean to glorify God?

● How can we glorify God at all times?

● How can we glorify God when bad things happen?

● How can we look for good in all things?

7. Close the session by distributing cups filled with Gatorade or juice. Say, "Remember, no matter what we eat, drink or do, it must be done to the glory of God."

Ask all runners to touch their cups together and say, "Cheers." After everyone has finished their drink have them shout in unison, "Amen!"

ACTION

Ask the group members to develop an eight-week exercise course to offer congregation members. It could be as simple as playing records and letting each person share an exercise he or she knows. Participants could begin slowly by walking a short distance, then gradually working up to running a longer distance. Before and after each session have participants read portions of 1 Corinthians 9—10. Focus on running the good race of faith. You also could focus on 1 Corinthians 6:12-20 (keeping your body fit because it is the temple of God).

---

1 CORINTHIANS 11:1-34 • *WORSHIP AND THE LAST SUPPER*

FOCUS
Worship traditions.

PREPARATION
Meet in the sanctuary for this study. Gather a Bible, a head scarf for each girl, Sunday bulletins, juice and bread or crackers. Prepare to role play Paul when reading the passage to the group members.

INSIGHT
Paul teaches about women and worship. He claims that the man is the head of the woman just as Christ is the head of the church. A woman must display modesty in public worship by covering her head. A man should not cover his head because he was created in God's image.

Some scholars contend that Paul is concerned about separating the reputation of the pagan temple harlot from the virtue of the Christian woman.

The apostle next turns to the Last Supper. He lists the abuses the Corinthians commit around the table of the Lord. When they meet, there are divisions. They eat when they desire and don't wait for those who don't have food. Some get drunk.

Paul tells how they should conduct themselves. He shares the account of the Last Supper, which has become the form for the words of communion for many Christian traditions.

In this study, group members will prepare a worship service typical of Paul's time.

BIBLE STUDY

1. Gather in the sanctuary. Say: "This Bible study is about the tradition of worship during Paul's time. Listen to his description and some guidelines he gives the Corinthians." Step to the pulpit and read the passage as if you were Paul delivering the message.

2. Summarize the passage by saying: "That's the situation in Paul's time. Women wore veils and were quiet. Men were allowed to bare their heads. Communion appeared to be a wild time. Christians had lost sight of its purpose." Ask:

● How is our worship service different from the one Paul describes?

● How would our church worship change if we literally followed Paul's teaching in this passage?

3. Give everyone a bulletin that provides the order of worship for a typical Sunday. Go over your church's order of worship. Ask:

● What instructions would Paul give us about each aspect of worship?

● How do you explain the difference between Paul's situation and ours?

4. Divide into small groups; distribute head scarves to the women. Assign each small group a portion of the worship service: opening prayer, songs, readings, sermon, offering, benediction. Ask each group to prepare to lead its portion according to Paul's teaching.

5. After several minutes, conduct a "Corinthian" worship service. (Group members will probably prepare the service so that men lead and women wear scarves and simply listen.) Afterward ask:

● How do you feel about the role of men in church during Paul's time? women?

● How did it feel to participate in this type of worship?

● How do you feel about the role of men in church today? women?

● Why do you think women weren't allowed to participate in church in Paul's time but are allowed to today?

● How do you feel about denominations ordaining women? How would Paul feel about this?

● Do you think Paul's feelings about women participating in church would change if he were alive today? Why or why not?

6. Close by celebrating the ministry of both men and women. If your church allows, have a love feast, which is an informal sharing of food to represent the Last Supper. Share juice and bread or crackers.

ACTION
If your church allows women to participate in leading worship, plan to attend a church that does not allow it. If your church doesn't allow women to participate in leading worship, plan to attend a church that does allow it. Come to the next session and compare your impressions of both services.

1 CORINTHIANS 12:1-31a • THE BODY OF CHRIST

FOCUS
Unique gifts.

PREPARATION
Use masking tape to outline a giant human body on the floor. Make it large enough so young people can stand inside it. On separate 3x5 cards, write one body part: head, eye, ear, nose, mouth, arm, hand, leg, foot and heart. You'll need one card for each person. On the back of the cards write a few verses of the passage. (Divide the passage according to the number of participants.) You'll also need a camera, black-and-white film, paper and pencils.

INSIGHT
Paul tackles one of the most important aspects of the church: spiritual gifts. We are called to many ways of serving with our different gifts. Although we may work in different ways, it is the same God who inspires us.

One person may have the gift of communicating wisdom or understanding; another person may be given faith; others may be blessed with the gifts of healing, miracles, prophecy, distinguishing between spirits, and speaking in and interpreting tongues. All these ministries have been given by the same Spirit, who gives as he wills.

Paul affirms the incredible reality that just as the human body is one while having many parts, so Christ calls many parts to make one body. Through baptism we were made one—despite nationality or geographical boundary.

In this study, group members will learn about their unique gifts.

BIBLE STUDY
1. Distribute the 3x5 cards as group members come into the meeting room. Ask young people to stand within the body outline according to the body part written on their card. Let the students read 1 Corinthians 12:1-31a according to the assigned verses on their cards.

2. Ask everyone to sit in a comfortable position, then discuss the verses they just read. Ask:

●What are the unique aspects of each body part? For example, the eye can see what's going on and visualize the beauty of God's world.

●How can each part be used practically in the church? For example: People with an eye for detail can prepare church bulletins. People who are gifted with their hands can repair church property or homes of the elderly.

●What does Paul mean when he says we are called in the Spirit as one body?

●How can different people with unique gifts function within one church body?

● According to this passage, does everyone have a unique gift or ability? Explain.

3. Encourage students to think of a body part that best describes their unique gift. Have them stand in an area of the body outline that represents their gift. Allow time for each person to describe his or her ability.

4. Have young people join hands where they are standing. Pray: ''Thanks for creating each of us as individuals. Help us use our unique gifts to serve you. Thank you for making us one through your Son. Amen.''

ACTION

Ask group members to sit in the body outline and hold hands. Take a picture of this physical representation of the passage. Ask students to write a report for the church newsletter about the session and its conclusions. Print the picture with the article.

1 CORINTHIANS 12:31b—13:13 • LOVE IS PATIENT AND KIND

FOCUS
Love.

PREPARATION
Cut several hearts out of red construction paper. Write one of the following characteristics on each: kind, patient, not boastful, not jealous, not arrogant, not rude, does not insist on its own way, not irritable, not resentful, does not rejoice at wrong, rejoices in the right, bears all things, believes all things, hopes all things, endures all things, never ends.

Prepare one red construction paper heart for each person. On each one write the word ''love.'' Post butcher paper along

INSIGHT
Paul explains God's gift that connects all believers: love. He does not mean the kind we sing about in popular love songs. He means love as in Jesus Christ.

Fancy speech, prophetic gifts, understanding mysteries, knowledge, enormous faith, generosity and martyrdom mean nothing without love. This love manifests itself in patience, kindness, and the lack of jealousy and boastfulness. Love is not arrogant, rude, irritable or resentful of others. It rejoices with the truth. Love never ends.

One scholar suggests that the closing triad of qualities represents past (faith), future (hope) and present (love). Whether Paul borrowed this poem from another source or prepared it another time and added it to this letter, it is a beautiful part of Christian literature.

In this study, group members will write descriptions of love and focus on this gift from God.

one wall of your meeting room. Be sure it is heavy enough so red markers or crayons won't mark the wall beneath. Gather a Bible, pencils, red markers or crayons, and red refreshments such as apples, Kool-Aid or Jell-O.

BIBLE STUDY

1. As students enter the room, give them each a pencil and a red construction paper heart with the word "love" written on it. Ask young people each to write a personal gift they possess that begins with each letter. For example:

- Listen.
- Open to new experiences.
- Very caring.
- Extra thoughtful.

Ask young people to share their gifts.

2. Give each person a red crayon or marker. Ask participants to go to the butcher paper and write slogans and phrases that describe the word "love." They also can draw pictures and symbols about love such as a heart with an arrow through it.

3. Seat the class by the wall. Encourage students to read aloud the different definitions.

4. Read 1 Corinthians 12:31b—13:13. Ask:
- How are the qualities listed in the passage different from some of the descriptions written on the butcher paper? How are they similar?
- Are there several kinds of love? Explain.
- Can we base life on a partial understanding of love? Why or why not?

5. Form pairs. Give each pair one or more of the characteristics you have written on the red hearts. Ask the pairs to think of an event from their own lives that illustrates their attribute. For example, a person might illustrate "kind" by telling about a neighbor who brought hot chicken soup to his mom when she was sick.

6. Let the pairs tell their real-life stories of love being expressed.

7. Close with a prayer of thanksgiving. Ask each person to use the word "love" in the prayer. For example, "Thanks for your love," "Thanks for my parents' love," "Thanks for the ability to love."

8. Serve the red refreshments.

ACTION

Ask each student to adopt one of the love characteristics Paul describes. Urge students to show this aspect of love to everyone they meet during the next week.

1 CORINTHIANS 14:1-40 • SPEAKING IN TONGUES

FOCUS
Intellect and emotions.

PREPARATION
Record two kinds of sermons from your television or radio. Select an intellectual and an emotional preaching style. Isolate a three-minute segment from each one. Gather a Bible, a pencil and three copies of the following form for each person. You also will need refreshments.

INSIGHT
Paul discusses the merits of prophecy (intelligible inspired teaching) and speaking in tongues (unintelligible inspired teaching). The context of this discussion is worship.

Paul states that both prophecy and speaking in tongues are of God. However, the person speaking in tongues edifies only himself or herself, because only God understands him or her. The person speaking prophecy builds up the whole church, because everyone understands.

He compares speaking in tongues to speaking a foreign language. If a stranger does not know the human language, how is he or she to understand an unknown divine language?

Paul says people who speak in tongues should limit the number of speakers, speak one at a time and have an interpreter for each

SERMON EVALUATION	
Words, phrases, stories that touch (or affect) my mind:	Words, phrases, stories that touch (or affect) my emotions:

Permission to photocopy this handout granted for local church use only. Copyright © 1988 by Dennis C. Benson. Published by Group Books, Inc., Box 481, Loveland, CO 80539.

message.

In this study, group members will listen to and compare intellectual and emotional styles of preaching.

BIBLE STUDY

1. Play a get-to-know-you game. Divide the group into pairs. Have pairs interview each other using these questions:

● What's the best thing you learned this week?

● When did you feel best this week? What happened?

Allow time for each person to introduce his or her partner and tell the acquired information.

2. Say: "We just discovered some things that happened to us this week that affected our intellect and our emotions. In 1 Corinthians 14:1-40, Paul discusses using intellect and emotions during worship. Worship needs to involve both mind and spirit. We need to be considerate of a variety of listeners when presenting the gospel." Read the passage.

3. Distribute a pencil and one evaluation form to each person. Tell the students you are going to play a three-minute segment of a recorded sermon. As they listen, have them write points from the sermon that affect their intellect (facts about Jerusalem in Jesus' time, or details about rules that governed Jewish people's lives) and points that affect their emotions (the disciples' joy at seeing the resurrected Jesus, or the release and freedom that come with forgiveness). Play the first tape.

4. Distribute a second form and play the second three-minute sermon segment. Ask group members to listen and take notes. Then discuss:

● Which sermon did you enjoy most? Why?

● Which sermon made you feel most uncomfortable? Why?

● Which sermon focused mainly on intellect? What did you like about it? dislike?

● Which sermon focused mainly on emotions? What did you like about it? dislike?

● Can God speak to you through both kinds of sermons? Why or why not?

● How can preachers be sure their message will be received and understood by the different people in the congregation?

● How can listeners be sure to receive the message—no matter what style is used?

5. Say: "Some listeners learn mostly through the intellect, some through emotions. Some preachers enjoy appealing to the intellect more than emotions and vice versa. This is just one example of the many different qualities God has given people. If we all were the same, life would be boring."

6. Close the session with a few games that illustrate our uniqueness as well as our similarity. Ask participants to race each other to form the following groupings. First group formed wins each race.

- Gather with people who have similar hair color.
- Gather with people who have similar eye color.
- Gather with those who were born the same month as you.
- Gather with those who are hungry for refreshments.

Serve the refreshments!

ACTION

Give the young people each one more evaluation form. Have them listen to a few more religious programs. Ask them to decide which preaching style they are most comfortable with and why. Discuss the experiences at the next session.

1 CORINTHIANS 15:1-58 • IN THE TWINKLING OF AN EYE

FOCUS

Resurrection.

PREPARATION

Gather a large bulletin board on wheels (most church education departments have these), construction paper of various colors, aluminum foil, glue, scissors, buttons, cotton, tape, yarn, string, and other odds and ends. Bring a Bible, a cassette tape or an album of classical music (or some other "heavenly sounding" tunes) and a cassette tape player or a record player.

INSIGHT

Paul talks about Jesus' Resurrection and our resurrection. Fortunately, Christ has been raised from the dead. Since we all died with Adam, we must all be raised by Christ.

Paul says we will be raised or changed in the twinkling of an eye. The trumpet will be heard, and the dead will be raised as changed, imperishable bodies. The last enemy Christ will destroy is death.

In this study, group members will create symbols of the resurrection.

BIBLE STUDY

1. Play the "heavenly" music as teenagers enter the room. Have them sit in a comfortable position and listen to the music for a few minutes. Read the passage as the music is played in the background.

2. Say: "Throughout this chapter, Paul tells about Jesus' Resurrection and our resurrection. I want to see how you visualize your own resurrection.'' Show the students all the odds and ends you have collected. Say that they have a chance to create a resurrection symbol. They can symbolize a specific verse or an idea. For example: A person could symbolize verse 52, which talks about the twinkling of an eye and a trumpet sound. He could cut a piece of blue construction paper into a cloud shape; cut aluminum foil into star shapes and glue them to the cloud; glue yarn in the shape of a trumpet; and add music notes made from black construction paper.

3. Encourage young people to use their imaginations. Allow 30 minutes for the artists to create their symbols. Then let the students describe them. You'll be amazed at their ideas and creativity.

4. Gather in a circle and have everyone fill in the following sentence for the person sitting on his or her right: ''It will be great being in heaven with you because of your . . .'' Ideas could be thoughtfulness, kindness, faith, love and care for new people.

5. Say, ''Our assurance of resurrection and a place in heaven is not guaranteed by any of our actions but on God's grace alone.'' Close with a silent prayer thanking God for grace and the gifts of resurrection and eternal life.

ACTION

Tape the resurrection symbols on the traveling bulletin board. Add a sign that says ''Resurrection Symbols'' or ''In the Twinkling of an Eye.'' Place it where congregation members can see it.

1 Corinthians 16:1-24 • *Greetings in the Lord*

FOCUS
Appreciation.

PREPARATION
This study will be held in two parts. The first part is a time for young people to plan an appreciation banquet; the second part is the banquet itself. Supplies you'll need for the first part are writing materials. Sup-

INSIGHT
Paul closes this letter with personal matters. He mentions the funds needed for the church at Jerusalem. He has been spending a lot of time trying to gather money for the poor. Paul promises to visit the Corinthians and perhaps spend the winter.

He asks them to accept Timothy and send him on his way back to Paul. Paul affirms their service and concludes with personal greetings.

In this study, group members will plan an appreciation banquet.

69

plies you'll eventually need are invitations, eating utensils, plates, napkins, food and awards.

BIBLE STUDY

1. As group members enter, greet each one by saying one thing you appreciate about him or her. Encourage the young people to express their appreciation of one another.

2. Read 1 Corinthians 16:1-24. Say: "In this last chapter of 1 Corinthians, Paul expresses his appreciation. Appreciation is an important—yet often overlooked—aspect of our relationships. Sometimes we are too busy or preoccupied to remember to say thanks. We are going to take time to thank special people in our lives; we're going to plan an appreciation banquet."

3. Host a group brainstorming session and ask questions such as:

● Who should be the honorary guests at this banquet? Should we invite parents? teachers? church staff? friends?

● Where should we have the banquet?

● What food should we serve?

● How should we pay for it?

● What activities should we plan?

● How should we publicize it?

4. Divide into small groups. Assign each group an aspect of the banquet to plan: invitations, awards, activities and food. Distribute writing materials.

5. Here's an example of an appreciation banquet for parents:

● Teenagers send invitations to their parents.

● On the designated night, youth group members and sponsors bring food—potluck style. (Hosts can bring one hot dish and one of the following: salad, vegetables, bread or dessert.)

● Several young people greet parents at the door; the others escort them to their seats.

● Teenagers dress in similar clothing. For example, white shirts, dark slacks and white aprons.

● Group members serve the meal.

● Host an awards ceremony. Each young person tells his or her parent(s), "You are the world's best parent(s) because . . ." The young person then presents parent(s) with a certificate that has those words written on it.

● Hold an affirmation time. Teenagers say one thing they appreciate about their parents; parents say one thing they appreciate about their teenagers.

● A massive group hug "wraps up" the evening.

ACTION

Host the appreciation banquet. You may want to make this a frequent event. Choose different people as guests of honor for each banquet.

2 CORINTHIANS

INTRODUCTION TO 2 CORINTHIANS

A wise, old pastor once told me, "Always remember—all you have is your reputation." This bit of advice proved to be vital to my survival as a freelance media consultant for over 20 years. You can't demand, fake or construct a good opinion from others. It's something others give you. What do you do when others attempt to destroy the public's understanding of the good you have done?

This is the problem Paul faced when he wrote this letter. He apparently had written several letters to the Corinthians—an important and demanding community of faith. In 2 Corinthians, he emphasizes some issues of previous communications while raising new ones.

One of the major themes of this Epistle is Paul restoring his good reputation after being falsely accused by certain critics in Corinth. Some people had fallen under the influence of false teachers. These false teachers had discredited him and challenged his authority.

In 2 Corinthians, Paul's words comfort many people who deal with similar problems and struggles. Second Corinthians is filled with comforting verses. Perhaps one of the most comforting is 2 Corinthians 5:17: "Therefore, if anyone is in Christ, he is a new creation; the old has gone, the new has come!"

2 CORINTHIANS 1:1-24 • CRITICISM FROM CORINTH

FOCUS
Leadership.

PREPARATION
Gather a Bible, finger paints, paper, tortilla chips, cheese, Kool-Aid, cups and napkins.

INSIGHT
Paul opens this letter with greetings. Apparently, after 1 Corinthians was written and before this letter was written, Paul had made a painful visit to Corinth. After that visit, Paul had promised to visit them again. But he changed his travel plans, because he was seeking to avoid a second painful visit. He hurts from the charge that he is wavering in what he says.

In this study, group members will discuss how to deal with the criticism that sometimes comes from being a leader and a servant.

BIBLE STUDY

1. Play "Follow the Leader." Allow time for as many group members as possible to lead the others around any path they choose. Ask:
- How did it feel to lead?
- How did it feel to follow?
- When you were a follower, did you sometimes want to direct or correct the leader's decisions? Why or why not?
- When you were the leader, did you feel responsible for the followers? Explain.

2. Say: "Paul is in a position of leadership. Like all leaders, he has been criticized for some of his actions. Paul is hurt by this and defends himself." Read 2 Corinthians 1:1-24.

3. Say: "Being a leader is being a servant. Good leaders are concerned about their followers. They want the best for them. Look at the palm of your hand. A hand is a good symbol of a servant and a leader.

"Look at the intersecting lines. A leader has to look at many options and choose the best route to follow. He or she has to consider the followers and what would be best for them.

"Look at the high points and the low points. Being a leader means experiencing the high points of affirmation and companionship and the low points of criticism and anguish.

"Look at your entire hand. Leaders are servants. They use all their resources to help others.

"How else can you compare your hand to a leader and a servant?"

Allow time for group members to say things such as "Hands are the instruments servants use to minister" or "Hands can heal."

4. Continue the discussion with these questions:
- What experiences have you had with leadership?
- How did you serve others with your position?
- How did you handle criticism?
- How did you feel about being a leader?
- What were some hurts or pains you experienced?
- What were some good times you experienced?

5. Get out the finger paints and paper. Let young people make palm prints and designs to symbolize their memories of leadership and servanthood. Allow time for young people to describe their designs when they've finished.

6. Ask students to stand palm to palm in a circle. Pray: "Thank you, God, for a chance to lead. Thank you, God, for a chance to serve. Help us withstand the criticism that sometimes comes. Thanks for the greatest example of a leader and a servant—your Son. Amen."

7. Let the group members use their hands to make refreshments. Have them melt the cheese, pour it over the tortilla chips and mix the Kool-Aid. Serve each other.

ACTION
Ask the young people each to think of one leader in their home, church or school. Have them thank the person for some specific aspect of his or her leadership. For example, a person could thank the minister for his strength and support through her parents' divorce, or a person could thank a science teacher for her ability to make the information interesting and understandable.

2 CORINTHIANS 2:1-17 • FORGIVING THOSE WHO CAUSE PAIN

FOCUS
Forgiveness.

PREPARATION
Bring a Bible to the study. Ask someone from another church or a person unknown to the group to role play a parolee. Ask him to come prepared to

INSIGHT
Paul continues to tell why he did not visit Corinth when he had promised. The last time he visited to correct their spiritual abuses had been difficult. Apparently a particular person criticized the apostle during his visit. Such divisive behavior is really an attack on the whole church. The majority had punished this person. Paul forgives him and encourages the church to forgive and comfort him also. This forgiveness is based on Christ.

describe his crime, punishment and feelings about the incident. Let him read the study so he knows what to expect.

In this study, group members will meet a "parolee" and practice forgiveness.

BIBLE STUDY

1. Gather group members in a circle and ask them to join hands and clasp them tightly. Ask a volunteer to stand in the middle. Tell the volunteer his or her task is to escape the "prison walls." He or she has to break out of the circle. The others have to contain the "prisoner." Let several people try this. Ask:

● How did it feel to be the prisoner?
● What was it like to escape? remain trapped?
● How did it feel to be the prison and contain a person?
● How is revenge like a prison?
● How is forgiveness like escape?

2. Say: "In 2 Corinthians 2:1-17 Paul asks the Corinthians to forgive a person who had wronged him. Paul had forgiven the person, now it is their turn." Read the passage.

3. Tell the students that shortly a person who is out from prison on parole will visit the study. They will have an opportunity to ask him questions. Encourage them to ask questions such as:

● What crime did you commit?
● How do you feel about committing the crime?
● How is the situation going to be restored?
● What do you feel is the proper punishment?
● Do you think society will forgive you for committing the crime? Why or why not?
● How does this forgiveness (or lack of forgiveness) make you feel?

Allow time for students to think of other questions. Let them discuss some of their anxieties and concerns about the upcoming meeting.

4. Invite the visitor into your meeting room. Introduce the person and allow time for questions and answers.

5. Reread verses 5-11. Ask the guest and students how Paul's message of forgiveness relates to their discussion.

6. Ask the parolee for a prayer request. Close with a prayer circle focusing on the parolee and his needs.

ACTION

Ask students to think of people who are sometimes forgotten and excluded from society's forgiveness. For example, alcoholics, prisoners and street people. Choose a way to actively show Christ's love to these people. As a group offer to serve at the city's soup kitchen once a month. Collect blankets and money to donate to an organization that helps needy people in your community. Go to the local city jail or state prison. Ask a facility administrator how your group could help. You may be able to raise funds for equipment or some other need.

2 CORINTHIANS 3:1-18 • GOD'S RECOMMENDATION

FOCUS
Affirmation.

PREPARATION
Gather a Bible, pencils, crayons, paper and tape. Make an inkblot by folding a piece of paper in half. Open it and place a drop of ink on the crease. Refold the sheet so that the ink spreads. Open it and let it dry. Copy the sheet so each participant will have one. Make one copy of the qualification form for each person.

INSIGHT
Paul had been criticized for commending—or praising—himself. He says that this is not the case. His readers are his letter of recommendation. What's happened in their lives is a living letter of recommendation from Christ. This recommendation is not written in ink but with the Spirit of the living God.

In this study, group members will complete a qualification form and affirm their gifts and abilities.

BIBLE STUDY
1. As each person enters the room, tape a blank sheet of paper to his or her back and distribute crayons. Ask students to write on one another's paper things that qualify him or her to be a group member. For example, enthusiastic, outgoing and interested in people. Give group members time to write something on each person's paper. Let participants read these qualifications.

2. Distribute the "My Qualifications" handouts. Encourage participants to *brag*—write anything and everything they have to be proud of. Share some of these qualifications.

MY QUALIFICATIONS	
Instructions: Brag! Write anything and everything you have to be proud of.	
● Education:	● Honors:
● Work experience:	● Accomplishments:

Permission to photocopy this handout granted for local church use only. Copyright © 1988 by Dennis C. Benson. Published by Group Books, Inc., Box 481, Loveland, CO 80539.

3. Say: "In 2 Corinthians 3:1-18, Paul had been criticized once more. Some people said he was commending—or praising—himself." Read the passage.

4. Compare the passage to their list of qualifications. Ask:
- What would the Corinthians say about your list of qualifications?
- What would Paul say about it?
- What did Paul say in defense of the charge that he was commending himself?
- How can you balance being thankful for your gifts and being overly boastful about them?
- If your qualifications have been given by Christ, how should you feel about them?
- How does God's love shine through your life? Could you show God's love through some of your gifts? If so, how?
- How can you use these gifts to serve God?

5. Give each person an inkblot. Ask the members to look at their papers while you reread verse 3: "You show that you are a letter from Christ, the result of our ministry, written not with ink but with the Spirit of the living God, not on tablets of stone but on tablets of human hearts."

6. Explain, "Paul says the Corinthians are his letter of recommendation, not written with ink, but with the Spirit." Ask students to write one qualification (or gift) their inkblot reminds them of. For example, the ability to teach or the gift of friendliness.

7. Close by silently thanking God for blessing the members with their unique gifts.

ACTION

Ask students to take home their inkblot gift symbols. Ask each person to tape his or her symbol to a mirror or place it in a prominent position. Ask young people to act on their gifts sometime this week. A person could act on the gift of friendliness by welcoming a new neighbor. A person could act on the gift of teaching by helping a friend with homework.

2 CORINTHIANS 4:1-18 • *JARS OF CLAY*

FOCUS
Overwhelming times.

PREPARATION
Borrow a clay jug and plate. Bring a bottle of fruit juice and a loaf of unsliced bread. You also will need a handful of clay for each person, a Bible, a piece of posterboard and a marker.

INSIGHT
Paul says we are simple jars of clay afflicted by attacks but never overwhelmed. We share in Jesus' death, but we also share in Jesus' life. Our outer nature wastes away and our inner nature is renewed daily. Present sufferings prepare us for the glory to come.

In this study, group members will form clay symbols of overwhelming times.

BIBLE STUDY
1. Play a game that displays teenagers' imaginations called "This Is Not." Young people take turns holding a clay jug and completing this sentence: "This is not a clay jug, it is a . . ." Answers could be: an ashtray, a Tupperware container for leftovers, an ancient birdbath. When the clay jug gets back to you say: "This is not a clay jug. It is a symbol of 2 Corinthians 4:1-18 where Paul talks about 'jars of clay.'"

2. Ask students to close their eyes and listen as you read 2 Corinthians 4:1-18.

3. Ask young people to paraphrase what Paul says in the passage. Pass the clay jug to each person who contributes.

4. Let each of the young people think of an experience that at first seemed overwhelming, but proved they were stronger and rougher than expected. For example, a grandparent died and a person was able to support his mother through her grief.

5. Distribute the clay. Ask group members to mold the clay into a shape that represents their experience. Then let everyone describe his or her symbol. For example: "This square represents a firm, solid foundation. I was the foundation of support for my mom when her dad died."

6. Place the bread on the clay plate and fill the clay jug with juice. Place them in the center of the circle. Say: "Christ promises to be with us through all our hard times. We will never be defeated or overwhelmed, because he is always by our side. Although we are clay vessels during this lifetime, we will live with Christ forever." Share the bread and juice.

ACTION
Create a display in the narthex. Place the clay jug and plate in the center of a table. Arrange the clay symbols around them. Place a sign on the table

that says "We're earthen vessels, made to hold something special—God's love."

---

2 CORINTHIANS 5:1—6:13 • AMBASSADORS FOR CHRIST

FOCUS
Helping others.

PREPARATION
Bring a Bible, piece of posterboard and marker. Make a sign that says "Needed: Christians Who Care." Ask two young people to be reporters for a TV show. Assign each young person one of the case studies to read during the study. Set up a "news table" for the two reporters. On front of the table attach the sign.

INSIGHT
Paul says each body is like an earthly tent. If the tent is destroyed, God provides a building that is eternal.

The apostle understands why some believers groan and long to leave the earthly tent and enter the heavenly house prepared for them. The perspective of being in an eternal dwelling place fills us with courage while we are still in the body. Paul says what we do in the body is important.

If a person is in Christ, he or she is a new creation. The old way of looking at things has passed away; the new has come. Christ has forgiven us and does not count our sins against us. We are his ambassadors—to reach out and help others.

In this study, group members will create happy endings for a TV show called "Needed: Christians Who Care."

BIBLE STUDY

●*Case study 1:* The minister has been at a medium-size church for five years. During this time there has been friction. Some of the older "charter" members are unhappy about some of the new members who are former alcoholics, parents with handicapped children, and divorced people.

The "power" people are being forced into early retirement and resent the way the world is treating them. They yearn for "the good old days" when life was simpler. They are embarrassed when the minister talks about Christ and evangelism. In fact, after one sermon about evangelism, a member yelled at the minister, "I don't want the word 'evangelism' used again in church!"

The minister is extremely intelligent and has a deep, biblical faith. He wants the church to push into the community with the gospel.

The pinches of misunderstanding and disagreement keep growing. The power group has asked the minister to leave. If he leaves, 250 members will leave the church with him.

●*Case study 2:* The mill has been in this town for almost 100 years. The presence of smoke in the sky gives the people a sense of security. One citizen says, "When I see the sky filled with smoke, I know that times are prosperous."

Three generations of people have worked in the mile-long sprawl of buildings. The company's motto always has been, "Enter the personnel office the week after high school, and you will have a place in the company when you're 62 years old."

The new chairman of the board recently told the union that if the workers wouldn't give up benefits, the mill would close. But the workers will not give up any more benefits.

The board retaliated by announcing that the plant will be permanently closed as of Monday.

They will tear down the buildings.

The town will become a ghost town.

Unemployment will soar to twice as high as the rest of the state.

1. Gather group members in front of the table. Say: "You are viewers of a TV show called 'Needed: Christians Who Care.' Let's turn on the show and watch for a while. Lights! Camera! Action!"

2. Ask a young person to read the first case study reporter style. After he or she finishes say: "We interrupt this broadcast to find Christians who care. Viewers? What we need is a reconciliation team to bring peace to this situation. What would you do in this situation?" Let group members think of ways to solve the disagreements.

3. Repeat the process with the second case study. Let the young people decide how they would bring peace and reconciliation to that situation.

4. Read 2 Corinthians 5:1—6:13. Emphasize 2 Corinthians 5:20: "We are therefore Christ's ambassadors, as though God were making an appeal through us. We implore you on Christ's behalf: Be reconciled to God." Ask:

●What does it mean to be an ambassador for Christ?

●How were you ambassadors when you tried to find alternative endings to the case studies?

●How can you be an ambassador today?

●Have you recently been an ambassador? Have you helped someone see an alternative that helped both sides concerned? If so, explain the situation.

5. Divide into groups of twos or threes. Tell the young people they are writers for TV commercials. They are to advertise their youth group as "Christians Who Care." For example: "Our Savior Youth Group. Kind. Caring. Fun. Friendly. Want someone to listen? Give us a call." Allow time for each small group to perform its commercial.

ACTION

Schedule the commercials for a few consecutive Sunday worships during announcement time.

2 CORINTHIANS 6:14—7:1 • MISMATCHING

FOCUS
Dating and marriage.

PREPARATION
Gather a Bible, pencil and three copies of the questionnaire for each student.

INSIGHT
Paul's defense of his ministry and talk about reconciliation seem to be interrupted with thoughts on relationships with pagans.

Paul tells the Corinthians not to mate with unbelievers. They shouldn't bring together things that don't belong together. Christ can't be joined with Satan. The temple of God has no relationship with idols.

In this study, group members will compare criteria for dates with criteria for marriage partners.

BIBLE STUDY

1. Ask group members to each take off one shoe and throw it in a pile at one end of the room. Form two teams. Have a race to see which team can ''re-shoe'' its members first. On ''Go,'' the first person in each line runs to the pile, finds his or her shoe, puts it on, ties it, runs back to the line, tags the next person, and so on.

2. After the race say: ''Just as we tried to find the right match for our shoes, we want to find the right match for a lifetime mate. Listen to what Paul says in 2 Corinthians 6:14—7:1.'' Read the passage.

3. Distribute a pencil and one ''Dating Preference'' handout. Ask the students to fill out the questionnaire without much reflection. The first response that enters their minds is the best indicator of their values.

4. Discuss the answers:

● Do you and your family agree with these choices? Why or why not?

● Which of your values differ from your parents'? Which are similar?

5. Distribute another copy of the questionnaire. Tell group members to rank each item according to this scale: 1 = would love to marry this person; 5 = would never marry this person.

6. Discuss the answers:

● Is there a difference between dating a non-believer and marrying him or her? Explain.

● Has the church's view changed since Paul's day? Why or why not?

● What dating guidelines can you give? (For example, "Listen to your parents" or "Don't get serious with a person of another faith.")

7. Close with a silent guided prayer. Say the following open-ended statements, allowing a few moments of silence after each:

● Help us do these things, Lord . . .

● Forgive us for these sins, Lord . . .

● Thank you for these gifts, Lord . . .

ACTION

Give the teenagers each another copy of the questionnaire. Ask them to have their parents (or brothers and/or sisters) take it. Compare the answers and be ready for some enlightening discussions.

DATING PREFERENCE

Instructions: Rank the following criteria according to this scale:
1 = would love to date him or her; 5 = would never date him or her.

	Would Love to Date				Would Never Date
Same race	1	2	3	4	5
Different race	1	2	3	4	5
Same religion	1	2	3	4	5
Different religion	1	2	3	4	5
Catholic	1	2	3	4	5
Protestant	1	2	3	4	5
Moslem	1	2	3	4	5
Hindu	1	2	3	4	5
Non-religious	1	2	3	4	5
Jewish	1	2	3	4	5
Same social class	1	2	3	4	5
Richer	1	2	3	4	5
Poorer	1	2	3	4	5
Same education	1	2	3	4	5
Better education	1	2	3	4	5
Less education	1	2	3	4	5
Uses drugs	1	2	3	4	5
Drinks alcohol	1	2	3	4	5
Smokes	1	2	3	4	5
Has a bad reputation	1	2	3	4	5
Parents are divorced	1	2	3	4	5

2 CORINTHIANS 7:2-16 • GODLY GRIEF

FOCUS
Criticism.

PREPARATION
Collect a pencil and two newspaper comic strips for each person. Choose comic strips that show people arguing. (For example, a Peanuts cartoon with Lucy shouting at Charlie Brown.) Use typing correction fluid to white out the conversation balloons. You also will need a Bible and several comic books.

INSIGHT
Paul is glad that his earlier tough letter drove the Corinthians to repentance. Their repentance proves they felt a godly grief. Paul rejoices because he has full, perfect confidence in the Corinthians.

In this study, group members will use comic strips to tell about a time they dealt with criticism.

BIBLE STUDY
1. Gather in a circle and distribute the comic books. Ask teenagers to thumb through them and choose one cartoon that symbolizes some aspect of their past week. A person could choose Superman and say: "My past week was so hectic. I had to be a Superman to get everything done."

2. Distribute a pencil and one comic strip to each person. Ask students to think of a time they were confronted by tough criticism from someone important. Ask them to write the dialogue in the conversation balloons.

3. Give participants a chance to share their comic strips and stories. Ask:
- How did you feel when you were criticized?
- How did the criticism affect your relationship with the critic?
- Is criticism easier to take if you feel it's deserved? Why or why not?

4. Give group members each another comic strip. Ask them to think of a time they had to confront someone else with tough criticism. Ask them to fill in the conversation balloons with the criticism.

5. Discuss the comic strips and the stories. Ask:
- Was it different to criticize someone else? Why or why not?
- How did the person react?
- Did this honest confrontation help the other person? Explain.
- Why is it difficult to confront a person?
- Do people react to criticism differently? Explain.
- How should we handle different reactions?
- What guidelines should we use when confronting others? (For example, confront out of kindness and concern.)
- What guidelines should we use when we are confronted with criticism

by others? (For example, listen to the criticism and see if there is a grain of truth to it.)

6. Read 2 Corinthians 7:2-16. Ask:

●How did Paul criticize the Corinthians?

●How did the Corinthians react? Did they feel they deserved the criticism? Explain.

●How does this passage help us deal with criticism? with confronting others?

7. Gather in a circle. Place all comic strips in the center. Pray for the ability to take and give constructive criticism and the ability to know when it is better to remain silent.

ACTION

Ask teenagers to think of one problem they'd like to confront at home, church or school. Ask them to think of a creative solution to the problem. A person's family may seem too busy to eat dinner together. The person could invite family members to a meal at a certain time and place. He or she could bring up the concern then discuss ways to hold each other accountable for regular meals as a family.

2 CORINTHIANS 8:1-24 • RELIEF OF THE SAINTS

FOCUS

Response to God's grace.

PREPARATION

Bring four charity posters that make an appeal for funds. Choose one with a starving or crippled child. Divide the passage into these four sections: 1-7; 8-15; 16-21; 22-24. Write each section on the back of each poster. Ask four young people to read the passage.

Gather a marker and a

INSIGHT

Paul does some serious work on stewardship. He reminds the Corinthians that although the churches of Macedonia had been faced with affliction, they gave with great generosity to the relief fund for Jerusalem. In fact, the Macedonians begged to participate in the relief fund.

Paul says the Corinthians have excelled in faith, speech and knowledge, so now they should excel in being generous. He doesn't command them to give to this fund; he invites them to respond to God's grace. Though Jesus was rich, he became poor that we might become rich.

In this study, group members will view charity posters and discuss stewardship.

piece of posterboard for each student. Bring one packet of material used by your church at its last stewardship appeal. You also will need two milk bottles (or containers with small openings) and 40 pennies.

BIBLE STUDY

1. Divide the group members into two teams. Give each team one milk bottle and 20 pennies. Ask one person on each team to be the counter and another person on each team to be the timer. Team members stand by the bottle one at a time and try to drop pennies into the container. The timer gives each person 30 seconds, and the counter counts the pennies that land in the container. The participants must stand straight and drop the pennies from waist level.

2. Introduce the session by saying: "You've just had a chance to see what we do with money. Sometimes we have a target. We know what items we want to buy, and we try to save enough money to purchase them. Other times we throw money away. During the study, we're going to talk about the charity appeals of Paul's time and the charity appeals of today."

3. Ask the four readers each to stand and hold their charity poster. Ask:
- Which of these charities would you donate money to? Why?
- Which poster appeals most to your pity?
- What else do you feel when you look at the posters?
- Is using guilt a good, effective way to motivate people to give? Why or why not?

4. Ask the four volunteers to read the passage. Ask group members to contrast Paul's message to the posters' appeals. Say: "Paul bases his message on the need for each person to respond with generosity to God's love. This is a different approach from today's posters. Paul didn't say: 'Give to the needy in Jerusalem. The Jerusalem believers are starving. They are wearing ragged, torn clothing. They have no shelter over their heads.' Paul just said to give as a response to God's grace. Jesus was rich, yet he freely became poor for our sake. We should do likewise."

5. Give each person a marker and a piece of posterboard. Ask students to design posters for Paul's request. Stimulate their creativity by asking questions such as:

● What pictures would Paul use to illustrate the need at Jerusalem? Would he use pictures of starving Jerusalem Christians? Would he use a picture of Christ? Would he use any pictures at all?

● What words would Paul use to raise funds? Would he describe the plight of the poverty-stricken Christians? Would he describe his response to God's grace?

6. Give group members a while to design their posters, then let them describe them to each other.

7. Bring out the stewardship packet. Ask:

● How is our stewardship material like Paul's message?

● Do we stress response to God's grace? Explain.

● Do we stress the poverty-stricken aspects of our church community? Explain.

● How would Paul revise our stewardship materials?

8. Ask students to analyze their time, talents and income. Say: "Tithing means giving 10 percent of these things. Even if you don't have any income, you still have time and talent to tithe. Choose one gift you'd like to give to the church."

9. Close with a silent prayer. Ask group members to join hands. Pray, "Lord, we give these gifts to you as a response to your love and grace . . ." Let each person silently say his or her gift.

ACTION

Ask group members to act on their tithes. If they can donate time, have them offer to type a Sunday bulletin or cook a meal for a grieving family. If young people have talent to donate, have them offer to play an instrument at a worship service, sing at a nursing home or lead games at a nursery school.

2 CORINTHIANS 9:1-15 • ABUNDANT BLESSING

FOCUS
Giving.

PREPARATION
Buy boxes of individually wrapped Ding Dongs (or other packaged goodies). Gather Bibles, four dozen napkins and several nice serving trays. (Bring extra Ding Dongs to give to your group members at the end of the study.) Arrange for transportation to and from an airport, bus station or mall—any area with many people.

INSIGHT
Paul continues to persuade the Corinthians to contribute to the church at Jerusalem. He doesn't want to be embarrassed by their failure to have the gift ready. God loves a generous giver. Those who sow (or invest) the most bear the greatest harvest. Generosity enriches the giver and glorifies God.

In this study, group members will give gifts to unsuspecting people.

BIBLE STUDY
1. Gather at your regular meeting place. Divide into small groups and assign each one to ride in an available vehicle. Go to the pre-arranged location. A certain excitement and fear will develop as you leave your usual setting.

2. On the way to the site, have someone in each car read 2 Corinthians 9:1-15. Talk about the blessings of generosity.

3. Once you arrive at the site, divide into small groups. Give each group a tray with napkins and several goodies on it. Tell the participants their mission is to give the goodies to strangers. They are to engage the strangers in conversation and ask them how they feel about receiving something for nothing.

4. After about 20 minutes, gather the students to discuss their experiences. Ask:

● What reactions did you receive when you tried to give something nice to another person?

● How did you feel when people would not accept your generosity? Did you feel they rejected you as well as your gift? Explain.

● How did you feel when people accepted your gift?

5. Reread 2 Corinthians 9:6-8: "Remember this: Whoever sows sparingly will also reap sparingly, and whoever sows generously will also reap generously. Each man should give what he has decided in his heart to give, not reluctantly or under compulsion, for God loves a cheerful giver. And God is able to make all grace abound to you, so that in all things at all times, having all that you need, you will abound in every good work."

6. Ask participants to describe how these verses apply to their experience. As young people are sharing, give out the goodies for them to eat. Say: "You have given generously, so now you will receive generously. Eat and be merry."

7. Travel back to your regular meeting area.

ACTION

Have young people perform this same act of generosity for the church members one Sunday morning. Group members buy goodies for the church members using their own donations or using money from their youth group fund. Afterward, let students compare church people's reactions with the ones they received at the public place.

---

2 CORINTHIANS 10:1-18 • *IT'S EASY TO BE HARD*

FOCUS

Strength and gentleness.

PREPARATION

Gather a Bible, newsprint, tape, markers, scissors, construction paper, two hats and 28 to 30 slips of paper. Bring newsprint (enough so each person can have a life-size drawing of himself or herself). Draw a life-size outline of a human being on a large piece of newsprint. Tape it to the wall.

Write the following body parts or pieces of clothing on separate slips of paper: hat, head, face, ears, neck, arms, hands, body, legs, feet, huge bow tie, beard. Make two sets. Place one set in each hat.

Tape two pieces of blank newsprint to a wall. Place a hat and a marker by each

INSIGHT

Paul returns to his critical comments. The apostle responds to an apparent accusation that his humbleness is a lack of boldness. He begs them not to do something to provoke his harsh side when he is among them.

Paul says that he is a bit uncomfortable with having to boast about his authority from Christ; yet he will not be weak. Paul claims some people say that his letters are strong, but that he is weak in person. He can boast about his ministry because he boasts in the Lord.

In this study, group members will trace their bodies on newsprint and define a strong personal quality.

BIBLE STUDY

1. Divide into two groups. Assign a piece of newsprint to each group. Say: "In each hat are separate slips of paper. On 'Go,' the first person in each line will run to the hat, pull a slip of paper from it, draw the item on the newsprint, run back to the line and tag the next person, who will repeat the process. The first team to complete the drawing wins." As a finishing touch, have each group name its

87

piece of newsprint.

———————————————

drawing, think of a description of the person and introduce him or her to the class.

2. Point to the life-size drawing of a human being. Ask the students to suggest qualities that make us strong. For example, the ability to speak out, the ability to lift heavy weights and the ability to remain calm under stress. List those qualities on one half of the sheet.

3. Read 2 Corinthians 10:1-18. Ask:

● What were the Corinthians complaining about Paul?

● What is their definition of strength?

● Do some of their definitions apply to us today? Explain.

4. Say: "The Corinthians complained that Paul was gentle and nice when he was with them but harsh in his letters. They complained that he was weak and boasted with empty phrases. Paul tries to explain that we can boast only in the Lord. He says we must be strong but also imitate Christ's meekness and gentleness." Ask:

● What is Paul's definition of gentleness? humbleness?

● What is your definition of gentleness? (Write these ideas on the second half of the newsprint. Ideas could be sensitive, caring and ability to listen to others.)

● Is it possible for a person to be gentle yet strong? Explain.

● To survive as a Christian in today's world, what strong characteristics do we need? gentle characteristics?

5. Divide the group in pairs. Give each pair two life-size sheets of newsprint and two markers. Have partners trace each other on the newsprint. Ask group members to write on their posters the strong and gentle characteristics they want to develop in their lives.

6. Gather in a circle and ask participants to hold up their posters. (Alternate—participant, poster, participant, poster—so all the posters are visible.) Close with a prayer asking God for the endurance it takes to be a Christian and for the ability to develop strong and gentle characteristics.

ACTION

Distribute construction paper and scissors. Ask group members to make a symbol of a characteristic they want to develop this week. A person could cut out a heart from red construction paper to symbolize forgiving a friend. A person could cut out a hand to symbolize putting a little effort into meeting a new person at school. Have young people tape their symbols to their posters and take them home as reminders to develop those characteristics this week.

2 CORINTHIANS 11:1—12:21 • STRENGTH IN WEAKNESS

FOCUS
Paul's legacy.

PREPARATION
Write the trials of Paul (listed in the "Insight" section) on separate slips of paper. Gather a Bible and writing materials.

INSIGHT
Paul continues to defend his ministry. His opponents in Corinth have a hold on some of the people. He must continually struggle to win them. Paul is placed in the difficult position of having to brag about his work. He knows that boasting is wrong, but he needs to strengthen his status as an apostle.

He lists the price he has paid to bring them his ministry: hard work, numerous imprisonments, countless beatings, close to death, five whippings, three beatings with rods, stoning, three shipwrecks, adrift at sea, dangerous river journeys, persecution from everyone, hunger and thirst.

Paul recalls an experience he had 14 years earlier on the road to Damascus. This experience gave him knowledge and changed his life. He apologizes for his need to boast of such an experience.

He tells his readers he was given a thorn in his flesh to keep him humble after such a blessing. We are not sure what this physical impediment is. He said that three times he asked the Lord to deliver him from this burden. He was not healed, but he was blessed with the strength to do his ministry.

In this study, group members will receive a legacy from Paul.

BIBLE STUDY

1. Tell the young people you are pleased to inform them of some great news. You have learned that they are blood relatives of Paul. He is a family member, an actual ancestor. He has left a legacy for them. Read portions of the letter Paul left for his kin (2 Corinthians 11—12).

2. Ask the students to give their initial reactions to the idea that Paul is a blood relative.

3. Distribute the slips of paper so each person has one of the trials faced by his or her relative. Say, "To inherit Paul's legacy, you must face a trial similar to the one written on the slip of paper you are holding."

Divide into small groups and let young people discuss their trials. Ask them to think of Paul and how he had to face those trials. Then have them think of a similar trial they could face today. For example, we may not be beaten physically, but our emotions may take a beating when friends ignore us because of our faith.

4. Distribute writing materials. Ask participants to write Paul a thank-you note for the trial he faced. For example, "Thanks, Paul, for showing me it is possible to suffer and still have a good attitude.''

5. Close by asking young people to read their thank-you notes.

ACTION

Publish the thank-you notes in the church newsletter, or arrange to have students read them during a Sunday morning worship service. Ask young people each to think of a person in their family or church who has helped them grow in the faith. Ask young people to write a thank-you note to that person.

---

2 CORINTHIANS 13:1-14 • EXAMINING FAITH

FOCUS
Tests.

PREPARATION
Gather one sticky gold star (like Sunday school teachers use), a pencil and two copies of the handout for each person. Also bring a Bible.

INSIGHT
Paul invites the readers to examine themselves to see whether they are holding to the faith. He bids them farewell by asking them to aim for perfection, listen to his appeals, agree with one another and live in peace.

In this study, group members will discuss tests they take in their lives and decide an area of their faith they'd like to develop.

BIBLE STUDY
1. Play games that test balance, speed and teamwork. Divide into teams. Ask members to close their eyes. On ''Go,'' they form a line from the oldest to youngest person and stand on one leg. First team done wins. No peeking! Another test is teams line up according to birthdays—no talking allowed. First team done wins.

TEST

Instructions: Choose one way we are tested today such as drivers license tests or school exams. List skills needed to pass the test.

_____
(Name)

Skills needed to pass:
1.
2.
3.
4.
5.

---

2. Say: "The games we played tested our balance, speed and team-work. Paul encourages the Corinthians to test themselves to see if they are faithful." Read 2 Corinthians 13:1-14.

3. Ask teenagers how we are tested today. For example, drivers license tests, dental exams, physicals, school exams, blood tests for marriage, psychological tests and eye tests.

4. Distribute one "Test" handout and a pencil to each person. Ask the students to choose one way we are tested today and list the skills necessary to pass that test. For example, to pass a drivers test a person needs to demonstrate an ability to drive safely, meet an age requirement and display a knowledge of the rules.

5. Allow time for group members to discuss the tests and necessary skills. Ask:

- How hard are some of the tests?
- Which of the tests have you experienced?
- How well did you do?
- Did you know that you were doing well during the test? Explain.
- If you failed, did you hesitate to tell others? Explain.

6. Say: "In 2 Corinthians 13, Paul doesn't explain how the Corinthians should test themselves. We're going to think of certain aspects or skills that tell us whether we're really following Christ."

7. Distribute another "Test" handout to each person. Ask group members to label the test "Following Christ." Have them list aspects or skills needed to pass the test. For example, daily devotions, quiet time and reaching out to others.

8. Discuss their listings. Ask:
- How well would you do on this faith-building test?
- What aspects are difficult? easy?
- What happens when you fail in one of these areas?
- What is Christ's role in our test of faith?

9. Say: "Tests in our lives show us areas we can improve. We always can improve certain areas of our faith. We can increase our daily devotion time, concentrate on serving others or attend worship. It's good to take an honest look at our faith and discover areas to improve so we can grow spiritually. Thanks be to God, grace is what saves us—not our works or anything we do. In God's grade book, we each receive an 'A+' because of Christ."

Go to each person and place a gold star on his or her hand and say, "You're a star in God's eyes."

ACTION

Ask group members to think about areas of their faith they'd like to develop. Have them choose one area and develop a lesson plan for improvement. A person could choose to change a complaining attitude to a thankful one. She could decide to start each day with a prayer of thanksgiving for all the blessings God has given her. Ask young people each to choose a partner and hold each other accountable to their lesson plans.

INTRODUCTION TO GALATIANS

The man aches. His body throbs from the brutalizing torture of burns and bruises. It won't be long now; his life is flickering away. As a political prisoner in a Central American jail, he can only suffer his physical pain and draw upon the memories of his loved ones. Juan needs this Epistle's message.

The depressed man paces the floor of his small room. Two years earlier, he had been forced to retire. Though healthy and able, he had been shoved out of his job so a young man could do the work cheaper. George needs this Epistle's message.

What these challenged Christians need is the timeless message of Paul's letter to the Galatians. This startling presentation of the freedom won for us in Christ shatters the world's demeaning values and evil practices.

Every Christian who has been oppressed by slavery, racial persecution, sexual or age bias can read Paul's letter to the Galatian church and receive hope and understanding. Indeed, every oppressor or persecutor is in need of the gospel as it is presented in this book. Christ has forged a kinship that heals all alienation between humans in different social and spiritual states. The family of God does not judge others according to race, age, sex, class or nationality.

In this letter, Paul offers the foundation for all Christian freedom: grace. We can't earn salvation by law or acts of piety. We are freed through the cross.

Galatians is sometimes referred to as the Magna Charta for Christian freedom. Believers are set free to let Christ live within them. Paul is facing a spreading blaze of false teaching within the Galatian church. These misled Christians are seeking a means of earning God's acceptance.

This letter has a contemporary ring to it. We are the Galatians. We want to earn God's acceptance and forgiveness. Galatians, with its message of hope, is for us.

GALATIANS 1:1-24 • THE CHRISTIAN MAGNA CHARTA

FOCUS
Freedom in Christ.

PREPARATION
Gather several strips of material to tie partners' ankles together. Gather a marker, a volleyball and net, newsprint, paper, pencils, Bibles, several water balloons and a squawker balloon. (A squawker balloon makes a loud noise as air escapes from it. You can purchase one at a party supply store.) Burn the edges of a piece of newsprint so it looks like an ancient piece of paper.

INSIGHT
Paul addresses the claim that a true apostle is one who has seen Jesus in the flesh. Paul believes he was called by Jesus on his Damascus road experience (Acts 9:3-6). The apostle often refers to his dramatic calling and believes God called him before his birth.

The apostle acknowledges his roots are Judaic. His reference to this heritage may indicate his opponents' character. They know about his former life as a hunter and abuser of Christians. The change in his life was based on God's work, not the others' arguments. He did not need to seek the blessing of the apostles in Jerusalem or other human agents. Cephas (Peter) was the apostle with whom he consulted during his short visit to Jerusalem.

In this study, group members will prepare a Magna Charta of Christian freedom.

BIBLE STUDY
1. Open the study by playing volleyball variations. Play with a squawker balloon instead of a ball, or gather outside (weather permitting) and play water-balloon volleyball. Another variation is to play partner volleyball. Each team consists of partners whose ankles are tied together. Play with a regular volleyball.

2. Untie the partners and discuss how nice it is to be able to move about freely. Say: "Galatians is sometimes referred to as a letter of freedom for Christians—the Magna Charta of Christian liberty. The Magna Charta is a charter that guaranteed civil and political freedom. It was written in 1215 by King John of England. We're going to look through Galatians' six chapters and discover some of the 'freeing' points mentioned by Paul. We're going to prepare our own Christian Magna Charta."

3. Divide into small groups. Assign each small group one chapter of Galatians. Give each group paper, pencils and a Bible.

Ask the groups to list some of Paul's points of freedom mentioned in their assigned chapter. A freeing point in the third chapter is verse 11: "Clearly no one is justified before God by the law, because, 'The righteous will live by faith.'"

4. Gather the groups and discuss their findings. Bring out the newsprint with burnt edges. Title it "The Christian Magna Charta." List the small groups' findings on the newsprint. Let each group member sign his or her name to the finished product.

5. Close by asking the kids to find their volleyball partners. Ask the young people to choose one freeing point on the Charta that means most to them and explain their choice to their partners. Have partners pray together after they share.

ACTION

Post "The Christian Magna Charta" in the sanctuary. Let congregation members discover freeing points of Paul's message. Prepare a devotion sheet for congregational members and insert it in the bulletin. It could look like this:

GALATIANS: THE CHRISTIAN MAGNA CHARTA

Instructions: The Magna Charta is a charter of freedom. What freeing points does Paul tell us in Galatians? List the freeing points you find in each of these chapters.

Chapter 1:

Chapter 2:

Chapter 3:

Chapter 4:

Chapter 5:

Chapter 6:

Permission to photocopy this handout granted for local church use only. Copyright © 1988 by Dennis C. Benson. Published by Group Books, Inc., Box 481, Loveland, CO 80539.

GALATIANS 2:1-21 • CRUCIFIED WITH CHRIST

FOCUS
Worship.

PREPARATION
Gather carrots, pencils, posterboard, songbooks, scissors, markers, 3x5 cards, newspaper, tape, nails, Bibles, bread, fruit, a hammer and two boards. Prepare a rugged cross by nailing together the two boards.

INSIGHT
Paul indicates that a long time had passed since his last visit to Jerusalem. He was accompanied by Barnabas and a Greek, Titus. He met privately with the Jerusalem leaders so they might understand his long and consistent ministry to the Gentiles—the non-Jews.

The apostle notes the leaders didn't require Titus to undergo circumcision as was the practice when a non-Jew became a Christian. This concession reflects their acceptance of Paul's ministry to the Gentiles. He tells of how Cephas (Peter) visited Antioch and ate with Gentiles but withdrew from them when those who favored circumcision came. Paul spoke publicly against this hypocritical action. Peter had not followed the inclusive truth of the gospel.

Paul affirms faith in Christ. A former master of the law, he rejects that salvation comes through following rules or acting a certain way. He has died to the law and now lives through Christ's crucifixion. Salvation is God's freely given, unearned gift to us.

In this study, group members will prepare a worship service based on the passage.

BIBLE STUDY

1. Open with a crowdbreaker called "Pass the Carrot" from *Quick Crowdbreakers and Games for Youth Groups* (Group Books). Divide into teams. Place a carrot between the knees of the first person in each line. On "Go," have team members pass the carrot to the end of their line then back to the front. No hands allowed. Award a fresh carrot to each person.

2. Let the kids munch on their carrots while you read Galatians 2:1-21. Say: "Carrots supposedly improve your sight. So eat your carrots while I read the chapter. Try to 'see' what Paul is telling the Galatians."

3. After you read the chapter, ask kids to list the main points. For example, acceptance, forgiveness, love, grace and unity in Christ.

4. Divide into small groups. Ask each group to prepare a segment of a worship service. The service must focus on the chapter's main points. Following are examples of worship segments and ideas from *Creative Worship in Youth Ministry* (Group Books).

• *The call to worship:* Cut footprints from posterboard. On each footprint, list one word of a key verse in the passage. Tape the footprints to the floor or hallway leading into the worship area.

● *Prayer:* Intercede for people all over the world—for Christians as well as non-Christians. Make a giant newspaper by taping together the edges of full sheets of newspaper. Tape both sides of the paper so it doesn't rip. Gather worshipers around the edge of the giant newspaper. Ask each group member to find a person or situation "in the news" and pray for God's intercession and help.

● *Music:* Choose songs about love such as "Love" or songs about the cross such as "Onward Christian Soldiers" from *Songs* (Songs and Creations). Ask members to play the guitar or piano.

● *Sermon:* Choose several volunteers to read the passage, or choose one volunteer to role play Paul speaking to the Galatians.

● *Offering:* Distribute 3x5 cards, pencils, nails and a hammer. Ask worshipers to think of what it means to be crucified with Christ. Have members each write one sin for which they need forgiveness on one side of their card. On the other side, have them write one gift they want to give God. Let kids nail their cards to the cross.

5. Participate in the worship after the small groups have prepared their segments. Conclude with a love feast of bread and fruit.

ACTION

Invite another church's youth group to your next meeting. Ask the kids to lead the worship service. Celebrate the groups' unity in Christ.

GALATIANS 3:1-29 • LAW AND FAITH

FOCUS
Rules.

PREPARATION
Gather a roll of toilet paper, a doll, a Bible and several board games.

INSIGHT
Paul realizes his opponents know the Old Testament well, so he bases many of his thoughts on Old Testament quotations and arguments. He says people are acceptable to God through their faith rather than through the things they do or the laws they keep.

The apostle depicts the law existing until Abraham's heir (Christ) came. The law was never against God. In fact, the law was a custodian—or babysitter—until Christ's coming. Now that Christ has come, the law is no longer our guardian. Since we are justified through faith in Christ, we are now God's heirs.

In this study, group members will discuss the purpose of rules and why we follow them.

BIBLE STUDY

1. Gather kids in a circle and play a get-to-know-you game. Pass around a roll of toilet paper, and ask kids each to tear off as much paper as they need to blow their nose. Once they have a strip of toilet paper, let each person say one thing about himself or herself for each square. For example, a person who tore off four squares could say four things such as "I like fried chicken and corn on the cob," "I enjoy reading mysteries," "My cat is at the vet" and "My cousin graduated from college." If your youth group is large, play this get-to-know-you game in small groups.

2. Say: "Now that we've gotten to know each other better, we're going to get to know the apostle Paul better. Paul was angry with the Galatians. He starts his third chapter with angry words. Listen." Read Galatians 3:1-5. After each sentence, have group members each hit the palm of their hand with a fist. This will help kids experience the emotional impact of Paul's words.

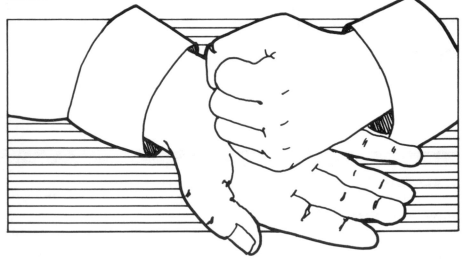

3. Say, "Paul was trying to tell the Galatians that people are acceptable to God through their faith rather than through the things they do or the laws they keep." Ask:

- What emotions did you feel as I read these verses?
- How do you think Paul felt?
- How important is the law?
- How important is faith?

4. Say, "Paul said the law existed as a custodian—or babysitter—until Christ came." Read Galatians 3:6-29. Ask:

●Why would we need a babysitter until Christ came?

●What roles do babysitters play? (For example, "Babysitters give guidance as to what's right and wrong.")

5. Pass a doll around the circle. Encourage kids to imagine they are babysitters for the child. Ask:

●What rules (or laws) would you issue to ensure the child's safety? (For example, "Don't put your finger in the electric socket," "Don't touch the hot oven" and "Don't put anything in your mouth.")

●What rules do parents enforce to ensure their children's safety?

●When do children no longer need a babysitter's rules? a parent's rules?

●If Christ frees us from the law, are rules still necessary? Why or why not?

●Do you ever reach a certain age when you don't need any more rules? Explain.

6. Say: "There is a balance between not following any rules and totally following all rules. Rules are given to us as guidelines. We can still follow them because they point us in the right direction. They make us aware of sin. We need to remember we aren't saved by how well we keep the rules; we are saved through Christ, through faith."

7. Close by having a game time. Play an assortment of board games and encourage kids to follow the rules!

ACTION

Further develop the theme of "custodian" or "babysitter." Ask kids to be a mentor to a younger person for a six-month period. Connect one high schooler with one elementary-age child. Encourage the high schooler to pray daily for the child, call him or her once a week, and plan an activity to do with him or her once a month (such as go out for a Coke, go bowling or attend a school play).

GALATIANS 4:1-31 • CHILDREN OF PROMISE

FOCUS
Our inheritance.

PREPARATION
Gather Bibles, markers, scraps of material, con-

INSIGHT
Paul explains that through God we are no longer slaves; we are God's children and heirs. Paul is concerned about the Galatians turning back to the pagan gods in their past. How can they do this? Paul feels his work has been for nothing.

struction paper, marshmallows, toothpicks, yarn, buttons, pipe cleaners, and one potato for each person.

Paul shifts from this discussion to his personal feelings about the Galatian church. They cared for the apostle during his illness. The nature of his illness isn't clear. Some people believe Paul had eye trouble since he refers to eyes in verse 15: "If you could have done so, you would have torn out your eyes and given them to me." Whatever his illness, Paul is grateful for their care and hospitality.

Paul talks to the Galatians as their father in Christ. He says we all are children of promise. We are like Isaac, not like Hagar's son who was born according to the flesh. We will inherit eternal life because of our faith in God's promise.

In this study, group members will create a symbol of inheritance out of potatoes and scraps of material.

BIBLE STUDY

1. Play a "sticky" relay race called "Porky-Mallow" from *Quick Crowdbreakers and Games for Youth Groups* (Group Books). Divide group members into two teams. Give each person a toothpick and each team a marshmallow. The first player for each team puts the marshmallow on his or her toothpick and the toothpick between his or her teeth. The rest of the team members place their toothpicks between their teeth. The object of the game is to be the first team finished passing the marshmallow to the end of the line. One catch: After each person passes the marshmallow, he or she must leave his or her toothpick in it. The last person in line faces an extremely sticky situation!

2. Say: "Paul faces a sticky situation. He has to reprimand the Galatians for their spiritual immaturity. He wants them to stay away from their old, elementary religious practices. The Galatians are no longer slaves. They are God's children, God's heirs."

3. Let each person read one verse of the passage. Ask:

● What does Paul mean when he refers to heirs? slaves? law? promise? inheritance?

● What does it mean to be a child of promise?

● What do we, as God's heirs, inherit?

4. Distribute a potato to each person. Show kids the scraps of material, pipe cleaners, buttons, yarn, markers, toothpicks and construction paper. Encourage them to design a child of promise—a person who will inherit eternal life. Ask them to be prepared to explain their child of promise to a partner. For example, a person could attach yellow yarn to the top of the potato, draw a face on it, attach pipe cleaners for hands and feet. The person could say: "This is my child of promise. His arms and legs allow him freedom to do God's will. His yellow hair will be even brighter when he inherits eternal life and is in heaven among the angels.''

5. Divide in pairs; explain the creations.

6. Roast the marshmallows left from the opening relay. Close with a prayer. Praise God for making us heirs; thank God for support during life's sticky situations.

ACTION

Ask group members to take their children-of-promise potatoes home. Encourage them to read a portion of Galatians 4 each day. Have them offer a daily prayer thanking God for our inheritance.

GALATIANS 5:1-26 • FRUIT OF THE SPIRIT

FOCUS

Christian freedom.

PREPARATION

Gather a Bible, plastic wrap, bows or ribbons, butter, knives, fruit jelly, aprons, and all the ingredients and utensils needed to bake bread.

Ask a cook in your congregation to help you with the study. Ask him or her to talk about the effects of yeast and to guide your class in preparing bread. Prepare enough dough for one loaf ahead of time. At the beginning of the study, place the prepared loaf in the oven. By the time the study is finished, the bread will be baked and ready to eat.

INSIGHT

Paul affirms that believers are free in Christ. He urges the Galatians to refrain from falling back under the yoke of legalistic slavery. The apostle condemns circumcision. He wishes those who demand this rite for salvation would completely mutilate themselves. Faith in Christ, working through love, is the only way to salvation.

Paul compares evil in their midst to leaven, or yeast. A small amount affects the entire loaf. The apostle warns that our human nature is at war with our spiritual side. The desires of the flesh are against the Spirit; the desires of the Spirit are against the flesh. Paul contrasts the works of the flesh to the fruit of the Spirit.

In this study, group members will bake bread and discuss the fruit of the Spirit.

BIBLE STUDY

1. Gather the kids in the kitchen. Give everyone an apron to wear. Introduce the cook. Have him or her explain how yeast works—how a little bit affects the whole loaf.

2. Divide into small groups. Give each small group the ingredients and utensils necessary to prepare bread dough. Ask the cook to guide the preparations.

3. When kids are through mixing and kneading and are allowing their dough to rise, read Galatians 5:1-26. Ask:
- How does yeast affect a lump of dough?
- How can a small amount of evil cause a large amount of damage?
- How can a small amount of goodness, care and help cause a large amount of happiness?

4. Reread the works of the flesh (verses 19-21) and the fruit of the Spirit (verses 22-24). Ask:
- What are the differences between the works of the flesh and the fruit of the Spirit?
- Why does Paul warn us away from the works of the flesh?
- How can we live by the Spirit?

5. Take out the freshly baked loaf of bread. Bring out butter and fruit jelly. Ask kids to help themselves to a slice of bread. As they add fruit jelly, ask them to say one fruit of the Spirit they want to include in their lives. For example: "I've been running on empty when it comes to patience. I want to add patience to my life and try to be more understanding of my family."

ACTION

Ask volunteers to add the finishing touches to the prepared loaves. (Bake them once they have risen.) Wrap the loaves in plastic wrap, place a bow or ribbon on each one. Give them to elderly people in your congregation or to people who are facing tough times.

GALATIANS 6:1-18 • THOUGHTS FROM PAUL

FOCUS
Faith.

PREPARATION
Gather butcher paper, tape, thick crayons, a bowl of water, a pad of newsprint, an album of soft meditative music, a record player, a tape recording of a person reading the passage and a tape player. Tape the butcher paper on

INSIGHT
Paul reminds the Galatians to bear one another's burdens. They should not deceive themselves by thinking they are beyond sin. The apostle says they will harvest what they sow. They are called to work for the good of others, particularly for their kin in the faith.

Apparently, Paul concludes his letter by taking the writing instrument from his scribe and writing his summary in big letters: "See what large letters I use as I write to you with my own hand" (Galatians 6:11). His concluding postscript reminds the Galatians that no law or practice counts for anything in light of Christ's

the meeting room walls.

Write five sets of instructions on separate sheets of newsprint. Leave the instructions on the pad so only one set will be visible at a time. Following are the instructions:

Sheet 1: Write your name in big letters on the butcher paper so others can see it. Draw a symbol to describe who you really are as a person.

Sheet 2: Draw a symbol of "Carry each other's burdens."

Sheet 3: Draw a symbol of "A person reaps what he or she sows."

Sheet 4: Draw a symbol of "Don't become weary in doing good."

Sheet 5: Gather in a circle. When a bowl of water is passed to you, give the person on your right a symbol of God's saving grace. Dip your finger in the bowl, then make the sign of a cross on that person's forehead.

saving work.

In this study, group members will draw symbols of faith—in silence.

BIBLE STUDY

1. Gather the students outside your usual meeting place. Say: "You will be entering into the world of the apostle Paul. He communicated with the Galatians through written letters. Therefore, the whole study will be conducted in silence through writing."

2. Give each person a thick crayon, then lead the students into the prepared room. All is silent except for background music.

Point to the newsprint with the first set of instructions. Allow time for kids to complete their symbols and walk around looking at other symbols.

3. Fade the background music and play the tape recording of Galatians 6:1-18. Play the music after the reading is complete.

4. Flip over the newsprint so the second set of instructions shows. Allow time for kids to draw the symbol. Continue in this manner until the fifth set of instructions.

5. Gather kids in a circle and pass around the bowl of water. After this last step, everyone will have a wet forehead and a silent feeling of closeness. Gather in a quiet group hug.

ACTION

Make the butcher paper symbols a permanent part of your meeting room. Get permission from your church property board and minister to paint one graffiti wall. This is a great way to build group unity. Repaint the wall each year with names and symbols of new group members.

EPHESIANS

"I'm the boss of this family. You will all do as I say! The Bible proves God wants it this way."

This insecure male is scrambling for support as he tries to bully and control his wife and children. He has taken out of context one of Paul's teachings in this letter: "Wives, submit to your husbands as to the Lord. For the husband is the head of the wife as Christ is the head of the church, his body, of which he is the Savior" (Ephesians 5:22-23). The man who tried to bully his wife did not first read verse 21: "Submit to one another out of reverence for Christ."

Ephesians is considered Paul's most majestic writing. The author focuses on the practical side of living a faithful life in an evil world. Paul deals with the nature of relationships between husbands and wives, children and parents, and slaves and masters—all who are in potential positions of conflict.

Ephesians is different from all of Paul's other letters, because he addresses no specific audience. He addresses everybody in general. Early manuscripts did not mention Ephesus. It is thought that copies of this letter were made and distributed to several churches. When copies of Paul's letters were collected, this copy was probably secured at Ephesus.

Written while Paul was a prisoner, the Epistle guides and encourages those who carry their faith into a troubled and distracting secular environment.

EPHESIANS 1:1-23 • THANKING GOD FOR BLESSINGS

FOCUS
Celebration.

PREPARATION
Gather a Bible, box and marker for each person. (Collect boxes from grocery stores or department stores.) Gather boxes of candy, cookies or dried fruit for refreshments and awards.

INSIGHT
Paul opens his letter in the normal pattern of self-disclosure and a general blessing. He next offers a high-powered, joyful, energetic stream of theology—a long creedal sentence about God's blessing. This non-stop volcano of praise supports the idea that Paul dictated his letters.

The apostle offers a prayer for the Ephesians. He lifts up the qualities of the Christian life. He paraphrases Psalm 8:6 as he calls upon God to bless them.

In this study, group members will decorate boxes with symbols of gifts.

BIBLE STUDY
1. Divide the group into two teams. Ask teenagers each to find a partner in their team. Ask the teams to form two lines; give a box to the first pair in each line. On "Go," one partner sits in the box while the other pushes or pulls him or her up to a certain point and back. Then the next pair goes. The teams must do this twice. The second time, partners switch positions. The rider is now the pusher; the pusher is now the rider. Award boxes of candy to the winners.

2. Give a box and a marker to each person. Ask teenagers to form a cross with the boxes as you read Ephesians 1:1-23. Say: "At the beginning of this chapter, Paul unleashes a joyous stream of celebration concerning the promise we are given in Christ. It's now your task to capture the stream of this message into shorter, manageable pieces. You will each be assigned a verse. Shorten your verse, but make sure it says the same thing. Imagine you are writing a bumper sticker and need to communicate the essence of the phrase in as few words as possible. For example, verse 3 could be shortened to 'Praise God for our blessings.' Write your shortened version on your box."

3. After group members finish, say: "There are 23 verses in the chapter. One at a time, you will read your shortened version, then place the box on the floor. By the time each person is finished, we should have a cross formed from the boxes."

4. Gather around the boxes. Say: "In verses 15-23, Paul tells the readers he remembers them in his prayers. Let's pray silently for someone who is special to us, asking God to bless him or her."

5. After the prayer say: "Paul celebrates and gives thanks for our spiritual blessings. He's joyous and happy for God's many gifts. Just like Paul, we're going to celebrate our gifts."

6. Divide the group into partners. Tell them to decorate their box with symbols of their partner's gifts. For example, a person could draw a sun and a rainbow to represent a partner's gifts of enthusiasm and ability to always keep a promise. Exchange the gift boxes.

7. Serve boxes of refreshments such as candy, cookies or dried fruits.

ACTION

To further celebrate gifts, ask group members to choose one friend or family member and think of his or her special qualities. Ask young people to decorate a box (or card or piece of paper) with symbols of the qualities and give it to the friend or family member.

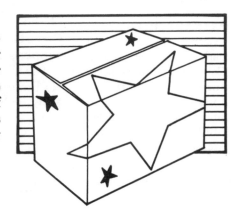

EPHESIANS 2:1-22 • SAVING GRACE

FOCUS

Grace and reconciliation.

PREPARATION

Gather a marker, candle and children's toy block for each person. Cover each block with construction paper so young people can write on it. Bring a Bible, an album of lively music, a record player, and a fairy tale of a princess who kisses a frog and turns him into a prince.

INSIGHT

Paul says believers have been transformed from death into life through Christ. We were once in sin, now we are crafted by God to perform good works. Yet this miraculous change has not been gained through our own efforts; it's God's gift to us. We are created to fulfill the good works God intends us to do.

In verses 11-22, Paul provides a great statement on how Christ brings peace. Christ tears down the walls of hostility that separate people and restores the reality of hospitality. The ability to transform hostility into hospitality is one of the greatest challenges for a Christian. This transformation is the basis for all peacemaking.

In this study, group members will build a wall of hostility and tear it down with Christ's peacemaking qualities.

BIBLE STUDY

1. Play lively music in the background. Organize a time for "Leap-frog." Let participants hop over each other in various directions around the room.

Divide the group into two teams. One team is the "Toads," the other team is the "Frogs." Give everyone a lighted candle. The object of the game is to blow out the other team's candles. If a person's candle is blown out, he or she must stand still and wait for another team member to relight it.

2. Gather participants in a circle and read a fairy tale of a princess who kisses a frog and turns him into a prince. Ask:

● How many of you have heard this story when you were younger?

● How would you describe the frog?

● How would you describe the prince?

● How would you describe the princess' reaction to the frog? to the prince?

3. Say, "As I read Ephesians 2:1-10, compare the frog-and-prince story to Paul's message." Read the passage. Ask:

● What compares to the frog? (For example, our dead selves—filled with sin and desires.)

● What compares to the prince? (For example, our new selves in Christ.)

● What compares to the princess? (For example, Christ's saving grace.)

● What does it mean to be saved by grace and not by our works?

4. Read Ephesians 2:11-22. After each verse, pause, then throw a children's block to a young person. By the time you've finished reading the verses, each person should have a block. Distribute markers.

5. Say: "In these verses, Paul talks about Christ tearing down the dividing walls of hostility. What specific things divide people today? Write your ideas on your blocks." Ideas could be fear, greed, jealousy.

6. Let the young people say the dividing qualities they listed. As they share, ask them to form a wall from the blocks.

7. Say: "Christ brings peace and unity. He is our cornerstone. What other characteristics of Christ tear down the walls of hostility?" Ideas could be peace, reconciliation, grace, acceptance.

8. Let the young people discuss Christ's reconciling characteristics. As they discuss, have them reshape the wall to symbolize what Christ has done to bring us together. For example, they could form a cross or a circle.

9. Gather around the block symbol. Pray: "God, thank you for changing our sinful selves to saved people. Thanks for the gift of your grace. Thanks for Christ's peace that tears down walls of hostility and makes us one. Thank you for Christ, our cornerstone of strength and support. Amen."

ACTION

Offer parents in your congregation a free night of babysitting. During the evening play "Leapfrog" and "Toads and Frogs." Read the fairy tale and discuss God's saving grace. Ask participants to bring a stuffed frog or other stuffed toy from home for "Show and Tell." Serve green refreshments such as lime Kool-Aid, lime Jell-O and grapes.

EPHESIANS 3:1-21 • *THOUGHTS OF WISDOM AND LOVE*

FOCUS
God's love.

PREPARATION
Gather red, pink and white construction paper, scissors, glue, markers and Bibles. You also will need candy hearts (the kind with messages written on them).

INSIGHT
Paul is a prisoner because of his work with the Gentiles. He made the Jews angry by stating the Gentiles were equal. God gives both Gentiles and Jews a saving legacy. The apostle bows his knees before God in prayer. He blesses his readers with God's gifts. God's power is at work in them.

In this study, group members will design construction paper messages of God's love.

BIBLE STUDY
1. Send pairs of participants on a hunt. They are to find the highest point of the church, the lowest point and the widest point.

Gather and discuss the findings. The highest point may be the top of the cross on the bell tower; the lowest point may be the drainpipes leading from the basement floor; the widest point may be from one end of the church to the next.

2. Say: "Paul describes God's love to us using the terms 'rooted,' 'grounded,' 'breadth,' 'length,' 'height,' 'depth.' God's love is higher, deeper and wider than all of the points we found on our church."

3. Distribute markers, scissors, glue, and red, pink and white construction paper. Assign one verse of the passage to each person. Have him or her use the passage and the materials to design a message of God's love. An example for verse 8 could be: "God's love makes even the least of people great." The construction paper design could have an arrow pointing from a small heart to a large heart. The phrase "God's Love" could be written on the arrow.

4. Discuss the designs of God's love.

5. Gather everyone in a circle. Give each person a candy heart with a message on it. Say: "Read your candy-heart message, then elaborate the message to affirm the person on your right. An affirmation for 'endless love' could be: 'You show God's endless love through your care and concern. Thanks for the phone call yesterday when I was feeling down.' "

6. Let each person affirm his or her neighbor. Eat the candy hearts.

ACTION

Contact a nursing home administrator. Tell him or her the number of members in your group. Work with him or her to assign the members each a resident. Have young people use the construction paper and other material to make their residents a message of God's love.

Go to the nursing home, visit with the residents and give the messages. Encourage young people to maintain regular contact with their nursing home partners.

EPHESIANS 4:1-32 • CHRISTIAN UNITY

FOCUS
Unique gifts.

PREPARATION
Gather a marker, Bible, pencil and piece of paper for each person. Make three copies of the "Job Description" for each person.

INSIGHT
Paul focuses on the unity of the church. This passage contains some of the most quoted lines in liturgy and preaching (verses 4-6; 26-27; and 31-32). The overwhelming image is the church as a body with different, but important, parts. The unity in diversity comes from Christ—the head.

The apostle underscores the need for Christians to live a life learned from Christ. He says to put off the old nature and put on the new. He lists practical guidelines for the new person in Christ:

- Tell the truth; don't lie.
- Be angry; don't let the sun go down on your anger.
- Work honestly to help the poor; don't steal.
- Offer encouragement; don't talk in an evil fashion.
- Be guided by kindness; don't feel bitter.
- Forgive; don't seek revenge.

In this study, group members will fill out a job description and list personal gifts and qualifications.

BIBLE STUDY

1. Give everyone a marker and piece of paper. Ask each person to write his or her name at the top of the paper and lay the paper on a table. Allow several minutes for young people to write one or two gifts on each person's paper. For example, caring, loving, fun to be with, creative, helpful, teacher and listener.

2. Let everyone read his or her gift list. Note the differences and similarities. Say: "Paul tells us each member of the body of Christ is blessed with different gifts. Listen as Paul tells of these gifts and gives guidelines for Christians." Read Ephesians 4:1-32.

3. Give the group members each a "Job Description" handout and a pencil. Assign each person one of the following jobs that Paul lists: apostle, prophet, evangelist, minister, teacher. Ask young people to think of qualifications for the jobs and write them on the handouts. Qualifications for a teacher could be caring for students, listening as well as teaching, knowing the subject.

JOB DESCRIPTION

Instructions: List one of the jobs Paul mentions. Add the qualifications necessary for the job.

_____
(Job)

Qualifications:

_____

_____

_____

_____

_____

Permission to photocopy this handout granted for local church use only. Copyright © 1988 by Dennis C. Benson. Published by Group Books, Inc., Box 481, Loveland, CO 80539.

---

4. After several minutes, share the qualifications.

5. Read each of Paul's guidelines from the "Insight" section. After you read each one ask, "Who does this guideline affect?" Encourage participants to shout out the position on their handout. After you read all the guidelines, students will realize the guidelines apply to all people, no matter what their job position.

6. Give each person another handout. Have participants decide which position they fill in the body of Christ—apostle, prophet, evangelist, minister, teacher. Ask them to list gifts that "qualify" them for that position. Gifts that qualify a person to be an evangelist could be friendliness, likes to meet people, remembers names, enthusiastic about faith.

7. Encourage group members to share their answers with one other person.

8. Gather in a circle and hold hands. One at a time say each person's name. Then pray: "Thank you for giving each one of us unique gifts. Thank you for making us one in you. Amen."

ACTION
Give each person one more handout. Have members complete the handout with a family member. Discover the role the family member fills in the body of Christ. Celebrate each other's gifts.

EPHESIANS 5:1-20 • CHILDREN OF LIGHT

FOCUS
Celebration.

PREPARATION
Send an invitation to each group member. Title each invitation "Celebrate Christ." Each person will need a balloon, pencil, candle, slip of paper and 3-foot piece of yarn. Prepare for the games and bring a Bible and refreshments.

INSIGHT
Paul continues to highlight the virtues of living the new life in Christ. He criticizes sexual sin, silly talk, impurity, false religious ideas, drunkenness and evil conduct. Christians are called to walk with the wise—those who share psalms, hymns and songs of thanksgiving.

In this study, group members will participate in a party to celebrate Christ.

BIBLE STUDY
1. Play party games such as "Pin the Tail on the Donkey." Play Bible variations of the game by changing it to "Pin the Tail on the Camel" or "Pin the Staff to the Shepherd."

2. Gather in a circle. Give everyone a balloon, pencil, piece of yarn and slip of paper. Read Ephesians 5:1-14. Ask group members to listen for things Paul says to avoid such as impurity, silly talk and envy. Ask them each to choose one item and write it on their slip of paper.

3. Go around the circle and let the students read their slips of paper. Ask each person to place the slip in the balloon, blow it up, tie it, attach one end of the yarn to the balloon and the other end of the yarn around his or her ankle.

Allow five minutes for participants to step on and pop each other's balloons—they're stamping out the things Paul tells us to avoid.

4. Read verses 15-20. Say: "God wants us to walk with other children of light. These people are filled with the Spirit; they sing songs and hymns and read psalms."

5. Sing songs such as "This Little Light of Mine," "We Are the Family of God" and "Walkin' in the Light" from *Songs* (Songs and Creations).

6. Read various psalms responsively. Ask girls to read one verse, guys to read the next.

7. Give everyone a candle. Light your candle and say: "We are children of light. We will give thanks to the Lord for all things." Light the person's candle to your right and say, "You are the light of the world." Pass the flame from candle to candle until all are lighted. Close by singing "Let My Light Shine Bright" from *Songs*.

8. Bring out party refreshments such as punch, nuts and a cake with the words "Celebrate Christ" written on it.

ACTION

Plan a party for someone who's ill or lonely such as a hospital patient, shut-in or congregation member who's recovering from surgery. Give the person a balloon bouquet, decorate the room with streamers, sing songs and tape a newsprint banner to the wall that says "Celebrate Christ."

EPHESIANS 5:21-33 • *HUSBAND AND WIFE*

FOCUS
Opinions.

PREPARATION
Gather paper, pencils, Bibles, concordances and refreshments.

INSIGHT
Volumes have been written about this passage. Paul is speaking to Christians living at a particular time in history. It is a time when most cultural patterns deal with wives, children and slaves as the property of husbands, fathers and masters.

We should be careful not to remove a teaching from its historical moment and its audience. Viewing a person's thoughts and actions out of his or her setting distorts the truth.

Paul wasn't speaking to the same issues concerning sexual equality as we are facing today. Yet Paul's message is vital to the contemporary Christian. We can apply his teachings to our relationships.

In this study, group members will debate the topic "Husbands have absolute authority over their wives."

BIBLE STUDY

1. When group members enter the room tell them you're going to warm them up for a debate. They can only agree or disagree with the following statements. Read each one and allow time for all those who agree to go to one side of the room and all those who disagree to go to the opposite side. Allow a few moments for teenagers to try to change each other's positions. Here are some statements. Add your own.

- Abortion is wrong.
- Smoking cigarettes is wrong.
- All lies are wrong.
- Murder is always wrong.
- All young people should go to college.
- All Christians should attend church regularly.
- Husbands have absolute authority over their wives.

2. Divide students into two groups according to their position on the last statement. Say: "We are going to debate this last statement. One group has to defend the position 'Husbands have absolute authority over their wives.' The other group has to defend the opposite position 'Husbands do not have absolute authority over their wives.' Use Ephesians 5:21-33 and other passages to support your view."

3. Distribute paper, pencils, Bibles and concordances. Allow 10-15 minutes for groups to prepare their positions.

4. Let each side present its position and support. Allow time for teenagers to debate, ask questions and refute each other's statements.

5. Close the study by asking young people to agree or disagree with these statements:

- We love each other because Christ loves us.
- We respect each other because we are God's children.
- We thank God for our friends in this Bible study group.
- We wish that our refreshments would be given to others, not ourselves.

6. Serve the refreshments!

ACTION

Ask teenagers to interview their parents and grandparents about this topic. Have parents and grandparents agree or disagree with the statement "Husbands have absolute authority over their wives." Ask for reasons why they agree or disagree. Discuss the interviews at the next session. Do parents' opinions differ from grandparents' opinions? teenagers' opinions?

EPHESIANS 6:1-9 • *PARENTS AND CHILDREN; MASTERS AND SLAVES*

FOCUS
Honor, obey and respect.

PREPARATION
Gather one large rubber band for each person, Bibles, writing materials and a box of rubber bands.

INSIGHT
Paul says children are to follow the commandment and honor their parents (Exodus 20:12). This is important if they are to have a happy life and live long on the earth. Christian parents' duty is to provide children with Christian instruction and discipline.

Slaves are to be obedient and serve their masters as if they were serving Christ. Everyone is free in Christ and will receive a just reward from God. Masters must treat slaves from the same perspective of serving the Lord. Threats and harshness must not be used. Both master and slave will be judged by the same God.

Paul says more to the slave than to the slave owner. Does this mean Paul's readers already know about owning slaves? Or does this mean they are mostly slaves themselves?

In this study, group members will make human sculptures to symbolize responsibility of parents, children, slaves and masters.

BIBLE STUDY

1. Play a fun game to loosen up the group. Put a large rubber band around each person's head. (Your own included!) Place the band so it's around the nose and over the ears. On ''Go,'' participants try to get the rubber bands down around their necks. No hands allowed. Award a box of rubber bands to the person who first succeeds.

2. Say: ''We just played a game where we were 'wrapped up' in a rubber band. Our study focuses on different relationships we're wrapped up in. Paul gives guidelines for us to follow in our relationships.''

Divide into four groups by having teenagers say one at a time: ''Parent,'' ''Child,'' ''Slave,'' ''Master.'' Group all ''Parents,'' ''Children,'' ''Slaves'' and ''Masters.'' Give each group writing materials and a Bible.

3. Tell the groups they are to read Ephesians 6:1-9 then list all the responsibilities for their person. For example, the group assigned to parents could list the following:
- Don't anger your children.
- Discipline them with love.
- Take them to church.
- Teach them about Christ.

4. Finally, ask each group to summarize its list of responsibilities by forming a human sculpture. Each group member must participate. For example, a group of six could form a human sculpture of three parent-child scenes: A parent holds firmly to her child's arm—portraying discipline; a parent and child walking to church; a parent reading the Bible to his child.

5. Share the lists and the sculptures. See if group members can guess the lists of responsibilities by viewing the sculptures.

ACTION

Ask each group member to do one thing to honor his or her mother or father. Members could clean the house, cook a meal, ask their parents about their day, go grocery shopping, do yardwork, leave parents a note of appreciation.

EPHESIANS 6:10-24 • THE ARMOR OF GOD

FOCUS
Strength during challenges.

PREPARATION
Gather Bibles, cardboard, crayons, tape, newspapers, scissors and refreshments.

INSIGHT
Ephesians concludes with an inspiring call to courage in the fight for truth. Paul uses the image of a warrior preparing armor for an actual battle. The armor of God protects Christians against the attack of evil.

In this study, group members will design armor for life's struggles.

BIBLE STUDY
1. Divide into small groups. Give each group tape and several newspapers. Ask each group to choose one member and dress him or her as a warrior ready for battle. Groups can use only the newspaper and tape for their creations. Host a warrior fashion show when the groups finish.

2. Read Ephesians 6:10-24. Say: "God provides Christians protective armor for the battle against evil. Armor around the waist for truth; armor around the chest and shoulders for righteousness; armor around the legs and feet for readiness to proclaim the gospel of peace; a shield for faith; a helmet for salvation; a sword for God's Word."

3. Assign one piece of armor to each small group. Distribute cardboard, scissors, crayons and tape. Ask the groups to design their pieces of armor. On one side of the armor, ask them to write the challenges they face today (such as school and disappointment); on the other side, have them list ways the piece of armor helps them withstand challenges (such as providing strength and protection).

4. Stand before the groups and ask them to protect you against the challenges you have to face. Let them put the pieces of armor on you as they present their conclusions.

5. Close with a prayer thanking God for support and strength in times of trials.

6. As the fully protected warrior, lead the group members to the refreshments. Attack!

ACTION

Coordinate with the minister for your group to lead a children's sermon one Sunday. You wear the cardboard armor, the group members explain God's support and protection during challenges and trying times.

INTRODUCTION TO PHILIPPIANS

The handwriting, personal-size envelope and special-issue stamp all suggested something personal. Sure enough. It was a note from the heart—a letter from a young mother. Her child was mentally handicapped and a challenge for her and her husband to raise. Yet Mary sought signs of God's love and kindness each day—and found them. Her words of happiness reached out and lifted my spirits. She gave me a special gift—a note from the heart.

When we read Paul's letter to the Philippians, we feel as if we've received a note from the heart. It's one of Paul's warmest and most affectionate letters. Paul doesn't preach to his readers about theological doctrines. He speaks of his personal needs and thanks the people who have helped spiritually and financially during hard times.

Paul talks to his beloved church and offers bits of advice, reflection and prayers.

PHILIPPIANS 1:1-30 • A WARM EPISTLE

FOCUS
Trying times.

PREPARATION
Gather a piece of poster-board, a marker, two chairs, two dice, pencils, Bibles and refreshments.

Prepare a poster with the following six commands on it:

1. Do 10 jumping jacks.

2. Crawl on your hands and knees around the chair.

3. Do five push-ups.

4. Whistle "Row, Row, Row Your Boat."

5. Clap your hands four times and yell, "I am happy."

6. Do all of the previous commands.

Place the poster at one end of the room. Set two chairs close by. Place a die on each chair.

Prepare two copies of the handout for each person.

INSIGHT
Paul greets and blesses the saints, bishops and deacons at Philippi. He plunges into a personal prayer for these beloved sisters and brothers. He expresses his longing for their presence during his imprisonment and suffering for the gospel.

The apostle explains that his trials have actually been a blessing. The guards and those with him have now heard the gospel. Other Christians have grown confident through his example.

Paul is unconcerned about what others do in their preaching of Christ, as long as they proclaim Christ.

He struggles to know whether Christ will use him as a martyr or as a living preacher. He is ready for either calling. It would be sweet to be with Christ for eternity, yet he knows his readers need him in the flesh at this time.

Paul urges the Christians to continue to battle the forces of evil on behalf of the gospel. There is no cause for fear.

In this study, group members will look at some of their past and current struggles, and they will give thanks for all things.

BIBLE STUDY
1. Welcome the group members and say: "Today's study is about trying times. Trials. Struggles. Giving thanks in all things. We're going to play a relay. Each one of you will overcome a struggle by the time we're through. Remember, give thanks in all things. No grumbling allowed. I'll divide you into two teams. Each team member runs to the chair, rolls the die, and follows the command on the poster that corresponds with the number. First team done wins." Form teams, then play the relay.

2. Divide Philippians 1:1-30 into six parts: 1-5; 6-10; 11-15; 16-20; 21-25; and 26-30. Divide into six small groups. Allow the groups to take turns rolling the die. Assign them a group of passages according to the number they rolled. A group who rolled a three would be assigned verses

11-15. If a group rolls a number that's already been rolled, have that group roll again. Read the passages according to the assignments.

3. Say: "Paul is in prison writing this letter to the Philippians. He has faced many struggles, but he continues to give thanks. We're going to look at some of our past and current struggles."

Distribute a pencil and a "Life's Trials" handout to each person. Let teenagers each mark an "X" on the line according to when they have faced struggles. Ask them to write a few words describing each struggle. For example, a person's parents divorced when he was 5 years old, a student's grandparent died when she was 10 years old, a student recently failed a course.

LIFE'S TRIALS

Instructions: Mark an "X" on the line to correspond to trying times in your life. Write a few words to describe each trial.

_____

Birth   Now

Permission to photocopy this handout granted for local church use only. Copyright © 1988 by Dennis C. Benson. Published by Group Books, Inc., Box 481, Loveland, CO 80539.

---

4. Discuss the struggles. Ask:
● How did you feel during these trying times?
● Did any good come from the struggles? Explain.
● How can you offer thanks throughout life's trials as Paul did even while he was in prison?
● Does God work for good in all things? Explain.

5. Ask young people to form a line from oldest to youngest. Say: "No matter what our age is, God loves us. No matter how hard life is, God gives us strength. No matter what struggles lie ahead, God will be with us and give us support. Thanks be to God."

6. Let the oldest person lead the way to the refreshments.

ACTION

Give students each another handout. Ask them to have their parents write in their past or present struggles. Discuss these times. Teenagers will be surprised at all they didn't know about their parents. Ask young people to share with their parents their past and present struggles. Encourage them to support each other during trying times. God is our strength and support, but God also blesses us with a family for strength and support.

PHILIPPIANS 2:1-30 • HUMILITY AND GREATNESS

FOCUS
Servanthood.

PREPARATION
Gather celery, peanut butter, bagels, cream cheese, juice, knives, cups and a Bible.

INSIGHT
Paul turns to the nature of the Christian life. We live in tension between greatness and humility. Christ provides the pattern we are to follow:

• Christ had God's power from the beginning.

• Christ gave up this status and took the form of a servant.

• Christ was humble and accepted his death on the cross.

• God raised him from the dead and made him Lord.

• All creation will worship Christ.

Paul pleads with his readers to pursue their salvation with fear and trembling. God is working within them. God urges them to maintain their innocence as pure children while they live in an impure and sinful world. They are called to be guiding lights in this darkness.

This chapter concludes with personal notes from Paul about his companions Timothy and Epaphroditus. He hopes to send Timothy to them shortly. Faithful Timothy will be able to bring news from the Philippians.

Epaphroditus also is anxious to visit them. He has been faithfully serving Paul and has just recovered from a severe illness. God spared him from death. He deserves to be honored for he risked his life for the work of Christ.

In this study, group members will experience servanthood by serving each other refreshments.

BIBLE STUDY

1. Open the study by playing a game of boasting called "I Can Do That." One at a time young people say a skill they can do. For example, "I can touch my nose with the tip of my tongue." Participants prove their boasts. Encourage them to try to outshine each other. For example, "I can touch my nose with the tip of my tongue and hop around the room on one foot." Let everyone have a chance to boast.

2. Say: "Christians live in tension between greatness and humility. We have reason to boast. We are God's children! God loves us and blesses us with many gifts! But our model is Christ. He emptied himself—denied himself—and became a human servant. The ultimate in sacrifice. We're going to practice this Christlike humility by serving each other for the rest of the study."

3. Play "Servant's Refreshments," a variation of "Servant's Lunch" from *Building Community in Youth Groups* (Group Books). Set out the food, utensils and cups. Tell participants: "You are servants. You can't fix refreshments for yourself. You can fix refreshments only for another person. You can eat the refreshments after someone serves you. Don't speak during this experience. While you're preparing the food, listen to Paul's words." Read Philippians 2:1-30.

4. After everyone is served and is eating, ask:

●How did you feel when you were served?

●In what ways was it hard to think of someone else's needs?

●What does it mean to humble yourself?

●What does Paul mean when he says to do all things without complaining or arguing? Why is this difficult?

●How can we remember to give thanks in all things?

5. Let each person say one thing he or she is thankful for.

6. Ask group members to continue their servant-like attitudes by cleaning up after they've finished eating.

ACTION

Continue the servanthood theme with your group. Volunteer to be Sunday greeters for one month. Volunteer to set up, clean up and serve coffee for the next church potluck.

PHILIPPIANS 3:1-11 • THE HOPE OF RESURRECTION

FOCUS
Death.

PREPARATION
Gather a copy of your church's funeral service,

INSIGHT
Paul notes he is repeating himself as he warns about false teachers who demand circumcision (and other works of human hands) as a means to earn salvation. Paul is reminded that he has gone through external works from his previous religion. He followed the law by

Bibles, writing materials, candles, matches, a tape recording of mellow organ music and a tape player. Prepare the room like a funeral parlor. Turn the lights low. Light some candles. Play the organ music in the background.

the book. It was in this form of understanding that he actually persecuted the church.

Paul has now given up all this law for the sake of Christ. Paul only seeks to know Christ and, through his suffering, share in the power of Christ's Resurrection.

In this study, group members will prepare thoughts about their own funeral services.

BIBLE STUDY

1. As students enter, ask them to be seated. Allow a few moments of silence so the mood is set. Read some words from your church's funeral service.

2. Allow a few more moments of silence, then read Philippians 3:1-11. Say: "Paul thinks back to his past struggles. He had been circumcised according to his faith. Now he knows circumcision is not a means of salvation. By sharing in Christ's sufferings, by becoming like him in his death, he may gain resurrection from the dead. Paul is hopeful. He looks forward to being with Christ for eternity." Ask:

●How would you describe a typical funeral service? Describe the atmosphere, feelings, music and service.

●How would you change a typical funeral service to reflect Paul's joy and anticipation of eternal life?

3. Turn on the lights and distribute writing materials. Ask each person to plan his or her funeral service to reflect celebration, the joy of the resurrection and the anticipation of eternal life. Guide group members with these questions:

●What hymns would be sung?

●What instruments would be played?

●What scriptures would be read?

●Would you celebrate with communion? Why or why not?

●What would you like the minister to say?

●What would you say to comfort the mourners? Write a paragraph to urge them to view death with hope.

4. Share the funeral services.

5. Close by asking group members to think of a friend, relative or acquaintance who has died. Pray: "God, thank you for blessing our lives with these people. Comfort us with the knowledge that they are with you for eternity. We will see them again. Thank you for the resurrection. Thank you for overcoming death through your Son. Thank you for eternal life. Amen."

ACTION

Although we realize we will inherit eternal life and see our loved ones again, we're still lonely. So ask group members each to think of someone in the church who has recently lost a loved one. Encourage group members to pray for the person, take him or her some food, call the person and listen to him or her. Maintain regular contact.

PHILIPPIANS 3:12-21 • *FORGET WHAT'S BEHIND; LOOK AHEAD*

FOCUS

Perseverance.

PREPARATION

Gather oranges, bananas, apples, juice, cups and a Bible. Ask participants to wear bike helmets and comfortable clothes and to ride their bikes to the session. Tell them ahead of time they will be taking a five-mile bike hike. Encourage all people to participate. Say that you will keep the pace slow and leisurely so all can enjoy it.

INSIGHT

Paul says the moment of perfection has not yet come. The journey along the road to eternal life is like a race toward a finish line. We can't be distracted by the past; we must look ahead. Eternal life is our prize.

In this study, group members will participate in a bike hike and receive a prize at the end.

BIBLE STUDY

1. Gather participants at the church. Lead them through stretches. Focus on stretching thighs, calves and ankles.

2. Read Philippians 3:12-21. Say: "Paul has a goal. He presses on because of Christ. He forgets what is behind and looks forward to what lies ahead. The goal is a prize of the heavenward call of Christ.

"We're going to press on toward a goal. We're going on a five-mile bike hike. We'll forget what lies behind and look forward to what lies ahead. We'll receive our rewards when we get back to the church."

3. Proceed with your biking. Keep the group together as much as possible. Keep the pace slow and easy. You want to accomplish a goal, not set a speed record. Head back for the reward.

4. Plan some cool-down exercises once you reach the church. Serve oranges, bananas, apples and juice. Say: "Congratulations. You pressed on toward the goal and received your reward." Ask:

• What obstacles are in our way as we run for the goal of eternal life?
• Why is it easy to get sidetracked from the course of Christianity?

123

● Why is it difficult to forget what's behind?

● Why is it difficult to focus on what's ahead?

● What encouragement can you give one another to stay in the race?

5. Let each person say one encouragement to the person who biked behind him or her. For example, "Keep your eyes on God," "You've done great so far; keep up the good work" or "Christ will help you through the tough times."

6. Ask participants to remember the bits of encouragement and continue pressing toward the goal of eternal life.

ACTION

Plan another bike excursion. Ask young people each to bring a friend and plan the reward for the end of the course.

PHILIPPIANS 4:1-23 • FILL YOUR MINDS

INSIGHT

Paul urges two women in the Philippian church to resolve their disagreement. He encourages his readers to rejoice. The Lord is at hand. They need only to pray to the Lord concerning their needs. Christ's peace will comfort and protect them.

Paul says to fill our minds with things that are true, noble, just, pure, lovely, gracious and deserving praise. He concludes his letter by thanking the Philippians for their gifts. While this means a great deal to him, he also acknowledges that Christ is sufficient in meeting all his needs. Christ strengthens him to face the good and bad times.

In this study, group members will fill their minds with good things, and they will thank each other for a special gift.

FOCUS

Receiving and giving.

PREPARATION

Gather two boxes, a pair of scissors and several magazines for each person. You also will need a Bible, 3x5 cards, pencils, two beach towels and two plungers. Meet in a room without carpeting.

BIBLE STUDY

1. "Plunge" into the session with a fun game. Divide into two teams. Give each team a beach towel and plunger. One at a time, team members sit cross-legged on their towel and use the plunger to scoot themselves to a line and back. First team done wins.

2. Say: "You have pressed on toward a goal and won. Just like Paul urged his readers in Philippians 3:14. Paul also asks people to fill their minds with things that are true, noble, just, pure, lovely, gracious and deserving praise.

"I'll give you each a box that represents your mind. Thumb through magazines and cut out pictures that symbolize things that are true, noble, just, pure, lovely, gracious and deserving praise. Fill your mind—or box— with these things."

3. Distribute the boxes, magazines, pencils and scissors. Read the passage while they are "filling their minds." Ask:

●What did you find that was noble? true? just? pure? lovely? gracious? deserving praise?

●How can you remember to fill your mind with these things?

4. Ask young people each to sign their name on the box. Place the boxes in a row. Distribute 3x5 cards. Say: "Paul concludes his letter by thanking the Philippians for their gifts. We receive gifts from each person we meet. On separate 3x5 cards, thank each group member for a gift he or she has given you. Gifts could be friendship and a listening ear. Place one thank-you note in each person's box."

5. Encourage young people to take home their boxes and read the thank-you notes.

ACTION

Ask group members to prepare one box for each of their family members. Have them ask their families to regularly give each other notes of thanks and encouragement.

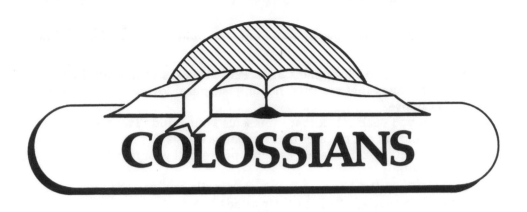

COLOSSIANS

"I'm doing hard time. I have a long time to go. I worry about my son. He's tempted to do some of the dumb stuff I did as a kid. How can I help him from here?"

The letter from the prisoner in the federal penitentiary touched me. Yet I didn't have any advice to give him. How could he provide much guidance to a child with whom he could not talk, walk or argue?

Paul felt this same kind of bind. He loved his spiritual children in the Colossian church. He wanted to offer them guidance while he was in prison. He knew they were falling down under the spell of false teaching. This sinister influence was particularly dangerous because it claimed to supplement the Christian faith; it distorted the gospel.

This letter deals with this problem and the ways the Christian faith affects lifestyle. The apostle focuses on how the Christian family should be organized. He offers guidance to his children at Colossae—through a letter.

COLOSSIANS 1:1-23 • GREETINGS, THANKSGIVING, INTERCESSION

FOCUS
Prayers.

PREPARATION
Gather doughnuts, string, coat hangers, paper, pencils, scissors, newspaper, construction paper, tape, markers and several Bibles. Ask three volunteers to read these verses:
● Greeting (verses 1-2).
● Prayer of thanks and intercession (verses 3-14).
● Christ's qualities (verses 15-23).

INSIGHT
The letter begins with the traditional greeting to the faithful at Colossae. Paul thanks God for his readers, then moves on to a prayer of petition for them. He asks God to fill them with knowledge of God's will so they may bear fruit.

Paul offers a poem or hymn to describe Christ. Christ is the visible likeness of God who can't be seen. Everything was created through him. He is the head of the church—the body of faith. The body's source of life is the Son who was raised from the dead. Paul urges the readers to avoid shifting from this foundation of the gospel.

In this study, group members will greet each other, offer prayers of thanksgiving and intercession, and make mobiles of Christ's qualities.

BIBLE STUDY

1. Gather the students. Ask the first volunteer to read Paul's greeting. Ask young people to change the greeting to fit their group. For example, "To the youth group members of Prince of Peace, grace and peace to you from God." Allow a few moments for participants to greet each other.

2. Ask the second volunteer to read Paul's thanksgiving and intercession (verses 3-14). Divide into small groups. Give each group a newspaper and writing materials. Ask participants to search through the papers and find things to be thankful for (such as good weather and good economy) and situations or people who need God's intercession (such as people suffering from poverty or famine). Encourage the small groups to write prayers of thanksgiving and prayers of intercession. Read the prayers.

3. Ask the third volunteer to read about Christ's qualities (verses 15-23). Give each group a coat hanger, string, tape, construction paper, scissors and markers. Tell each group to design a mobile to hang from the ceiling. The mobiles should proclaim Christ's qualities. For example, a group could shape the coat hanger into a cross, then the members could cut several crosses from construction paper. On each one they could write qualities such as creation, authority, head of the church, beginning and mediator. They could tape string to the crosses and attach them to the hanger.

4. Let each group explain its creation and hang it from the ceiling.

5. Make doughnut mobiles for a refreshment-time game. Attach one 3-foot piece of string to each doughnut. From one wall to the other wall, tape a stronger long piece of string about 7 feet off the floor. Attach all doughnuts to the longer string. Invite the teenagers to eat the doughnuts— no hands allowed. This game is even more fun if you use gooey, chocolate doughnuts.

ACTION

Compile group members' prayers of thanksgiving and intercession into a flier. Make copies and distribute them at church. Ask congregation members to pray for the items and add their own.

COLOSSIANS 1:24-29 • SUFFERING FOR CHRIST'S SAKE

FOCUS

Living in Christ.

PREPARATION

Prepare a mystery sack by placing a bag of licorice inside a brown paper bag. Close the top by stapling it. Gather a pencil and a copy of the handout for each student. You'll also need a Bible.

INSIGHT

Paul describes himself as being a servant. He has gladly endured suffering as an extension of Christ's pain. His calling is to proclaim the message: Christ is in us. We are partners in God's glory.

In this study, group members will imagine Christ lives within them and complete a handout.

BIBLE STUDY

1. Gather group members in a circle and pass around the mystery sack. Let each one guess its contents. No peeking allowed.

After each person guesses, reveal the mystery! Distribute a piece of licorice to each person. While teenagers eat, read Colossians 1:24-29.

2. Ask each student to describe a time when he or she had to keep a secret. Participants don't have to tell the secret, just the feelings and the situation.

3. Whisper, ''Paul tells the readers a secret (or mystery) that has been hidden for ages is now revealed: Christ lives in us.''

4. Distribute a handout and pencil to each person. Ask young people to imagine Christ lives within them and fill out the handouts from this perspective.

WHAT CHRIST SEES FROM WITHIN ME

Instructions: Paul tells us the ''secret'' hidden from generations is that Christ lives within the believer. Imagine Christ is looking at your life from inside you. Answer the following questions from his viewpoint:

● I am proud of you because you are doing _____

_____

_____

● I see your biggest worry is _____

_____

_____

● I see your biggest stumbling block to being faithful is _____

_____

_____

● I want you to develop these gifts I have already given you

_____

_____

Permission to photocopy this handout granted for local church use only. Copyright © 1988 by Dennis C. Benson. Published by Group Books, Inc., Box 481, Loveland, CO 80539.

---

5. After a few minutes, form pairs and discuss responses.

6. As a large group, discuss these questions:
● What does it mean to have Christ living in you?
● How do you feel when you think Christ is continually present in you?
● How can this thought guide your life?

7. Close with a prayer time. Ask students to say: ''Christ lives in me. I am a new creation. Amen.''

ACTION

Ask young people each to choose one gift they listed on the last question of the handout. Encourage them to develop this gift. A gift of thoughtfulness could be developed by thinking of a different person each week and sending him or her a note to ''Have a good day. God loves you.''

COLOSSIANS 2:1-23 • STAND FIRM IN THE FAITH

FOCUS
Praising God.

PREPARATION
Gather paper, pencils, glue, ribbon, scissors, four 3-foot-by-1-inch dowels four 3-foot-by-5-foot pieces of burlap, and various-colored scraps of felt. Fold over the top 3 inches of each piece of burlap. Sew it so that a dowel can slip through the loop. Gather several of the church's banners that are used throughout the year.

INSIGHT
Paul states he is a servant of God on the Colossians' behalf. He works so they can be knit together into one body of love. The readers must not be deceived by clever teachings that oppose Paul's teachings. Paul is present with them in the spirit and rejoices that they have stood firm in their faith.

In this study, group members will prepare banners to praise God.

BIBLE STUDY
1. Show the church banners to the students. Ask them to notice the messages, designs and construction. Encourage them to remember their thoughts, because they will be designing banners during this study.

2. Divide into four groups. Ask students to read Colossians 2:1-23 and answer these questions:

- What was Paul's message to the Colossians?
- What is his message to us?
- What one theme of praise does this chapter highlight?

3. Give each small group a piece of paper and pencil. Ask group members to design a banner to highlight a theme of praise from the chapter. Group members could symbolize true teaching. They could draw a large cross with sunbeams streaming from behind it. The banner could be titled "Jesus Died So We Could Live."

4. Distribute the materials and dowels. Let small groups create their banners.

5. After group members finish, ask them to explain what Paul meant in the chapter, how his words apply to us today and the main theme depicted on their banner.

6. Display the finished products in the meeting room. Offer a closing prayer using each banner's message of praise.

ACTION
Present the banners to the church. Display them in a processional one Sunday.

COLOSSIANS 3:1-25 • *CHRISTIAN LIFE AND DUTIES*

FOCUS
Christian qualities.

PREPARATION
Gather 25 3x5 cards. Write one verse of this passage on each card. Hide the cards around the church area. Bring two large shirts, two sweaters, two pairs of pants and two pairs of shoes.

INSIGHT
Paul urges his readers to remember they have been raised in Christ and must seek things in heaven where Christ is. They should forget earthly things and focus on things above.

The apostle expands on the concept of a new being in Christ. He lists the marks of the earthly person and the contrasting qualities of a person who puts on the clothing of God.

Paul reminds wives to acknowledge that the husband gives the orders. Husbands are ordered to love their wives and refrain from being harsh with them. Children must obey their parents. Parents should not nag their children or discourage them. Slaves are to obey their masters out of reverence for God. They can work hard because Christ is their real master.

In this study, group members will hunt for scripture verses and clothe themselves in Christian qualities.

BIBLE STUDY

1. Invite students to participate in a scripture hunt. Encourage them to search the church grounds for scripture verses. Tell them there are 25 verses. Once they find the cards, ask them to arrange them according to the order they feel they belong.

Read Colossians 3:1-25 and see how close group members came to the real order.

2. Say, ''Paul tells us to take off what is earthly (such as passion and envy) and clothe ourselves in compassion, kindness, lowliness, meekness, patience and forgiveness.''

3. Play a relay to emphasize this teaching. Form two lines. Ten feet in front of each line place a shirt, pair of pants, sweater and pair of shoes. Tell team members to, one at a time, run to the clothes, put them on, take them off, run back and tag the next person, who repeats the process. First team done wins.

4. Discuss the experience. Ask:
● What does it mean to put to death—or take off—what is earthly in you?
● What does it mean to clothe yourself—or put on—good things?
● What qualities should Christians ''wear'' to reflect they are God's

chosen ones?

5. Close by asking group members each to choose one quality they want to wear this week to reflect the fact they are God's children. Share the qualities with partners and close with prayer.

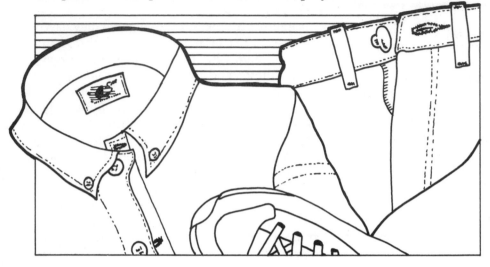

ACTION

Verses 18-25 speak about the roles of wives, husbands and children. Ask teenagers each to sit down with family members, read the verses and compare how their family functions. What are the differences? similarlties? How does Paul's message speak to us today? Bring the insights back to the next session.

COLOSSIANS 4:1-18 • ADDING SALT TO YOUR SPEECH

INSIGHT

The apostle continues with bits of advice for living the Christian life. He tells his readers to season their speech with salt and be gracious.

Paul concludes this letter with news concerning his party of missionaries. He urges the Colossians to read his message to other Christians. They must not forget the chains he bears on behalf of the gospel.

In this study, group members will eat an unseasoned meal and discover the need for salt.

FOCUS

Witnessing.

PREPARATION

Gather all the ingredients to make spaghetti. One note: Don't add any seasoning. Save salt, pepper and seasoning for later. Gather ice cream, chocolate syrup, peanuts, whipped cream and cherries for dessert. Prepare for the dinner: Set tables with plates, glasses, utensils and napkins. Invite teen-agers to the dinner. Warn them to come hungry.

BIBLE STUDY

1. Seat the group members at the tables. Fill their glasses with water. Open with prayer.

2. Serve each one a portion of the unseasoned spaghetti. Ask group members to wait until everyone is served, then allow them to eat.

3. Watch for looks of surprise and sounds of distaste as the students discover the bland food.

4. Distribute salt, pepper and other seasonings. Let the students season their food and then eat it.

5. After the meal read Colossians 4:1-18. Say: "In Paul's final chapter to the Colossians, he tells them to witness in bright and tasty ways. They need to season their speech with salt." Ask:

●How did the unseasoned food taste?
●How would an "unseasoned" speech, witness or sermon sound?
●How did the seasoned food taste?
●How would a "seasoned" speech, witness or sermon sound?
●Is it possible to overseason our message? Explain.
●How can you add just the right amount of seasoning to your speech (or witness)? (Allow time for young people to come up with ideas such as using personal stories, not talking too long, being sensitive to timing, getting to know a person and inviting a person to a fun youth group activity.)

6. Close by eating ice cream sundaes for dessert. Be sure to top them with lots of salty peanuts.

ACTION

Ask each person to share a "salty" message of faith with a friend. This could be as simple as inviting him or her to attend a Sunday worship service, lock-in or retreat.

1 THESSALONIANS

INTRODUCTION TO 1 THESSALONIANS

As a pastor in a small church, I taught young people and helped them prepare for their public affirmation of faith. Yet it was only when my oldest daughter publicly confessed her faith that I fully understood the change in the life of a new Christian. When Amy stood after kneeling before the congregation, she was a different person. The child was gone, the Christian woman had emerged. Her mother and I knew Amy would have to reaffirm her faith as she made future tough decisions; however, she was a different person after that moment.

Paul helped people experience this kind of transformation. After the new Christians accepted their faith, Paul still had to nurture their spiritual development. Accepting Christ into our lives is only the first step. Developing our faith is a daily process.

In 1 and 2 Thessalonians Paul helps those who are putting on Christ during confusing times. Paul is well into his ministry when he encourages and instructs these new believers. These two letters are among the earliest preserved.

How do we guide new Christians? How much can we instruct through criticism? How much must we guide through affirmation? Any parent knows the balance between criticism and affirmation is tough to achieve. The apostle also is walking along this fine line.

1 THESSALONIANS 1:1—2:16 • *PAUL'S WORK WITH THE THESSALONIANS*

FOCUS
End-of-the-year evaluation.

PREPARATION
Ask group members to bring any pictures or slides from the past year's youth group activities. Gather refreshments and a Bible. You'll also need a piece of paper, pencil and an evaluation for each person. Use the sample and create one to fit your own situation.

INSIGHT
Paul gives thanks for the Thessalonians' perseverance. These young Christians have held firm to Christ and resisted their former worship of idols. The apostle talks about his ministry among his readers and the situation facing them. The nature of his love for them shines through these verses.

In this study, group members will evaluate the youth group at the end of the year.

BIBLE STUDY
1. Greet the students and say: "Paul opens his letter to the Thessalonians with a traditional greeting and prayer of thanks. We're going to open this study with a time of greeting and thanks.

"Each person will say his or her name and one blessing he or she is thankful for. The blessing must rhyme with the name. For example: 'Hi. My name is Mike. I like to bike and hike. God blessed me with the ability to do both' or 'How do you do? My name is Sue. I'm thankful for you, and you, and you, and you.' " Allow time for each person to contribute.

2. Say: "This meeting wraps up a year of youth group activities. We're going to take some time and talk about the past year's memories." Let everyone talk about past fun memories.

3. Tell the students that Paul reminisces with the Thessalonians about his life and work with them. Read 1 Thessalonians 2:1-16.

4. Distribute a piece of paper and pencil to each person. Have group members each write a letter describing their memories of the past year. Ask them to address the letters to you.

5. After students finish, ask a few to read their letters.

6. Distribute the evaluation forms. Allow time for young people to complete them. Collect them when young people finish.

7. Celebrate the year and the good memories. Look at everyone's pictures and slides. Munch on favorite snacks such as popcorn, chips and dip.

8. Pour everyone a glass of pop. Ask participants to raise their glasses for a toast. Say: ''Thanks be to God for a great year. Thanks be to God for a good year to come.'' Let everyone drink.

END-OF-THE-YEAR EVALUATION

Instructions: Fill in this evaluation with your thoughts and feelings about the past year's youth group activities.

1. How would you rate the following activities? (1 = great; 5 = lousy)
   - Weekly Bible studies   1 2 3 4 5
   - Bimonthly retreats   1 2 3 4 5
   - The New Year's lock-in   1 2 3 4 5
   - Service projects   1 2 3 4 5
   - Fund raisers   1 2 3 4 5
   - Other: _____   1 2 3 4 5

2. What meeting topics did you enjoy most?

3. What meeting topics did you enjoy least?

4. What meeting topics would you like to cover in the future?

5. What activities (retreats, lock-ins, parties, fund raisers) did you enjoy most?

6. What activities did you enjoy least?

7. In what activities would you like to participate in the future?

8. Overall, how would you rate this year?   1 2 3 4 5
   Explain:

ACTION

Ask several group members to help you summarize the evaluations. List strengths, weaknesses, and high and low points of the past year. Ask the young people to serve as a planning committee. Plan activities and meeting topics for the next year according to the evaluations.

1 THESSALONIANS 2:17—3:13 • PASTORAL CONCERN

FOCUS

Qualities of a good congregation.

PREPARATION

Gather a marker, a Bible, a thank-you card, posterboard, some newsprint, construction paper and writing materials.

INSIGHT

Paul desires to visit the Thessalonians. They have been in his thoughts continually. They are his hope, joy and reason for boasting.

The apostle expresses his pastoral concern for them. He was prevented from coming to them, but he sent Timothy. His aide reported they had developed beautifully in their faith. Paul's concern reveals spiritual and emotional depth—the marks of an authentic pastor.

In this study, group members will list qualities of a good pastor and characteristics of a good congregation.

BIBLE STUDY

1. Open with an affirmation time. Gather everyone in a circle. All group members say each person's name five times, then complete a sentence about him or her using three affirming, descriptive words. For example: "Kim, Kim, Kim, Kim, Kim. Kim is cute and friendly and fun. David, David, David, David, David. David is athletic and enthusiastic and bright." Give everyone a chance to be affirmed.

2. Say: "We've just affirmed each other and shown our appreciation. Paul does the same with the Thessalonians." Read 1 Thessalonians 2:17—3:13.

3. Say: "Paul reveals several marks of a good pastor. He loves the Thessalonians, he's concerned about them and he maintains contact with them. What are other qualities of a good pastor?" Give young people a few minutes to say these qualities. List them on a piece of posted newsprint.

4. Tell group members to imagine they have been appointed to the board of directors for a seminary—a school that trains people to become clergy.

5. Form groups of threes. Distribute writing materials. Have each group outline the courses and experiences seminary students should take in order to become quality pastors. Encourage group members to write the courses and experiences as specifically as possible.

6. Share the necessary courses and experiences. Ask, "How would Paul pass some of the courses?"

7. Ask the small groups to list five attributes of a good congregation. For example, members are enthusiastic about faith, they care for each other and they reach out to others.

8. Share the qualities. Ask:

●What does a minister look for when he or she considers a church or parish?

●How does your church compare with these characteristics?

●Is more or less expected of clergy than church members? Explain.

●What happens when these expectations are mismatched or unfulfilled by one party or the other?

9. Pass around the thank-you card. Say: "We're going to show our minister our appreciation. Write a note of thanks on the card and sign your name. I'll mail it to the minister."

10. Pass around a piece of paper. Say: "We're also going to show our appreciation to the congregation. Write a note of thanks on the piece of paper. For example, 'Thanks for supporting our youth ministry.' We'll print the note of thanks in the next Sunday bulletin."

11. Close with a prayer of thanksgiving for the minister and the congregation.

ACTION

Ask students to prepare a poster. Title it "A Quality Congregation." Add the lists of qualities the group members developed. Add an arrow made from construction paper. Point it toward the qualities. Write on it "What qualities does our church do well in? What areas do we need to improve in?" Post it where congregation members can see it. Then involve young people in areas they could help improve. For example, in mission outreach teenagers could serve on a special task force to promote local or world outreach.

1 THESSALONIANS 4:1-8 • *LIVING IN HOLINESS*

FOCUS
Sexuality.

PREPARATION
Gather a Bible, a bottle of mouthwash, two pieces of posterboard, several magazines, scissors, newsprint, markers, glue, and a cup of water and refreshments for each person. Videotape segments of various soap operas. Capture those moments that focus on today's view of sexuality.

INSIGHT
In this passage, Paul warns against sexual immorality. Today, some churches rarely speak about sexuality other than in the prohibitive sense. Paul, however, is not shy about addressing the sexual immorality of his time.

Someone once said soap operas are media brothels masquerading as TV entertainment. A cultural brothel certainly seems a fair description of Thessalonica in Paul's day.

The increase in teenage pregnancies, AIDS and herpes indicates a need for the Christian model of fidelity and chastity.

In this study, group members will contrast the media's view of sexuality and God's view of sexuality.

BIBLE STUDY

1. Give each student a cup of water as he or she enters the room. On ''Go,'' have group members begin gargling. The one who gargles the longest wins a bottle of mouthwash.

2. Say: ''The gargling contest leads us into our study. We're going to look at what the media says about sexuality and what God says about sexuality. Commercials focus on the cleanest hair, brightest smile, prettiest face and freshest breath. What else do they say?'' Allow time for students to contribute.

3. Distribute magazines, scissors, glue, markers and one piece of posterboard. Have students make one poster of the media's view of sexuality. They can cut out pictures of bright smiles, shapely bodies, healthy hair, clean skin and seductive smiles. Title the poster ''The Media's View of Sexuality.'' Ask:
● What pictures did you find to illustrate the media's view of sexuality?
● What messages do these pictures give us?

4. Play the video segments of the soap operas. Ask:
● What messages about sexuality do these soap operas give us?
● How do these messages compare with the ones given in magazines?

5. Read 1 Thessalonians 4:1-8. Ask:
● What does Paul say about sexuality?

●How does Paul's message differ from the media's message? Are there any similarities? Explain.

6. Give students the other piece of posterboard. Title it "God's View of Sexuality." Ask them to find pictures or draw symbols to portray this message. Discuss the poster.

7. Ask students to imagine they are offering advice and guidelines to a younger sibling concerning sexual matters. Let them tell their guidelines. Write them on a piece of newsprint. Ask:

●Are these guidelines similar to Paul's standards? Explain.

●Are Paul's standards practical for us today? Explain.

●How can you say no to temptation?

●How would you sum up this lesson in one sentence? (For example, "Sex is a gift of God for two people who have committed themselves to become one.")

ACTION

On a bulletin board in the education area, post the two posters and the list of guidelines. Use this study as the opening study to a sex-education course for upper-elementary children. Encourage the teenagers to lead the session.

---

1 THESSALONIANS 4:9-12 • WORK WITH YOUR HANDS

FOCUS
Work.

PREPARATION
Gather several 3x5 cards, scissors, the want ads section from several newspapers and a Bible. You'll need equipment to record interviews. Decide whether you want to record on cassettes or videotape.

Type the role descriptions in the study on separate 3x5 cards. Feel free to create your own descriptions.

INSIGHT
Paul advises the Thessalonians about day-to-day living. He encourages the readers to love one another, live a peaceful life, take care of their own obligations and work to support themselves. The example of this Christian life will command respect from non-Christians.

The concept of work has taken a beating during the past few years. Cultural critics of the '60s and '70s felt people were possessed by work. The Protestant work ethic was seen as destroying other important values. Today, however, a substantial portion of the population can't find work. American productivity has fallen.

The concept of work is needed more than ever. There is value in earning your own way.

In this study, group members each will portray an unemployed or employed person.

BIBLE STUDY

1. Pass out the want ads to the students. Ask them to find one job they'd like to have. Let each person share the job and explain why it attracted him or her. Ask:
- Is work satisfaction important? Why or why not?
- What are you looking for in a job?

2. Distribute one of the following role descriptions (on a 3x5 card) to each student.
- A middle-aged, unemployed, uneducated laborer: "I can do anything a mule can do. Just give me a chance."
- A high school dropout: "The minimum-wage jobs are terrible. They never give you enough hours to qualify for the benefits. I now work two of them."
- An unemployed steelworker: "I'm not going to take one of those fast-food jobs. I made a lot more money when I worked in the mill a couple of years ago. The mill will come back sometime. I'll wait and live off my benefits—and my wife's income."
- An unemployed, 50-year-old miner: "We lost our home and car. I have been unemployed for three years. My union friends ignore me. My wife keeps us alive. She works in a fast-food restaurant. I don't know what I can do. I want to work. I just can't learn to run computers."
- A wife of an unemployed railroad worker: "We've been without a job for two years. I keep urging my husband to try for another kind of job. He says he doesn't want to give up his benefits. He's sure he'll be called back. It hurts me most when I can't get clothes for our children or buy them little treats. We stopped going to church. It's hard to give an offering when we barely have enough money to put food on the table."
- A college student: "I hate my summer job. The work is so stupid. I count the hours until I get back to school. It's so depressing to know exactly how much I'll make for the hours I work."
- A retired businessman: "My retirement is terrible. My life is a huge vacuum. It seems as if I lost a limb during these six months away from the company. No one calls or values me anymore. There isn't much reason to live."
- A high school junior: "My buddy and I have a good deal. We mow lawns. I know it sounds like a lousy job. But we've been able to get a whole bunch of lawn jobs lined up for weekly cutting. We found we can make more money than our friends who work in the grocery store. I like being my own boss."

3. Ask students each to focus on their person described on the card. Ask:
- What past events have molded the man or woman?
- Why does your person say those things?
- How do you feel about the person?

●Does he or she match your work attitude? Explain.

4. One at a time, have students portray the character by communicating the attitude on the card. The class interviews each person about the meaning and importance of work. Let everyone have a chance to be interviewed.

5. Read 1 Thessalonians 4:9-12 and ask:

●What is Paul's recommendation about work?

●What were your reactions to some of these role-play situations?

●How do you feel about someone who works hard? someone who's lazy? someone who's unemployed? someone on welfare?

●What would Paul say about some of these situations?

6. Distribute scissors. Have students each cut out the shape of a cross from the want ads. Place the crosses on the floor and gather around them. Reread 1 Thessalonians 4:9-12 as a closing prayer.

ACTION

Ask each person to interview adult church members and other youth group members about their jobs. Tape these interviews either on cassette tapes or videotapes. Discuss these insights at the next session. Then form a tape library for other young people and adults to learn about vocations.

1 THESSALONIANS 4:13—5:11 • THE COMING OF THE LORD

FOCUS
Priorities.

PREPARATION
Gather writing materials, construction paper, a marker and a Bible. Using the marker and construction paper, make a fake $10,000 check.

INSIGHT
Paul addresses death, resurrection and eternal life. He says Christ will descend from heaven with an archangel's call and with the sound of trumpets. He will gather the host of believers into an eternal communion. The Thessalonians and all believers should not grieve as others who have no hope.

Paul says the day of the Lord will come like a thief in the night. Sudden destruction will come like birth pains to a pregnant woman. He calls upon believers to stay awake. Christians are assured of God's forgiveness and eternal life.

In this study, group members will imagine they have only 15 minutes to live and must set priorities accordingly.

BIBLE STUDY

1. Gather students in a circle. Pass around the fake $10,000 check. Let each person complete this statement: "If I could buy anything with this money, I would buy . . ." Let each person contribute and explain the reason for his or her choice.

2. Distribute writing materials. Say: "Good news. You each have won 10 times $10,000. You've won $100,000. List 15 things you'd want to buy with your money." Let young people explain their choices.

3. Read 1 Thessalonians 4:13—5:11. Say: "Paul is answering some questions concerning Christ's second coming. He tells the Thessalonians to stay awake—to keep their priorities straight. The day of the Lord will come unexpectedly like a thief in the night.

"Imagine you were to die unexpectedly in 15 minutes. Knowing this, how would you spend $100,000?" Let young people list some ideas on the opposite sides of their papers. Ask:

●How are your lists similar? different?

●How did knowing you were going to die affect your priorities?

●What does Paul mean when he says to stay awake?

●How can we remember to prioritize our hopes and desires as if Christ were coming soon?

4. Say: "Paul tells the Thessalonians God has given Christians eternal life. He says not to worry but to simply be prepared and encourage one another—build one another up."

5. Pass around the fake $10,000 check. Ask each young person to build up (or encourage) the person on his or her right by completing this statement: "If I could buy anything for you with this money, I would buy . . ."

ACTION

Ask young people to begin each day this next week with the thought: "Christ could come today. I'll live my life accordingly." At the next study, discuss whether or not this thought affected their actions.

---

1 THESSALONIANS 5:12-28 • CONCLUDING THOUGHTS

FOCUS
Christian attributes.

INSIGHT
Paul concludes this Epistle with general instructions and greetings. He tells the Thessalonians to do several things:

PREPARATION

Gather pencils, refreshments, a bag of candy, a Bible and two blindfolds. Make two copies of the handout for each person.

- Honor their leaders.
- Extend peace among members.
- Warn the lazy.
- Encourage the timid.
- Support the weak.
- Be patient with everyone.
- Live with justice.
- Do good for others.
- Be joyful.

- Pray constantly.
- Give thanks in all things.
- Don't quench the Spirit.
- Hold fast to good.
- Abstain from evil.

The apostle bids them farewell and asks them to greet each other with the kiss of peace.

In this study, group members will rate the church and themselves according to certain attributes.

BIBLE STUDY

1. Play a game called "Hot and Cold." Divide into two groups. Blindfold one person in each group. Place the bag of candy somewhere in the room. Tell each group to guide its blindfolded team member to the bag of candy. Members yell "Hot" if the person is heading in the right direction or "Cold" if the person is off target. The team member who reaches the candy first shares it with his or her team members (and the other team too)!

2. Read 1 Thessalonians 5:12-28. Say: "Paul concludes his letter to the Thessalonians by telling them several Christian attributes—things they should strive for. I'll give you a pencil and a handout. Rank our church 'Hot' if it follows each item to perfection, 'Cold' if it doesn't follow it at all, or between the two extremes." Distribute a handout and pencil to each person.

3. After young people finish, discuss their rankings. Ask:
- What areas are hot?
- How can our church keep doing these things?
- What areas are cold?
- How can our church "warm up" in these areas?

CHRISTIAN ATTRIBUTES—HOT OR COLD?

Instructions: Rate your church according to how well it follows each item. Color in each thermometer with your answer.

	Cold/ Not so good	Hot/ Excellent
1. Honor your leaders.		
2. Extend peace to others.		
3. Warn lazy people.		
4. Encourage shy people.		
5. Support weak people.		
6. Be patient.		
7. Don't repay evil with evil.		
8. Do good for others.		
9. Be joyful.		
10. Pray constantly.		
11. Give thanks in all things.		
12. Be open to the Spirit.		
13. Hold fast to good.		
14. Avoid all evil.		

4. Play "Hot and Cold" once again. Blindfold two other team members. Each group must guide its team member to the table of refreshments. First team there gets to be first in line for refreshments.

ACTION

Give students each one more handout. Ask them to rank themselves according to how well they follow each item on the list. Ask students to choose one cool area and heat it up (develop and improve it). They may be cool on their patience; they could practice counting to 10 when they're angry. They may be cool on being joyful; they could thank God every morning for five blessings and every evening for one good thing that happened that day.

2 THESSALONIANS

INTRODUCTION TO 2 THESSALONIANS

"I'm proud of you, son. You've done a great job." The father praises his son for his excellent grades on his report card.

Paul is proud of his readers. He praises them for standing firm amidst trials and persecution. Paul's second letter to the Thessalonians closely followed the first. He continues to explore several themes.

The Thessalonians thought the day of the Lord had already come. Paul tries to erase that belief and explains more about the Lord's second coming. Nobody knows the exact day. Believers should not drop out of day-to-day living to wait for the end. They must live each day to the fullest and not be a burden to others.

2 THESSALONIANS 1:1-12 • A SPECIAL PEOPLE

FOCUS
Affirmation.

PREPARATION
Gather a Bible, chair, marker, writing materials and newsprint.

INSIGHT
Paul affirms the Thessalonians. He doesn't threaten or scare them. He gives them a clear picture of judgment: Those who ignore the Word will be separated eternally from God; those who believe will live with God for eternity.

The apostle prays that God will make them worthy of God's call so Christ is glorified. The readers are permitted to bask in the light of Paul's love and pride.

In this study, group members will experience affirmation.

BIBLE STUDY

1. Place the Bible on a chair. Form a circle of students around it. Say: "Paul loves the Thessalonian Christians and affirms them in his letter. Listen to his words of praise and encouragement." Read 2 Thessalonians 1:1-12.

2. Hand the Bible to one of the group members. Tell him or her, "I give you this gift because you have blessed me in a special way." Use specific blessings such as kindness to others, faithfulness to the group, honesty and courage to do what is right.

3. Ask that person to give the Bible to another group member and offer words of appreciation and affirmation. For example, "I give you this Bible as a sign of thanksgiving for your friendliness and care for others."

4. Repeat this exercise until everyone is affirmed. Reread verses 3-4.

5. Discuss the experience. Ask:

● How did it feel to be personally affirmed by other Christians?

● Do you sometimes feel that nobody affirms or appreciates you? Explain.

● What critical comments—or lack of comments—hurt?

6. Form small groups of twos or threes. Give each group writing materials. Ask the groups each to create five ways their church can tell members that God is proud of them. For example, offer an honors banquet for all members and give a "God-loves-you" award to each person.

7. Discuss the thoughts as a large group. Write the ideas on newsprint.

8. Gather everyone in a circle around the chair. Ask one group member to sit in the chair. Go around the circle and have group members affirm the person by completing this statement: "God is proud of you because . . ." Give everyone a chance to sit on the "affirmation seat."

9. Divide in pairs. Ask each person to offer a prayer of thanks for his or her partner. For example: "God, thank you for the gift of Corry. Thanks for blessing him with musical talent and ability. He brightens every worship service and event he participates in. Amen."

ACTION
Ask young people to choose one way to affirm church members. For example, create certificates that say "God loves you for being you," and distribute them after a Sunday worship service.

---

2 THESSALONIANS 2:1-17 • JESUS' FINAL RETURN

FOCUS
Trust.

PREPARATION
Gather a Bible, blindfold and sack of fruit—one piece for each person. Videotape a segment of a horror film. (If this isn't possible, cut out newspaper ads for horror shows.)

INSIGHT
Paul explains what must happen before Jesus' final return. Paul urges the Thessalonians to live as if the kingdom of God is at hand. Christians will not know the exact time of Jesus' return. The signs will be confusing. There will be persecutions and false prophets. But believers are held securely in God's hands. God will destroy the ungodly and be faithful to those who believe. Believers are chosen by God from the beginning of time to be saved.

In this study, group members will experience trust in unknown times.

BIBLE STUDY
1. Form a circle of students. Have them stand shoulder to shoulder.

2. Choose one person and blindfold him or her. Place the person in the center of the circle. (If you have a large group, form several tight circles.)

3. Ask the blindfolded person to fall back and trust the others will catch him or her. Say: "The group members will catch you and gently push you in another direction. Keep your body stiff and your legs together. Allow yourself to be caught and tossed." Let others try this game of trust.

4. Read 2 Thessalonians 2:1-17 as each person experiences the group's support. After everyone has tried this, ask:
- How did it feel to fall while blindfolded?
- How did it feel to trust others to catch you?
- How did you feel when others caught you?

5. Show a videotaped segment of a horror film. (Or distribute newspaper ads of horror shows.) Ask young people to choose scary parts of the message—ones that frighten them most. Ask:

● Why are these parts scary? (For example, they portray things that are unknown.)

● How do the images from the horror show compare to what Paul is describing? (For example, they're unknown; nobody has experienced them.)

● Why are we afraid of the unknown?

● Why is little known about the end times?

● What words of hope does Paul give his readers? (Reread verse 13.)

● If God chose us from the beginning to be saved, how should we feel about the unknown?

6. Say: "God has chosen us from the beginning to be saved. God will protect us from evil. God loves us and gives us eternal comfort and hope. Trust him."

7. Play another game of trust. Pass around the sack. Ask each person to reach in and pull out a surprise (no peeking). Encourage students to trust it'll be a good surprise. Eat the goodies.

ACTION

Ask students to focus on trust for their daily devotions this next week. They can read Psalm 25:2; 37:3; Proverbs 16:20 and other passages that highlight the value of trust.

2 THESSALONIANS 3:1-18 • CLOSING APPEALS

FOCUS

Work versus laziness.

PREPARATION

Gather a Bible, a loaf of sliced bread, butter, jelly, honey and knives. Ask one person to read "A Story for Our Times" (a version of a Mother Goose story).

INSIGHT

Paul again addresses the issues of work and laziness. Many of the Thessalonian Christians had stopped working and were living on others' generosity. Paul says if anyone won't work, he or she shouldn't eat. No good can come from people who are idle and busybodies.

He closes this Epistle with his blessing. Paul guarantees the readers this greeting comes from him because of his handwriting. The strokes are the same ones he makes on all of his letters.

In this study, group members will listen to a story and discuss work versus laziness.

BIBLE STUDY

1. Invite students to sit in a comfortable position. Ask a young person to read the story.

A STORY FOR OUR TIMES

There once lived a small man. He wasn't much of a sight. He was ordinary and plain, but he was a busy, busy person. His neighbors often stood around and watched him work hard on various tasks. The neighbors were bored with life. They received a little enjoyment by teasing the man: "You're a busy little thing"; "Yeah. You'd give the Road Runner a run for his money."

They'd all laugh at the way he was so serious about his work. They'd say: "Ease up. Relax. Enjoy life."

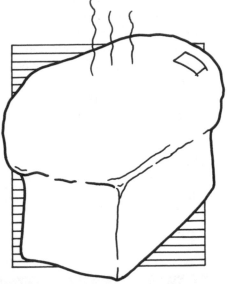

One day, the man found a sack of wonderful, enriched flour. This meant he could bake a fresh loaf of bread. With the butter, jelly and honey he'd saved, he'd have a marvelous meal. However, he needed help. He knew the neighbors made remarks about him. Their teasing hurt. However, this project was too important and wonderful to pass up. He asked: "Would you neighbors lend a hand? I have something fun and tasty to do. We can make a beautiful loaf of bread."

They all laughed and said: "Who needs the work? We don't want dough all over our hands. The hot oven makes us sweat."

The man went away sad. The job would be hard alone. Yet he was determined to transform his find into a wonderful feast. He mixed and worked. His neighbors were right. He became covered with dough. His muscles ached and his face sweat from the difficult labor.

Finally he placed the bread in the oven. The whole neighborhood filled with the fragrance of fresh bread. The lazy neighbors became a bit restless as their senses filled with the aroma of the baking.

The man took the loaf from the oven and set it on a bench to cool. The hungry neighbors gathered around. "Hey, little man. Share your feast with your neighbors," they said.

He took the loaf. "I'm sorry, but you can feast on the wages of your laziness," he said as he moved away from them.

That was one sad, hungry neighborhood.

2. Ask:

●How do you think the neighbors felt when they saw the busy man working?

●How do you think the busy man felt about his neighbors?

●What did the neighbors miss by not helping the man?

●How do you think the neighbors felt at the end of the story?

●When were you like the lazy neighbors? What did you miss by not using your time better?

●When were you like the busy man? What did you gain from working?

3. Pass around a loaf of bread. Set out the butter, jelly, honey and knives. Encourage students to take a slice and add butter, jelly or honey. While they do this, read 2 Thessalonians 3:1-18.

4. Say: "Many of the Thessalonian Christians were not working. They were living on other people's generosity. Through some misunderstanding, they thought the end was upon them—so why work? Paul tells them to work and not be a burden to others." Ask:

●What do you think people thought of the Thessalonian Christians?

●Was their lack of work a good example to others? Why or why not?

●Why does Paul say to work and not be a burden to others?

●While we wait for Christ's return, what work can we do?

5. Let participants eat their slices of bread. Pray: "God, help us put aside any laziness and actively work to better our world. Amen."

ACTION

Brainstorm jobs that need to be done around the church. For example, vacuum carpet, clean windows, paint walls and polish furniture. Set aside one day as a workday. Encourage young people to put away non-activity and work to better the church.

1 TIMOTHY

INTRODUCTION TO 1 TIMOTHY

When I was a college student, I served as a youth adviser in a small church. Rev. D. Andrew Howey from that church was my mentor and friend. He guided me through those first days of serving Christ.

Rev. Howey received an invitation to speak at another church one Sunday. It was my responsibility to host the visiting pastor. My instructions were to read the call to worship and let the visiting pastor do the rest. Well, the guest preacher didn't show. At first I didn't know what to do, but it didn't take me long to figure out I needed to preach my first sermon. I'm not sure how much I contributed to the service that morning; all I know is I read the call to worship *and* preached the sermon.

I can still feel the warmth of Rev. Howey's affirmation: "I knew you wouldn't let me down. Here's the honorarium for the sermon. Thanks." His kindness, love and affirmation strengthened me to continue on the road to ministry.

This encouraging, affirming, "mentor" spirit wells up from the books known as the Pastorals (1 and 2 Timothy and Titus).

A good deal of scholarly discussion has occurred about who is really the author of these books. They are ascribed to Paul, but many internal points make this possibility unlikely. For example, vocabulary, style and expressions. For the sake of these studies, we will use Paul's name.

This first Epistle is addressed to Timothy. Timothy is a young man who received Christian training from his grandmother, Lois, and mother, Eunice. His father was a Greek, and his mother was a Jewish woman who had converted to Christianity.

The letter provides practical advice about the church's life and activities. The writer addresses scattered problems and concerns that evolve from Christians' daily lives.

1 TIMOTHY 1:1-7 • *RELIGIOUS SPECULATION*

FOCUS
Astrology and cults.

PREPARATION
Bring a Bible and a trash can. Collect astrology columns that match students' birthdays.

INSIGHT
The author of the Epistle opens with the usual greeting; however, this letter is addressed to a person, Timothy, rather than to a church. Paul urges his "child" to guide people who are wandering after false teaching back to the true path. These backsliders occupy themselves with myths, genealogies and other pagan diversions. This leads to disputes and division. Paul directs Timothy to focus on true teaching and not become involved in debating such speculations.

In this study, group members will examine astrology columns and discuss Paul's warnings against religious speculation.

BIBLE STUDY

1. Affirm each other with an opening game. Gather in a circle. Each group member completes this sentence for the person on his or her right: "I foresee . . ." For example, "I foresee success in college for you since you get such good grades" or "I foresee a huge family for you since you're so good with children."

2. Say: "We just affirmed each other with forecasts. In reality, only God knows the future. Throughout the ages, people have tried to foresee events. That's one reason astrology is so popular today."

3. Pass out the astrology columns. Ask each person to find his or her sign (according to his or her birth date) and read the prediction. Ask:
- What is your forecast?
- Do you believe it? Why or why not?
- How accurate is your forecast compared to the events in your life?
- If the stars and planets control your behavior, what does that say about God's work in your life?
- If the minister printed these forecasts in the church bulletin, how would people react?

4. Read 1 Timothy 1:1-7. Discuss what Paul tells Timothy concerning such discussions in the church. Ask:
- What teachings is Paul warning against?
- What myths or cults are distracting people from the gospel today?
- The passage advises us not to enter into vain discussions when confronted with off-base teachings. We are to offer love from a pure heart, good conscience and sincere faith. How can you apply this advice to your life?

153

5. One at a time, have students wad the astrology columns and toss them in a trash can. As they do, have them complete this sentence: "I trust God for my future because . . ."

ACTION
Offer a course on the dangers of cults. Gather data on cults in your community. Ask a police officer or school official to speak to your group.

---

1 TIMOTHY 1:8-20 • LAWLESS LOVE

FOCUS
Forgiveness.

PREPARATION
Gather paper, pencils, Bibles, 3x5 cards, notebooks, hand lotion and a Nerf ball. Write one of the following "lawless" people on each 3x5 card:

- Lawbreakers and rebels.
- Ungodly and sinful.
- Unholy and irreligious.
- Murderers of their fathers and mothers.
- Killers.
- Adulterers.
- Liars.

INSIGHT
This letter addresses the place of the law. The author moves away from the belief that the law alone brings salvation. He confesses there is a role for the law—it gives boundaries for the weak and the lost. However, the law is not a substitute for the gospel.

Paul describes how God chose him for service in the midst of his ignorant sinfulness. God's grace overwhelmed him. God chose Paul to show God's love. Christ came into the world to save all sinners.

In this study, group members will decide whether certain "lawless" people are outside of God's forgiveness.

BIBLE STUDY
1. Play "Prisoner Dodge Ball." Gather in a circle and give one person a soft Nerf ball. Ask another group member to be the prisoner and stand in the center of the circle. He or she is to dodge the ball as others throw it. Once the prisoner is hit, another group member goes in the center.

2. Form pairs. Give each pair a Bible, piece of paper, pencil and one of the examples of a lawless person written on a 3x5 card.

3. Read 1 Timothy 1:8-11. Ask pairs to use their Bibles to compare their examples with the commandments (Exodus 20:2-17 or Deuteronomy 5:6-21). Have the pairs answer these questions:

●What commandments does your sinner break?

●Are lawless people beyond forgiveness? Why or why not?

●What punishment does your sinner deserve?

4. Discuss what life would be like without laws to guide us. For example, we'd have no curfews, traffic laws or court orders. Ask:

●Are some laws necessary? Why or why not?

●If laws are for disobedient people (as Paul tells Timothy), why do we need them?

5. Invite the students to reflect on their past sins as you read 1 Timothy 1:12-20. Ask:

●How do you feel knowing you don't have a dramatically sinful background?

●Have you missed something in life? Explain.

●Are you less of a sinner than someone else (like the people on your 3x5 cards)? Explain.

6. Say: "We all are sinful by nature. It's only Christ's saving act that cleans us. Sin is more than murder or stealing. Sin is turning from God and our neighbor. In Christ's presence everyone knows he or she has fallen short of God's glory. There are no big and little sins. We all need Christ's saving action."

7. Put some hand lotion on each person's hand and say: "(Name), Jesus' soothing and cleansing love erases all your sins. He forgives you."

ACTION

Ask students to daily seek God's forgiveness and to daily receive God's love. Have them keep track of their prayers in a notebook. Each night have them pray: "God, forgive me for . . . God, thank you for . . ."

1 TIMOTHY 2:1-15 • MEN AND WOMEN

FOCUS
  Equality.

PREPARATION
  Gather Bibles, concord-
ances, paper, pencils and
refreshments.

INSIGHT
  Paul discusses the universality of Christianity. God seeks all people through Christ, our
mediator.

  The author then offers some controversial
concepts about worship. He teaches that
women must be modestly dressed in worship.
They must be silent and submissive. No
woman can teach or have authority over men.
He bases his reasoning on Eve's creation after
Adam and the story of Eve in the Garden. She
was easily deceived by Satan. Women will be saved through bearing
children and continuing in faith, love, holiness and modesty.

  In this study, group members will debate whether a woman should be
ordained.

BIBLE STUDY

1. Divide into two groups. Make sure each team has the same number
of girls. Girls take off their shoes and mix them in one huge pile. On "Go,"
guys (or princes) search the pile and "re-shoe" the girls (or Cinderellas).
No talking allowed. First team with re-shoed females wins. Girls serve
refreshments to the guys.

2. Say: "These activities illustrate traditional thoughts about men and
women. Men are the princes who rescue the Cinderellas. Women serve
food and refreshments. Times are changing, however. Both men and
women work outside the home. Men share the housework. Women are
ministers and have authority over men. When 1 Timothy was written there
was a different view of women." Read 1 Timothy 2:1-15.

3. Divide into two groups. Give each group paper, pencils, Bibles and
concordances. Say: "You represent committees that will call a new pastor
to your congregation. The first group wants the new pastor to be a woman;
the members want to give a woman pastor a chance. The second group
wants the pastor to be a man; the members think women should never be
ordained. You have 15 minutes to write reasons for your position. Support
your ideas with scripture.

  "Although ordination of women isn't specifically mentioned in the Bible,
some verses explain women's role in worship. The group against the ordination of women could support its view with these verses: 1 Corinthians
14:34-35; Ephesians 5:22-33; 1 Timothy 2:8-15. The group for the ordination of women could support its view with these verses: Genesis 2:18;

1 Corinthians 11:11-12; Philippians 4:3; 1 Timothy 3:11.''

4. After the groups complete their positions, allow time for presentations and questioning. Ask:

●Did you agree with your committee's position? Why or why not?

●If you didn't agree, how did it feel to search for facts to support an opposing view?

●If our church were to hire a new minister, would it consider a woman? Explain.

●Why did the author of this passage feel this way about women participating in worship?

●Why can you find support for both views in the Bible?

●Why are opinions changing today?

●Rather than being male or female, what characteristics really qualify a person for ministry?

5. Ask students to develop a litany that illustrates their conclusions. For example:

For making women as helpers for men.

Thank you, God.

For making men as helpers for women.

Thank you, God.

For erasing all barriers such as sex, race and social status.

Thank you, God.

For your Son who died for all.

Thank you, God.

6. Close by reading the litany.

ACTION

Secure permission from your minister and worship coordinator to print the litany in a Sunday bulletin. Read the litany as an entire congregation.

---

1 TIMOTHY 3:1-16 • CHURCH LEADERSHIP

FOCUS
Qualities of a good pastor.

PREPARATION
Gather Bibles, paper, pencils, butcher paper,

INSIGHT
The author discusses the practical life of the church—the offices of bishops and deacons.

The office of bishop is a noble one. A person aspiring such a position must be above reproach, the husband of one wife, temperate, self-controlled, respectable, hospitable, a good teacher, not violent or quarrelsome. He can't

157

balloons, streamers, markers and refreshments.

be a drunkard and he must not love money. The aspiring bishop must manage his family well and keep his children respectful. He can't be a new Christian and he must be well-thought-of by outsiders.

Deacons can be male or female (verse 11). They are required to have character strengths similar to bishops. They must be serious, sincere, not greedy or addicted to wine. They must have faith and a clear conscience. There is no clear indication whether a bishop or a deacon has superior position.

In this study, group members will list qualities of a good pastor and make an affirmation banner for their pastor.

BIBLE STUDY

1. Ask students to find a partner with the same color of eyes. Tell them to follow your directions:
- Nose to nose (partners touch noses).
- Elbow to elbow (partners touch elbows).
- Knee to knee (partners touch knees).
- Switch partners.

Add other directions such as hip to hip, shoulder to shoulder and back to back. Switch frequently so participants get several partners.

2. Ask students to remain with their last partner for the next activity. Give each pair a Bible, paper and pencil. Tell young people to read 1 Timothy 3:1-16, then create a list of 10 qualities a good minister needs to have. For example, compassion, love, care for members and faith in God.

3. Ask pairs to present their qualities in a "pastor fashion show." One partner is the model pastor, the other is the announcer. The announcer describes the pastor as he or she walks in front of the group. For example: "A pastor sports a friendly smile and knows everyone's name. (Pastor smiles and waves.) A pastor cares for the congregation members when they're sad. (Pastor takes a handkerchief out of his or her pocket.)" Let each pair participate in the fashion show.

4. Play another round of the opening game. Use the last direction to lead the young people to refreshments. For example:
- Foot to foot.
- Head to head.
- Knuckles to knuckles.
- Teeth to food.

5. Serve refreshments.

ACTION

Ask students to make an affirmation banner for the pastor. Use markers to decorate a strip of butcher paper. Add the qualities your pastor shares in his or her ministry. Surprise your pastor by decorating his or her office with the banner, balloons and streamers.

1 TIMOTHY 4:1-16 • *FALSE TEACHING*

FOCUS
Nutrition.

PREPARATION
Gather oranges, apples, construction paper, markers, five pieces of poster-board and a Bible. Write each of the following food philosophies on a separate piece of posterboard. Post the signs around the room; place construction paper and markers under each sign.

● Fast-Food Frank: Eats burgers and fries, drinks shakes and colas. Philosophy: "I love the grease, salt and calories. It's the Western way of life. What tastes good is good."

● Vegetarian Marian: Abstains from eating meat of any kind. Philosophy: "God loves all living things. In Genesis we were given herbs, vegetables and fruit. Meat is no good for us."

● Dieting Diane: Focuses on artificial sweeteners, liquid diets, low-calorie foods and drinks. Philosophy: "I want my body

INSIGHT
The author discusses false teaching. The Spirit foretold that people would fall away and follow the teachings of demons and deceitful spirits. These false leaders forbid marriage and reject certain foods. God has created everything to be good when blessed by believers with prayers of thanksgiving.

Paul reminds Timothy that if he teaches these things he will be a good minister. The younger man must stay away from heresies. He must train himself in godliness. Christians' one hope is the living God.

Timothy should not let people look down on him because of his youth. He should set an example in faith, life, love, speech and purity.

In this study, group members will eat fruit, look at various food philosophies, and discuss nutrition and diets.

BIBLE STUDY
1. Play a few relays using fruit. Divide in teams. Give the first member of each team an apple to place under his or her chin. On "Go," players each pass their apple to the next person who takes it under his or her chin. No hands allowed. If the apple drops, the team must start over.

Ask people to find a partner within their team. For each team, place an orange between two people's hips. The pairs go to a point, return to their team, and pass the orange to the next pair, who repeats the process. No hands allowed.

159

slim and fit, like models and movie stars. I eat only enough to keep going.''

● Fad-Diet Doug: Eats all protein, all carbohydrates or all bananas. Philosophy: ''The latest way to lose weight is the best. I want to lose weight fast and easy.''

● Eat-Everything Eric: Eats all foods in great quantities. Philosophy: ''I was born to eat. Treats with lots of chocolate and sugar are the best.''

2. Let participants eat the fruit while you read 1 Timothy 4:1-16. Say: ''In the first five verses, Timothy is told about false teachers who were urging people to stay away from marriage and abstain from eating certain foods. Food was an issue then as it is today.

''People race to try the latest diets. Some starve themselves nutritionally while others overdose on unhealthy food. Bulimia, anorexia and other eating disorders abound.

''Posted around the room are five philosophies about food. Choose one poster you find most interesting. Beneath the poster are construction paper and markers. Draw a picture of how such a person might look. For example, Fast-Food Frank might have his mouth full of french fries, a burger in one hand, a shake in the other. Let your creativity go.''

3. Ask participants to describe their drawings. Ask:

● What should we avoid concerning our diets? (For example, overeating, eating unbalanced meals and using too much salt.)

● What should we strive for concerning our diets? (For example, eating balanced meals, maintaining a consistent weight, and eating plenty of fruits and vegetables.)

● Why do so many people suffer from eating disorders today? (For example, they're unhappy with themselves.)

● What guidelines can you think of concerning diet? (For example, eat a good breakfast each day, don't overeat, monitor your weight daily and don't compare yourself to others.)

4. Say: ''Remember these guidelines. Also remember God says all things are created good. Nothing is to be rejected if it is received with thanksgiving and consecrated with prayer.''

5. Distribute more fruit for refreshments and offer a prayer of thanksgiving before you eat.

ACTION

Later in this chapter Timothy is encouraged to be a good minister and teacher in spite of his youth. Encourage the students to be ministers and teachers. Let them develop dietary guidelines and find more information on eating disorders and nutrition. Have them teach a nutrition course to younger children at church.

1 TIMOTHY 5:1-25 • *WIDOWS*

FOCUS
Helping needy people.

PREPARATION
Search magazines for a picture of an elderly woman who is living on the streets. Glue the picture to a piece of cardboard. You'll also need a Bible.

INSIGHT
Paul continues with practical advice about the life of the local church. The old and young should be treated as family in all purity. Widows over 60 years old deserve support if their children do not help them. Young widows should remarry. Faithful women raise their children, show hospitality, honor the saints, help those in trouble and devote themselves to good works.

Elders who rule well deserve extra honor, especially those who preach and teach. One should never bring charges against such a leader except on the strong evidence of two or three witnesses.

Timothy is encouraged to drink a little wine when his stomach hurts.

In this study, group members will describe memories of grandmothers and decide how to help elderly people in their community.

BIBLE STUDY

1. Begin the study with a few minutes of reminiscing. Ask students to remember when they were 5 years old or younger. Have them describe a memory of their grandmother or favorite older aunt.

2. Say that Paul advises Timothy on how to help elderly women who are widows. Read 1 Timothy 5:1-25.

3. Pass around the picture of the street person. Give her a fictitious name and location (nearby city).

4. Ask students to imagine as many aspects as they can about this person's life. For example, having no money, no family, no husband, mental problems. Ask:
- How would Timothy help this person?
- Would you be willing to help this person? Explain.
- Would you be willing to take her home? Why or why not?
- What if she were your grandmother (or mother in a few years)? Would you help her then? Explain.

5. Say that we are urged to treat all women as family members (verse 2). Pray the following prayer. Pause after each line and let students repeat it:
God, open my eyes that I may see
the needs of people all around me.
Bless all people no matter their age.

Keep them safe from day to day.
Amen.

ACTION

Develop a plan to help elderly women in your community. Visit a near-by nursing home. Students can talk with the residents and express their love in Christ to them. Meet with the administrators to discover needs you can help with. They may need money for equipment, or food and blankets for the residents. View and discuss *The Shopping Bag Lady* (available from Mass Media Ministries, 2116 North Charles Street, Baltimore, Maryland, 21218).

---

1 TIMOTHY 6:1-21 • THE LOVE OF MONEY

FOCUS
Possessions.

PREPARATION
Bring a penny for each person, a quarter, a Bible and a bag of chocolate candy coins. Ask students to bring one thing from home they'd like to keep forever. (For example, a favorite doll or a keepsake from a grandparent.)

INSIGHT
Advice about Christian living fills this passage. Paul urges slaves to respect their owners so God's name won't be defamed. Timothy is urged to continue teaching sound doctrine.

Verse 10a is often misquoted. Money is not the source of all evil; the *love* of money is a source of all evil. Rich people are not to be proud. They are not to set their hopes on riches but on God who gives all good things. They are responsible for using their wealth to do good.

In this study, group members will bring a favorite possession and discuss helping those who are less fortunate.

BIBLE STUDY

1. Begin the study with a show-and-tell time. Ask students to describe their favorite possession and tell why it has this honored position in their lives.

2. Ask young people to look at their prized possessions while you read 1 Timothy 6:1-21.

3. Say: "In the last chapter of 1 Timothy, Paul says we brought nothing into this world and we can take nothing out of it. He warns us against setting our hopes on possessions. He talks about the love of money being a source of evil. Money, when kept in proper perspective, can be used for good.'' Ask:

●Why do we value our possessions?

●What does Paul mean when he says we brought nothing into this world and we can't take anything out? How does this make you feel?

●How can the love of money be a source of evil?

●How can money be used for good?

4. Pass around a quarter. Ask each person to complete this sentence: ''If I could use this money to help people in need I would . . .'' For example, ''I would buy a treat for the neighbor kid down the street; his family is really poor,'' ''I would save it until I had over $100 then give it to a hunger organization.''

5. Give each person a penny and say: ''Let this penny remind you of those thoughts. Use your money and your possessions to help the needy.''

6. Pray: ''God, help us remember not to love money and possessions but to use them for good. Help us fight the good fight of faith while we live. Open our eyes to those who are less fortunate. Amen.''

7. Serve chocolate candy coins for refreshments.

ACTION

Choose a charity that helps the needy such as a hunger organization, community children's hospital or soup kitchen. Raise money for the organization with a fund raiser called ''Penny Chain.'' Advertise your fund raiser well in advance. Ask church members to donate all their pennies. Tell them you will be trying to form as long a chain as possible from the collected pennies. (Also accept nickels, dimes and quarters. Go to a bank and exchange them for pennies.)

At an assigned time, gather the group members and go to work. Place the pennies end to end around the church parking lot. Call your local newspaper to cover the event. Not only will the charity receive money from you, but the publicity may bring in more donations.

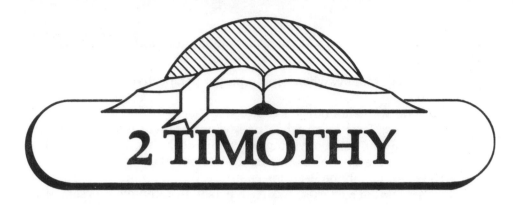

2 TIMOTHY

INTRODUCTION TO 2 TIMOTHY

The mentor advises his friend on a problem: "Why don't you try it this way? It worked for me last year in my job."

Paul, now imprisoned in Rome, continues to advise Timothy as to the life of the church. Although various scholars wonder whether Paul really wrote 1 and 2 Timothy, the material is still helpful. The practical advice about ministry helps Christians with their own concerns.

2 TIMOTHY 1:1-18 • SOUND WORDS

FOCUS
Faith.

PREPARATION
Make an equal number of construction paper stars, circles, triangles and squares. Make enough so each student receives one symbol. Bring a Bible, markers and straight pins.

INSIGHT
Paul greets Timothy, thanks God for him and mentions his family. Timothy can rest assured of his calling because he has been commissioned through Paul. Paul urges Timothy to stand firm on the apostle's teaching. God doesn't make us timid. God gives us a spirit of power, love and self-control.

In this study, group members will create a chant for different faith expressions and discuss their upbringing in the faith.

BIBLE STUDY
1. As young people enter the meeting room, give each one a construction paper symbol. Divide into groups according to symbols. (All the circles are one group, all the squares are another and so on.) Distribute markers and pins.

2. Ask students to design name tags to represent themselves. A person who likes to play football and eat pizza could draw a football and a steaming pizza. Explain the name tags in the small groups. Ask students to pin them to their shirts for the remaining time of the study.

3. Assign each group one of the following faith expressions:

(☆)The New Now Movement: This group denounces all ties with family and serves the leadership of Prophet Joe. The members sell items on street corners and give the prophet all their money.

(○)The Religious Order of Poverty: Men and women enter this faith and take vows of poverty, chastity and silence.

(△)The Commune of People Who Care: People live among the poor and serve them with care and love. They rebuild old homes. They seek to live in Christ's footsteps.

(□)Positive People: This self-improvement group uses positive thinking and self-improvement goals to gather followers. After attending a three-day course, students help set up other such meetings.

4. Ask groups to create a chant that summarizes their beliefs. A chant for The New Now Movement could be: "Prophet Joe. Prophet Joe. Here you go. Here's some dough."

5. Share the chants and discuss the different beliefs. Ask:
- Which of these religions would you be most willing to accept? Why?
- Which one would you be most unhappy with? Why?
- How would your parents react if you dated someone of each religious

165

expression?

- What values and beliefs have been entrusted to you?
- How are they different from these other religious expressions? similar?
- Are your beliefs similar to your parents? Explain.

6. Read 2 Timothy 1:1-18. Say: "God sent Jesus to die for our sins. God blesses us with a spirit of power, love and self-control—not of timidity. The Spirit will guard the truth that is in us."

7. Pray: "God, help us follow your true teaching, through faith and love in Christ. Thank you for blessing us with a spirit of power, love and self-control. Amen."

ACTION

Ask students to sit down with their families and discuss their faith. Answer these questions:

- What do we believe?
- Why do we believe it?
- What would we do if a brother or sister dated someone of another religion? married someone of another religion?
- How do we accept our parents' faith and make it our own?

---

2 TIMOTHY 2:1-26 • IMAGES OF FAITH

FOCUS

Advice for Christians.

PREPARATION

Gather a Bible, a canteen filled with a beverage, yogurt, fruit, bowls, spoons and cups.

INSIGHT

Paul uses the images of a soldier, athlete and farmer to illustrate that there's a price to be paid for rewards. Paul says he is suffering in chains for preaching the gospel. But God's Word is not chained.

Timothy must remind those in the church that they can't be distracted by disputing over words. It does no good and only confuses and ruins the hearers. Believers must avoid youthful desires and aim at righteousness, faith, love and peace. Believers must have nothing to do with arguments, but be kind and good teachers, gently correcting opponents.

In this study, group members will portray soldiers, athletes, and farmers and discuss the work and rewards of being a Christian.

BIBLE STUDY

1. Ask students to march in place. Say: "We are soldiers for Christ. Listen to God's Word." Pass a Bible from person to person. Have young people each read a verse of the passage. (Keep marching!)

2. After the passage is read yell, "Halt, soldiers." Say: "Paul uses the image of a soldier whose desire is to please the one who enlisted him. A Christian's desire should be to please God."

3. Ask young people to jog in place. Ask them to shout out characteristics of an athlete. For example, strong, enduring, healthy and keeps eyes on a goal. Yell, "At ease, athletes." Say: "Paul uses the image of an athlete who is not rewarded unless he plays by the rules. A Christian's reward for living as a servant is eternal life."

4. Ask students to pretend they're hoeing a field. Say: "Paul uses the image of a hard-working farmer who should have the first share of the crops. A Christian holds nothing back in commitment to Christ."

5. Divide into three groups: soldiers, athletes, farmers. Tell each group to think of five ways to persevere through life by hanging tough in Christianity and looking for the reward of eternal life. For example, pray daily, keep thoughts focused on Christ and help others.

6. Ask groups to portray their assigned person (soldier, athlete, farmer) and present their pieces of advice. The soldiers could march in single file. The leader could yell, "Pray daily." The rest of the soldiers could repeat, "Pray daily," and so on for each piece of advice.

7. Serve refreshments. Give the soldiers a canteen filled with a beverage, give the athletes yogurt and give the farmers fresh fruit. All groups share. Mix the fruit and yogurt and fill cups with the beverage.

ACTION

Teach the preschool-age Sunday school children this lesson. Ask participants to pretend they're soldiers—march in place and follow the leader. Pretend they're athletes—jog and touch their toes. Pretend they're farmers—play "Farmer in the Dell."

2 TIMOTHY 3:1-17 • FROM GENERATION TO GENERATION

FOCUS
Parents.

INSIGHT
Paul reminds Timothy that there will be stress in the last days. He lists the evils of people who love pleasure rather than God.

PREPARATION

Gather paper and pencils. Make two copies of the handout for each person.

Paul tells of his work. He suffers for the gospel as must all who bear this faith. Timothy's upbringing in the faith will keep him strong. The scriptures will complete and prepare him for the ministry ahead.

In this study, group members will list positive characteristics of their parents and discover how they are similar and different from their parents.

OUR BELIEFS		
Instructions: Fill in your parents' beliefs for each item, then fill in your own beliefs.		
	Parents	*You*
God		
School		
Work		
Drugs		
Drinking		
Sex		

BIBLE STUDY

1. Gather group members in a circle. Give each one a piece of paper and pencil. Ask students to list five positive qualities of their parents such as hard working, dependable and fun loving.

2. Ask a young person to read his or her list. Let others affirm him or her by saying a quality he or she shares with his or her parent. For example, "Sandy, you're dependable—just like your mom." Let each person read his or her list and experience affirmation.

3. Read 2 Timothy 3:1-17. Say: "Paul urges Timothy to hang on to what he has learned from his childhood. Timothy learned a lot about Christianity from his mom and his grandmother."

4. Distribute an "Our Beliefs" handout to each person. Ask teenagers to fill in their parents' views and their own beliefs about each item.

5. Discuss their answers. Ask:

● Which beliefs are similar? different?

● Why are some beliefs similar? different?

● In the future, will you move closer to or further away from your parents' views? Explain.

6. Close with a prayer. Ask each person to complete this sentence: "God, thanks for my parents because . . ."

ACTION

Give everyone another handout. Ask teenagers to have their parents complete the form. Discuss and compare the answers.

---

2 TIMOTHY 4:1-22 • *FAITHFUL MINISTRY*

FOCUS

Memories.

PREPARATION

Gather a Bible, 3x5 cards, paper and pencils. Serve a snack such as chocolate milk or root beer floats that will bring back childhood memories. Ask group members to bring scrapbooks from home (ones that contain pictures and mementos from their growing-up years).

INSIGHT

Paul urges Timothy to be faithful in his ministry. Timothy must preach the Word constantly and convince, admonish, and urge his listeners to repent and serve Christ. He also needs to be patient in his teaching. The writer predicts a time when people will have "itching ears" for new and different teachings. Paul encourages Timothy to focus on his ministry—to be steady and endure suffering.

Paul knows the time is near for his death. He has fought the good fight and run a good race of faith. God will reward him for this faithfulness. He closes the letter with personal notes about various relationships. When Timothy comes, he can bring Paul's cloak, books and other things.

Paul says that at his trial no one stood with him; however, God did not desert him. His heavenly reward is undeniable. He bids his reader farewell.

In this study, group members will bring scrapbooks from home and discuss memories.

BIBLE STUDY

1. Allow 15 minutes for group members to look at each other's scrapbooks.

2. Gather participants and say, "Keep these memories in mind as you listen to the passage." Read 2 Timothy 4:1-22.

3. Say: "Paul is imprisoned and facing martyrdom. He says he has fought a good fight of faith throughout his life." Give each person a piece of paper and pencil. Have participants title their papers "My Race of Faith."

4. Ask students to think of their past memories and write some thoughts about their race of faith. They can address points such as their first memory of church, the first time they brought a friend to church, early thoughts of God, the first time they talked to someone about Christ.

5. Share memories.

6. Serve a childhood snack such as chocolate milk or root beer floats. Take another look at the memories preserved in the scrapbooks.

ACTION

Give each person a 3x5 card and pencil. Have young people paraphrase 2 Timothy 4 and keep it for a bookmark in their Bible. A paraphrase could be: "Help me be patient and teach others of you. Let me look back on my life and be able to say: 'I fought a good fight. I finished the race. I kept the faith.'"

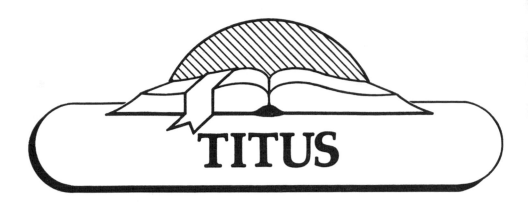

INTRODUCTION TO TITUS

I was caught up in the power of the worship service. God's Word seemed to fill me. I turned to look at those around me. On my left was a small child. He was rocking back and forth keeping perfect time with me! He was mimicking my emotional reaction—a bad habit of rocking. I was a model for this young person.

Titus is one of the Pastoral Epistles (along with 1 and 2 Timothy). The writer has modeled and is passing on ministry qualities to a young pastor named Titus. Titus is referred to in many of Paul's letters. He went with Paul and Barnabus to the apostolic council in Jerusalem. His parents were Gentiles.

Some scholars believe no Pastoral Epistle was actually written by Paul. The vocabulary is different and some of Paul's main theological ideas are missing. A few scholars believe a disciple of Paul's expanded some of Paul's unpublished material. Other scholars say Paul is the author; circumstances made him write differently. For our purposes in these studies, we'll refer to Paul as the author.

The personal quality of Titus touches all who are part of a Christian community. The advice is consistently helpful. The material gives an important glimpse into the life of the early church.

TITUS 1:1-16 • *SPIRITUAL PARENTS*

FOCUS
Mentors.

PREPARATION
Gather one candy bar, 3x5 card, piece of paper, envelope, pencil and stamp for each person. Divide the passage according to the number of teenagers. Write the verses on separate 3x5 cards. Tape each card to a candy bar. Number the cards in the order the verses appear in the passage. If you want a healthier snack, supply oranges instead of candy bars.

INSIGHT
Titus is seen as a spiritual son who has been sent to appoint elders and properly organize the church. The ruling people of the church must have their family life in good order. They need to be blameless and free from drunkenness, temper and greed. They must be hospitable, upright, holy and self-controlled. The bishop also must be girded with sound theology. Those who offer false teaching must be silenced.

In this study, group members each will choose one person who's made an impact on their life and write an appreciation letter to him or her.

BIBLE STUDY
1. Distribute candy bars as group members enter. Tell them God's Word is food for our faith. Invite the person with the first verses to read them, unwrap his or her candy bar and begin eating it. Invite the second person to read, unwrap and begin eating. Do this until the entire passage is read and participants are munching on the goodies.

2. Say: "Paul is a model for Titus. He's passing along instructions and guiding him in his ministry. Think of one person who has made the most impact on your life. He or she could be a schoolteacher, Sunday school teacher, parent, grandparent, brother, sister or friend." Ask:

- Who is the person?
- What qualities do you admire?
- How did he or she affect your life?

3. Distribute paper, pencils, envelopes and stamps. Have students write an appreciation letter to this mentor.

4. Close by praying: "God, thank you for giving us these models in our lives . . ." Let group members say their mentors' names one at a time.

ACTION
Have students search for the addresses then mail the letters. Wait for the responses. Chances are the mentors never realized they made an impact on the teenagers' lives.

TITUS 2:1-15 • THE YOUNG MINISTER

FOCUS
Understanding older adults.

PREPARATION
Gather a Bible, 3x5 cards, pencils, refreshments and background music (such as an album and record player, a cassette tape and tape player or a radio). Invite your church's retired group of adults (65 years and older) to the study. Tell them to anticipate a question-and-answer time.

INSIGHT
Titus, the young minister, is told to teach moderation to the older men and women. The senior women are to teach the young women to be good wives and mothers. The young men also must control themselves and be sensible in behavior. The minister is to be the example of these virtues. The Christian way of life is for all in the community.

In this study, group members will participate in a question-and-answer time with older adults from the congregation.

BIBLE STUDY
1. Form two circles, one inside the other. Youth group members form the inside circle; older adults form the outside circle. Play background music. Ask young people to move in a clockwise direction, older adults to move in a counterclockwise direction.

Explain: "When the music stops, the person you're closest to in the other circle is your partner. Introduce yourself to your partner. I'll ask a ques-

tion, you'll both answer it. When the music starts again, start walking. When the music stops, grab a different partner, introduce yourself and answer the question." If there's not an equal number of people in each age group, pair two young people with an older adult or vice versa. Ask questions such as:

● How long have you been a member of this church? What do you like about it?

● What's your favorite hobby?

● If you could do anything you want to next weekend, what would you do?

● Who is your favorite Bible character and why?

2. Ask everyone to sit. Read Titus 2:1-15. Say: "Paul gives Titus instructions on teaching older men and women in his church. He encourages respect and learning between young people and older people. We're going to learn from each other during this session."

3. Distribute 3x5 cards and pencils. Ask young people to write any questions they have for the older adults. For example: "What was life like when you were a teenager?" "How did you handle pressure to drink?" "How did you find out about the facts of life?"

Ask older adults to write any questions they have of the young people. For example: "Is the pressure to drink and experiment with drugs as bad as everyone says? If so, how do you handle the pressure?" "How do you feel growing up in a world like ours today?"

4. Collect the cards. Keep the two groups' cards separate. Proceed with a question-and-answer time. Draw one question from the teenagers' pile, ask the older adults to answer it. Allow time for more questions and clarification. Draw a card from the older adults' pile, ask young people to answer it. Limit discussion to three to five minutes per question so participants can answer as many as possible.

5. Regroup in the two circles. Play the opening game using these questions:

● What's one thing you learned from this study?

● What's one thing you want to remember from this study?

● How does God want teenagers and older adults to react to each other?

● If you could give your partner one bit of advice, what would it be?

6. Encourage participants to keep talking while they enjoy refreshments.

ACTION

Continue to interact with older adults. Plan an activity every two months such as a Bible study, potluck, picnic or bowling. You may want to plan an annual intergenerational retreat.

TITUS 3:1-15 • OBEY AUTHORITIES

FOCUS
Avoiding arguments.

PREPARATION
Gather paper plates, markers, tape and Popsicle sticks. Place these supplies on a table. You also will need a Bible and a bag of jellybeans. A good resource for this study is *Controversial Topics for Youth Groups* (Group Books).

INSIGHT
The author concludes the Epistle with more advice about the Christian life. He focuses on living in the midst of the secular world. Christians must obey authorities and be willing to do honest work. Believers must speak evil of no one, avoid arguments, and be calm, gentle and courteous.

In this study, group members will discuss controversial topics calmly and gently.

BIBLE STUDY
1. Gather students around the table with supplies. Have them each take a paper plate, marker and Popsicle stick; tape the stick to the plate; and draw a happy face on one side and a sad face on the other side.

2. Tell them you are going to ask a few questions. They answer by holding up their plates. Happy faces mean they agree, sad faces mean they disagree. Pause after each question and have the group members discuss their responses with a neighbor. Use these questions:
- Did you have a good day today?
- Did you have a good week?
- Are you ready to participate in a good study?

3. Read Titus 3:1-15. Ask, "How do you feel about Paul's words to Titus?" Let them show their signs according to how they feel. Say: "Paul tells Titus that Christians need to be submissive to authority, be obedient, work hard, speak evil about nobody and avoid arguing. We're going to discover how people feel about various controversial topics. We'll discuss our feelings gently and without confrontation. After I read a topic, signify your feelings by showing your plate. Happy faces mean 'yes,' sad faces mean 'no.' Discuss your feelings with the people sitting closest to you." Use these ideas and add your own:
- Should young people always obey their parents?
- Is it right to have sex outside of marriage?
- Should abortion be outlawed?
- Should homosexuals be ministers or other church leaders?
- Is the end of the world near?
- Did God create life on other planets?

● Should school authorities have the right to search students' lockers?

● Should Christians view R-rated films?

4. Discuss how easy or hard it was to calmly discuss these topics.

5. Ask group members to show their signs on the appropriate side when you pause during the prayer. Pray: "God, no matter if we're happy (pause) or sad (pause), help us to keep our eyes on you. No matter if we agree with each other (pause) or disagree with each other (pause), help us be gentle and courteous and avoid arguments. Amen."

6. Serve the jellybeans by placing a handful on the happy side of each person's plate.

ACTION

Encourage teenagers to take home their plates as reminders to calmly and gently work through disagreements with their family and friends.

INTRODUCTION TO PHILEMON

"I don't want to go back home. I don't like the rules I have to follow there." The young runaway struggles with the inevitable. He'll be better off if he lives at home until he gets older.

It's hard to accept certain controls in our lives. People in Paul's day had to accept certain controls. Slavery was a necessary part of society. Strict laws dealt with those who interfered with slave owners.

In his letter to Philemon, Paul makes a moving appeal to a fellow Christian who owns a runaway slave, Onesimus. Paul befriended the slave and converted him to Christianity. Paul begs Philemon to forgive Onesimus. If Onesimus has done anything wrong, Philemon is to charge it to Paul's account. Paul hopes Philemon will release Onesimus to assist in the ministry.

New Testament scholar John Knox provides a convincing case for the possibility that Onesimus was returned to Paul and later became bishop of Ephesus. As bishop he could have overseen the collection of Paul's letters, including this short one, which deals with his life. Onesimus, then, becomes the important link between Paul's ministry and our inheritance of his writings.

PHILEMON 1-25 • A CHRISTIAN APPEAL

FOCUS
Forgiveness, love and compassion.

PREPARATION
Gather a Bible, crackers, peanut butter, Kool-Aid, 3x5 cards, paper, pencils, napkins, cups and knives. You also will need one newspaper advice column for each student. Cut off the answer to each request for help.

INSIGHT
Paul is not denying Philemon's right to claim his slave. In fact, the owner has the right, under the law, to have Paul killed for interfering. Paul urges Philemon to act out of love for another Christian. He asks him to forgive Onesimus. Paul offers to pay for any of the slave's wrong-doings.

Many people are amazed that New Testament Christians tolerated slavery. According to Christ's teachings, early Christians *did* deal with slavery. They emphasized God's love for all and the need for Christians to serve others. Those who truly followed Christ's teachings would know something was wrong about one person owning another.

In this study, group members will respond to requests for advice.

BIBLE STUDY

1. Play a game called "Slaves and Masters." Divide the group into pairs. Appoint one partner to be the slave and the other to be the master. The masters order the slaves to prepare their refreshments. For example: "Get the crackers out of the box. Spread peanut butter on the cracker. Place it on a napkin. Prepare a glass of Kool-Aid." The slaves respond after every order, "Yes, master."

Then switch positions. Slaves are now masters, masters are now slaves. Ask, "How did it feel to be a slave? master?"

2. Encourage young people to keep those feelings in mind (and keep eating their snacks) as you read Philemon. Tell them some of the background information found in the "Insight" section and the "Introduction." Ask:

● Do you think early Christians should have revolted against the institution of slavery? Why or why not?

● Why do you think slavery lasted so long throughout history?

● What was Paul's advice to slaves and slave owners? (Refer to Ephesians 6:5-9; Colossians 3:22-25; Titus 2:9-10.)

3. Say: "Paul appeals to Philemon as one Christian to another. He appeals to his compassion and sense of forgiveness. He encourages reconciliation and love."

4. Distribute advice columns, paper and pencils. Ask young people to read the situations and offer advice as they think Paul would have responded.

5. Read the situations and share the responses.

6. Give each person a 3x5 card. On one side of the card, have each young person write a problem he or she needs help with. Collect, mix and redistribute the cards. Let group members respond to the problems by writing their answers on the other side of the cards. Read the situations and solutions and allow time for other suggestions.

7. Ask students to outdo each other in love, compassion and servant-hood for the last few minutes of the study. Students could say to each other: "Please sit down. Let me clean up the crumbs from your snack." "No, please sit down. Can I get you a glass of water?"

ACTION

Ask students each to think of a person they need to forgive. Has a friend hurt them with biting gossip? Did a parent embarrass them in front of their friends? Did a brother or sister break a favorite possession? Ask young people to forgive the person and intentionally do something nice such as invite the friend to lunch, clean the parent's car, or help a brother or sister with homework.

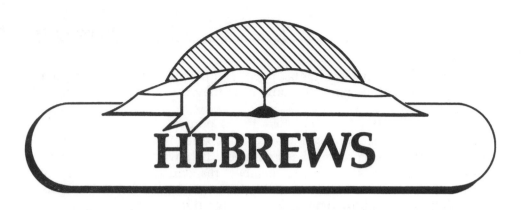

INTRODUCTION TO HEBREWS

The young man stands in the busy airport hallway, clutching an armful of books. His body is taut; his eyes focus on a passing traveler. He lunges toward him. "How are you today? Tired of the materialism in your life?"

An impatient rejection doesn't faze him. He's ready to spring at the next person. These zealous young people can be found in airports and on street corners. They seem to cluster around mysterious, modern religious leaders who offer them a simple new life of dedication.

The anonymous author of Hebrews speaks to readers who also desire a special call. He focuses on the new priesthood of Christ. He strives to prove Christianity over Judaism.

This book doesn't open with a greeting like many of the other Epistles. Yet it concludes like a letter. Scholars suspect the last chapter may have been added after the letter's composition.

The author draws heavily on the Old Testament and carefully builds a case concerning the importance of the Christian faith. He stresses that Christ is superior to the prophets, to angels and to Moses. Christ's priesthood and sacrifice are superior to Old Testament priests and animal sacrifices.

Christ's priestly work is important to an audience facing persecution. They must take a stand and be faithful.

Hebrews was written to show them that believing in Jesus Christ is greater than all their jewish traditions and practices

HEBREWS 1:1—2:18 • *CHRIST'S SUPERIORITY TO ANGELS* week 1

FOCUS
Angels.

PREPARATION
Decorate the room like heaven—use silver tinsel, white construction paper clouds, and silver stars made from aluminum foil and cardboard. Check out an album of harp music from the library. Bring a record player, Bibles, paper, pencils, markers, and construction paper name tags cut like stars. You also will need a picture of Christ, a picture of angels, and heavenly refreshments such as angel food cake and divinity.

INSIGHT
The author reminds this audience that God spoke through the prophets. However, in these last days God spoke through Christ, the radiance of the Creator's glory.

The author strings together seven quotations from the Old Testament to show that angels do not take away from Christ's glory. Angels are sent to minister to those who will inherit salvation.

Christ suffered death for all of us. Christ is above the angels, the one for whom and by whom all things were made. Christ is our salvation.

In this study, group members will compare Christ's qualities to angels' qualities.

BIBLE STUDY
1. Play the heavenly harp music as students enter. Give each young person a star-shaped name tag and marker. Ask young people each to write their name on their name tag and lay it on a table. Encourage everyone to write on each person's name tag one angellike quality he or she possesses. For example, compassion, kindness or love. Allow time for students to sign all the name tags.

2. Read some of the participants' angelic qualities. Pass around the picture of angels and ask:
- How would you describe an angel?
- What Bible stories do you remember about angels?
- Are angels real today? Explain.

3. Pass around the picture of Christ and ask:
- How would you describe Christ?
- How are Christ's qualities similar to angels' qualities? different?

4. Divide in small groups by having participants spell "a-n-g-e-l-a-n-g-e-l." All A's form one group, N's form another, and so on. Give each group a Bible, paper and pencils. Assign each group a part of the passage such as 1:1-4; 1:5-14; 2:1-4; 2:5-9; 2:10-18.

5. Say: "The author of Hebrews tells his readers that Christ is superior to angels. Some believers were giving up their Christian faith and turning back to Judaism. He wants to convince them of Christ's superiority. Read your passage. List any qualities of Christ and qualities of angels you find."

6. Allow five minutes for students to complete this activity, then compare and discuss the findings.

7. Ask the small groups each to compose a prayer using the words "heaven," "Christ" and "angel." For example: "God, thanks for sending Christ from heaven to earth to save us from our sins. He is greater than the angels, yet he gave his life for us. Amen."

8. Gather students in a circle. Place one group member in the center. Invite everyone to tell him or her the Christlike qualities he or she possesses. Give everyone a chance to be affirmed.

9. Read the composed prayers, then serve heavenly refreshments such as angel food cake or divinity.

ACTION

Print the passages and prayers in the church bulletin. Encourage church members to use them for daily devotions. Ask students to demonstrate one Christlike quality this next week. They could show love to a parent by hugging him or her. They could show servanthood by completing a household chore without being asked.

HEBREWS 3:1-19 • CHRIST'S SUPERIORITY TO MOSES

Week 2

FOCUS

Faith journey.

PREPARATION

Gather songbooks, small stones, refreshments and a Bible. Find three locations in or around your meeting area to lead participants to during the study. Use these ideas or add your own:

●Represent a first commitment—meet at a baptistery or baptismal font.

●Represent hard or difficult times of faith—meet

INSIGHT

The writer identifies Jesus as an apostle and a high priest. He was faithful to his calling like Moses; however, Jesus is above Moses. Moses was a faithful servant in God's house, but Jesus is the faithful Son in a family home. We are part of this family if we hold on to our faith.

The author uses Psalm 95 to prove that the readers must be careful of unbelief. Because of unbelief their ancestors died in the wilderness and did not enter the promised land.

In this study, group members will participate in a "wilderness journey" through faith.

BIBLE STUDY

1. Gather the students in the regular meeting room and say: "Moses was a faithful ser-

near a rough stone, brick or cement-block wall.

● Represent the promised land—meet in a tower room, in the balcony or on a hill near the church.

vant who followed God's call. Moses led his people out of Egypt through the wilderness. Because the people took their eyes off God and didn't believe, they couldn't enter the promised land.

"We're going to travel along our wilderness journey of faith. Follow me to three different locations."

2. Lead students to the first stop. Read Hebrews 3:1-19.

3. Invite group members to dip their hands in the water. Ask:

● Do you remember your baptism? If you were baptized as a child, what stories have your parents told you?

● When did you consciously decide to follow Christ? (For example, at confirmation or during a confession of faith.)

4. Dip your finger in the baptismal water and form a cross on each person's forehead. Say: "You are a child of God. Remember your baptism."

5. Lead students to the second place in their wilderness journey. Line students along the rough wall. Say that it represents difficult times of faith. Have them close their eyes and move along it—feeling the texture with their hands.

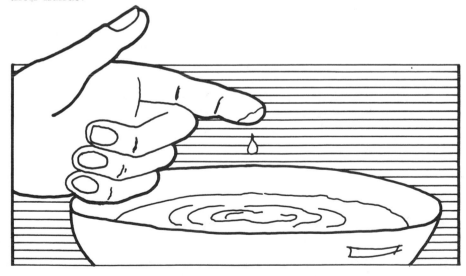

6. Let each student share how the rough wall symbolizes a tough time in his or her faith. A person could say: "The cold, hard wall reminds me of how I felt when my mom and dad divorced. I felt cold and alone. It was hard to believe in God."

7. Lead young people to the third location. Invite them to view their surroundings as the promised land. Ask:

●What are we promised as Christians?
●How do you feel about your faith journey?
●Will you reach the promised land? How do you know?
●How does Christ help you in the face of uncertainty, disbelief or difficult times?

8. Sing a song such as "Promised Land" from *Songs* (Songs and Creations).

9. Lead participants to the final stop—refreshments.

ACTION

Give each student a small stone. Say: "Remember, Christ is our cornerstone and support through life's ups and downs. He's with us during tough times of unbelief." Ask group members to keep the stones as reminders of Christ's strength and support during their journey of faith.

HEBREWS 4:1-13 • THE PROMISED REST

week 3
vbc.

FOCUS
Rest.

PREPARATION
Bring a Bible and a children's book containing the story of Moses leading the Israelites through the wilderness. Ask students to bring their pillows from home.

INSIGHT
The author continues to use the image of the unbelieving people who did not enter the promised land. These people failed to reach the goal of this promised "rest." The promise of rest remains for us today.

The readers must not harden their hearts to God's invitation. They can enter God's rest if they are obedient. God's Word is sharper than any sword. Nothing is hidden from God's eyes.

In this study, group members will relax and discuss the rest God promises us.

BIBLE STUDY
— How do you get that rest?

What rest is author referring to?

1. Ask students to bring their pillows and gather in a circle. Let each group member describe a bedtime memory from when he or she was little. For example: "I shared a room with my brother. My mom would tuck us in bed each night. First she'd kiss my brother, then she'd kiss me. The next night she'd kiss me first then my brother. She'd leave a night light on in the hall so we could see our way to the bathroom."

2. Ask students to lie down, place their heads on their pillows, relax and close their eyes. Read Hebrews 4:1-13. Pause at each punctuation mark.

Let the words about rest slowly enter the students' minds.

3. Read a children's story of Moses leading the people to the promised land. Discuss their lack of faith and how it must have felt to get so close to the land without being able to enter it. Ask:

● How does this story compare to our journey through life?

● What is the promised rest for Christians?

● How will it feel to reach our final rest?

● When have you felt grateful for rest and relaxation? (For example, after a long day of work or after a hard test at school.)

● How does this compare to living a hard life and resting in heaven?

4. Remind students how good it feels to rest after a lot of exercise or a hard day's work. Encourage them to keep the faith, work hard to serve others, and anticipate rest and eternal life.

5. Play games with the pillows. Divide into two groups. See who can make the most creative pillow structure. Run a pillow relay: Participants run to a line, lay their pillow on the floor, lie down, place their head on the pillow, snore loudly three times, run back and tag the next person.

ACTION

Let students experience the need for sleep. Plan an all-night lock-in. Base all activities and Bible studies around this theme of working hard in the faith and the promise of rest and eternal life.

Relationship of Faith + obedience?

HEBREWS 4:14—5:10 • CHRIST IS THE HIGH PRIEST   *Week 4*

, Dick

FOCUS
Selfless love.

PREPARATION
Gather a Bible and several newspapers.

INSIGHT
The author explains the traditional role of a priest. A priest represents the people before God and offers gifts and sacrifices for sin. A priest is understanding because he is subject to the same weaknesses of the people. A priest is called by God.

Jesus was appointed by God. He is God's Son. He is a priest forever in the order of Melchizedek. The author compares Christ to Melchizedek—the "priest of God Most High" (Genesis 14:18b). Melchizedek offered Abraham bread and wine upon his return from defeating the kings. Melchizedek is mentioned again in Psalm 110:4.

During Jesus' life on Earth, he appealed to God with loud cries and tears during his suffering. He learned obedience. He is the source of salvation.

185

Christ was chosen by God to be a high priest in the order of Melchizedek.

In this study, group members will search newspapers for examples of selfless love—people risking their lives for others.

BIBLE STUDY

1. Distribute the newspapers. Ask young people to thumb through them to find a word, phrase, story or cartoon that symbolizes how their week has gone. A person could show a weather forecast and say her week was mostly sunny with overcast skies on Wednesday because of a math test. Another person could show a movie section and say his week was entertaining.

2. Ask students to look through the newspapers to find a story of selfless love—a story of someone who risked his or her life to save another.

3. Read the newspaper examples of selfless love. After everyone has shared, read a biblical example of selfless love—Hebrews 4:14—5:10.

4. Say: "Jesus became human. He suffered as we suffer. He was tempted as we are tempted. He gave his life to save us from our sins. He was selfless in his love for us." Ask:

● How would you describe selfless love?

● Has any person shown selfless love to you? If so, explain.

● Have you shown selfless love to someone else? Explain.

● Why is it difficult to forget our concerns and welfare and focus on another's welfare?

● How can we model Christ's life and focus on others' needs and concerns?

5. Ask each person to search the papers one more time to find one person or situation to pray for. Close by asking God to bless each person or situation.

ACTION

Ask young people to do one intentional act of selfless love this week. A person may notice his sister staying up late one night studying. Even if he's tired and wants to go to bed, he could offer to help her study.

HEBREWS 5:11—6:20 • MILK TO SOLID FOOD

FOCUS
Spiritual growth.

INSIGHT
After warning his readers about their immature faith, the author says they must leave elementary teachings and move on to maturity.

PREPARATION

Bring a Bible and the following materials; make four stations for this study:

● *Station 1:* Make a sign out of posterboard that says "Infant Faith." Supply cups, chocolate milk and a children's Bible story.

● *Station 2:* Make a sign out of posterboard that says "Elementary Faith." Supply cookies, paper and crayons.

● *Station 3:* Make a sign out of posterboard that says "Adolescent Faith." Supply peanut butter, jelly, bread and knives.

● *Station 4:* Make a sign out of posterboard that says "Adult Faith." Supply crackers, juice, cups, napkins, paper and pencils.

He mentions repentance from acts that lead to death, faith in God, instruction about baptism, the laying on of hands, the resurrection of the dead and eternal judgment.

It's impossible to bring to repentance those who once have been enlightened (baptized) but have fallen away. They subject Christ to public disgrace.

The author compares this situation to an agricultural image. Rain falls upon the land and helps it bring forth food. If the land accepts the water but gives forth only thorns and thistles, it is worthless and deserves to be burned.

After this dire warning, the author relents a bit and assures the readers that God will take into account their past work and love. They must have the full assurance of hope until the end. They must overcome laziness and imitate those who inherit the promise through faith and patience. The promise given to Abraham is offered to an even greater degree through Jesus, who is a high priest in the order of Melchizedek.

In this study, group members will experience these spiritual stations: "Infant Faith"; "Elementary Faith"; "Adolescent Faith"; and "Adult Faith."

BIBLE STUDY

1. Introduce the session by saying: "The author of Hebrews explains spiritual growth. Christians must progress from milk to solid food. Listen to his thoughts." Read Hebrews 5:11—6:20.

2. Lead young people to the first station. Say: "New Christians feed on milk. They learn the basics." Serve the chocolate milk and read the story. Ask group members to share early memories of their faith.

3. Take students to the next station. Say, "As we grow spiritually, we learn more about God." Serve the cookies. Give everyone a piece of paper and crayon. Ask students to draw their view of God when they were young. Share the drawings.

4. Proceed to the next station. Say, "As we grow spiritually, we realize God is the Three in One." Symbolize the "Three in One" by supplying three ingredients. The bread represents Jesus who is the bread of life. The jelly represents the fruit of the Spirit. The peanut butter represents God who holds all things together. Have each young person make one sandwich.

5. Proceed to the final station. Say: "An adult faith realizes Christ's body was broken for our sins (break the crackers). His blood was shed for us (pour the juice). We realize that just as Christ came as a servant, so too we must serve." Distribute paper and pencils. Have young people brainstorm ways to reach out and serve others. Let them eat the crackers and drink the juice.

ACTION
Choose one of the ideas and put servanthood into action. If you need help with this, ask the minister for ideas. He or she may know several people in the hospital who'd like visitors. Or the minister may know of some new families who need help settling in a new home.

HEBREWS 7:1-28 • MELCHIZEDEK, THE HIGH PRIEST

FOCUS
The function of a high priest.

PREPARATION
Gather 3x5 cards, pencils, paper, Bibles, Bible dictionaries, concordances, videotape equipment and a robe.

INSIGHT
The author compares Melchizedek to Christ. Melchizedek was superior to the Levitical line of priests. Abraham greatly honored him by giving him 10 percent of the booty won in his victory over the kings.

Jesus is superior to Melchizedek. Death prevents other priests from continuing in office, but Jesus lives forever. Jesus is a new high priest who is sinless. He is pure and perfect.

In this study, group members will write a screenplay about the Old Testament high priest Melchizedek.

BIBLE STUDY
1. Give everybody a 3x5 card and pencil. Ask young people to guess the meaning of the word "Melchizedek." You'll get a variety of meanings: "It's the name of a pharmacy," "It's a new brand of jeans," "It's a rare disease that makes a person sneeze."

2. Collect the cards and read the responses. Tell students to find the true definition by listening as you read the passage. Read Hebrews 7:1-28.

3. Divide students into small groups. Tell them they are responsible for writing a screenplay about Melchizedek's life. A screenplay could be a simple narration of the facts about the high priest's life. Give each group several sheets of paper, a Bible, concordance and Bible dictionary. Have group members search the following scriptures for facts about Melchizedek: Genesis 14; Psalm 110; Hebrews 7.

4. Gather the groups and have the students read their screenplays. Combine the facts into one narration.

5. Ask someone to read the narration as you role play this interesting character.

6. As Melchizedek, hold a press conference. Invite young people to ask you any questions about your life as a high priest. For example: ''What does a high priest do?'' ''Why is Jesus considered a high priest?'' or ''How can I be assured of God's acceptance when I sin?''

7. Say: ''A high priest was a human mediator. He knew our temptations and sins because he too was tempted and sinned. Christ is the true high priest. He became human and is our mediator, though he did not sin. He suffered as we suffer. He sacrificed his life. Through him we live forever.''

8. Close by asking students to define Christ as our high priest. Have group members complete this sentence: ''Christ is our high priest; he . . .'' Answers could be: ''He loves us,'' ''He died for us'' and ''He suffered as we suffer.'' Offer a silent prayer of thanksgiving for Christ's saving work.

ACTION
Videotape your narration and press conference. You play Melchizedek and dress in a long robe. Group members pretend they're reporters and ask you questions. Show the videotape to other Bible study groups.

HEBREWS 8:1-13 • THE NEW COVENANT

FOCUS
God's promise.

PREPARATION
Gather newsprint, markers, Bibles, scissors, an old favorite sweater and yarn that's the color of the sweater.

INSIGHT
The author continues to develop the idea of Jesus' priesthood. Jesus is a high priest who was appointed by the Lord, not by human authority. His role is much more excellent than that of ordinary priests.

God made the old covenant with the Israelites when Moses led them out of Egypt. The people didn't remain faithful to the covenant. God gives us a new covenant. We are God's people. Jesus serves from the new covenant that supersedes the first covenant.

In this study, group members will learn about the new covenant.

189

BIBLE STUDY

1. Show the students an old sweater. Tell them it's one of the most comfortable pieces of clothing you have ever had. Tell a few stories about the good times you have had in that sweater.

2. Ask young people to share similar stories. Encourage them to tell about something old they just can't throw away.

3. Ask students to examine your sweater and find reasons it should be thrown out. Ask:

● When does a person know when to let something go?

● Does the memory of good times have anything to do with an item's value? Explain.

● Is comfort the most important factor in deciding whether to keep an item or not? Explain.

● How does appearance become important in such a decision?

4. Say: "God talks about giving a new covenant to replace the old one from Sinai days. The new covenant promises everyone knowledge of God." Read Hebrews 8:1-13.

5. Divide into pairs. Give each pair a piece of newsprint, marker and Bible. Ask the pairs to paraphrase the new covenant (verses 8-12). For example: "God wants to make a new promise. God wants to update the Israelites' promise when they came out of Egypt. The Lord says: 'I will be their God. They will be my people. I will forget their sins.' "

6. Share the paraphrases.

7. Say: "God threw away an old covenant and gave us a new one. Think of one thing you want to throw away from your life to replace with something new. You may be ignoring a friend because he or she hurt you. Throw away your pain and forgive the person. You may have a bad habit such as biting your nails or eating away your stress. Throw away the bad habit; replace it with a good habit."

8. Ask young people to hold hands, bow their heads and pray silently for what they want to change. Start with one person. When he finishes, he squeezes the hand of his neighbor on his right. When she finishes, she squeezes her neighbor's hand. When the squeeze reaches the original person, he says, "Amen."

ACTION

Tie a piece of yarn that's the color of your sweater around each person's wrist. Ask students to wear the bracelets to remind them to throw away something old and replace it with something new.

HEBREWS 9:1-28 • CHRIST'S GIFT

FOCUS
Sacrifice.

PREPARATION
Ask group members each to bring a picture of a pet from home. If they don't have a pet, have them bring a stuffed animal. You also will need a Bible. If you're really daring, you could have parents bring the live pets for the final 15 minutes of the study for a real-life pet show.

INSIGHT
The author compares the sacrifices of the old and new covenants. Priests of the old covenant offered animal sacrifices on behalf of the people. Christ did not sacrifice animals; he sacrificed his life. If the old covenant helped sinful people through its animal sacrifices, how much more will the new covenant purify people—through Christ's sacrifice. He is our sinless high priest.

In this study, group members will participate in a picture pet show and discuss sacrifice.

BIBLE STUDY
1. Sponsor a youth group picture pet show. Have group members bring a stuffed animal or a picture of a favorite pet. Let each one tell the pet's name, how he or she got the pet and any tricks the pet can do.

2. Read Hebrews 9:1-28. Explain that the ancient world used simple animals as blood sacrifices to take on the people's sins or guilt. An animal was killed in place of the worshiper as a way of paying for sin. Ask:

● How would you feel if your pet was punished for something you did?

● When did someone take the blame or punishment for something you did?

● Did you ever take the blame or responsibility of another person's pain or action? If so, explain. How did it feel? Did it seem unfair? Explain.

● What does Christ's sacrifice for us mean?

3. Invite students to repeat each line after you:
Christ is our high priest.
Christ sacrificed himself for our sins.
Christ forgives our sins.
We are saved.
Through Christ, our sinless high priest. Amen.

4. Invite parents in with the live pets. Sponsor a real-life pet show. Let young people introduce their pets and show the amazing animals' tricks!

ACTION

Ask students to experience self-sacrifice. Have them skip one meal each ✓ day the following week. Collect the money they would've spent on the meals. Give it to a charity or world hunger organization, or donate it to the church.

HEBREWS 10:1-39 • AFFLICTION ९

FOCUS

Keeping faith through trials.

PREPARATION

Meet in a huge furnace room. Gather a Bible, bread, water, butter, jelly, cheese, peanut butter, cups and knives. Write "Survival Kit" on the outside of a bag. Inside place three messages, each contained in an envelope. Number the envelopes.

✓ ●*Envelope 1:* "You are a prisoner. You are charged with being a Christian. You are threatening our world."

●*Envelope 2:* "You are imprisoned for life. You lose your car, home and job."

●*Envelope 3:* "Be compassionate with one another. Joyfully accept the punishment. Keep your confidence. Don't hold back on expressing your faith."

INSIGHT

The writer contends that the law is a shadow of the promises to come. Priests under the old covenant had to repeat the sacrifices each year. Those sacrifices were annual reminders of sin. It's impossible for the blood of bulls and other animals to take away sins. Christ's sacrifice—his death—is the final act of sanctification.

Since we are forgiven through our high priest, Christ, we must hold fast to the hope we possess. We must encourage one another to love and to do good works.

If we sin willfully after receiving the knowledge of truth, we face judgment. The punishment under the old covenant was terrible. Imagine what it will be under the new covenant. "It is a dreadful thing to fall into the hands of the living God" (Hebrews 10:31).

The readers are encouraged in their struggles. They have been faithful during times of abuse, persecution, imprisonment and loss of property. Christians do not pull back and retire. They are confident and faithful. They believe and are saved.

In this study, group members will be imprisoned and talk about keeping faith through tough times.

BIBLE STUDY

1. Take the students to the furnace room. Tell them to imagine they have been imprisoned for their faith. There are a number of places around the world where this is a reality. Close the door and gather the group members by the "Survival Kit."

2. Invite one person to open the bag and find the first envelope. Ask him or her to read the charge. Ask:

●How does it feel to be imprisoned for your faith?

●Is this happening to some people today? Explain.

●If you had to choose between renouncing (denying) your faith and being imprisoned for life, which would you choose? Why?

3. Ask another person to open the second envelope and read the message. Ask:

●How do you feel about this punishment?

●What five things would you want to take with you to jail?

●How would it feel to lose all your possessions and give up your current lifestyle?

4. Ask another person to open the third envelope and read the message. Ask:

●How are you going to express your faith in prison?

●How are these bits of advice difficult to follow?

5. Free the prisoners and take them back to their usual meeting place.

6. Read Hebrews 10:1-39. Debrief their experience. Ask:

●What was the hardest aspect of the experience?

●What are the implications for your day-to-day living?

●How would your faith in Christ help you through this situation?

●How does the knowledge of Christ's sacrifice for us help?

7. Serve the ex-prisoners a meal of bread and water. Since they're freed from prison they can celebrate by adding butter, jelly, cheese or peanut butter.

ACTION

Ask students to remember this lesson when they encounter a tough trial—when everyone seems against them and they feel lost. Have them remember to be compassionate with others, joyfully accept the trial as a time of growth, keep confidence and express their faith. *(check up*

HEBREWS 11:1-40 • *CONVICTION OF THINGS NOT SEEN*

FOCUS
Faith.

INSIGHT
This chapter is probably one of the best-known parts of Hebrews. The author discusses practical aspects of a Christian's life. By faith

PREPARATION

Gather watercolors, paintbrushes, markers, paper and Bibles. Tack an old bed sheet to an open doorway. Cut a 3-inch-in-diameter hole in the center.

we are called to embrace what we can't see. The writer describes several faithful human witnesses to God's act of salvation: Abel, Enoch, Noah, Abraham and Sarah, Isaac, Jacob, Esau, Joseph and Moses.

In this study, group members will paint a symbol of faith.

BIBLE STUDY

1. The study will focus on faith—the conviction of things not seen. Illustrate the theme by playing a game called "Guess Who?" Ask several volunteers to stand behind the sheet. Say, "Although we can't see them, we have faith that several group members are back there."

2. Have volunteers one at a time place one body part through the hole. For example, a nose, ear, tongue or toe. Have young people guess who the body part belongs to.

3. Say: "Faith is being sure of what we hope for and certain of what we do not see. Just as we were sure volunteers were behind the sheet even though we couldn't see them."

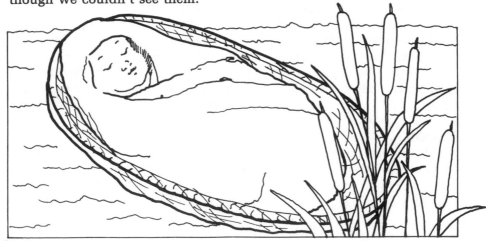

4. Divide into pairs. Give each person watercolors, paper and a paintbrush. Give each pair a Bible. Instruct them to read Hebrews 11:1-40 and paint symbols of faith. They could paint old Abraham holding a baby or Moses in a basket on the river.

5. Ask each "artist" to complete this sentence: "Faith is . . ."

6. Give each person a marker. Have students each write their definition of faith on their painting.

7. Invite young people to describe their completed paintings and display them on a meeting room wall.

ACTION

Ask students to keep their eyes and ears open this week for examples of faith. For example, a grandparent who hasn't missed a Sunday worship service in 70 years, or a neighbor who tends to his wheelchair-bound wife's needs. Bring back the examples and discuss them at the next meeting.

HEBREWS 12:1-29 • THE RACE BEFORE US

FOCUS

Perseverance.

PREPARATION

Gather a Bible, fruit, juice and cups. Ask young people to wear comfortable clothes and sturdy shoes. Hike in the mountains, woods, park or around the neighborhood. Plan three stops along the way.

INSIGHT

The author says we are surrounded by a great cloud of witnesses (those mentioned in the previous chapter). We must throw off everything that hinders us and run with perseverance the race ahead. Jesus is the source and perfecter of our faith. For the joy set before him, he accepted the cross. He now sits at the right hand of the throne of God. The readers should consider Christ so they won't grow weary and lose heart.

They endure some suffering. God is simply disciplining them. They are being treated as children are treated by a parent. Discipline is unpleasant but helps prepare the child for greater maturity.

Believers must make every effort to live in peace with all people. If a person misses God's grace, bitter roots can spring up and cause trouble.

The author writes about Moses' fear when he encountered God on the mountaintop. Christians await an even more awesome experience: the heavenly city at the final day.

In this study, group members will go on a hike, stop at various spots along the way and discuss the passage.

BIBLE STUDY

1. Prepare students for the hike. Lead stretching exercises to warm up the muscles and prevent injuries.

2. Say: "The author of Hebrews tells us to run with perseverance the race that is ahead of us. We're not racing during this study; we're hiking. Let's stay together at an easy pace."

3. Proceed to your first stop. Ask a young person to read Hebrews 12:1-11. Ask:

How did Jesus' faith sustain him?
Why does God allow us to go thru hardship?
How can I be ready to endure hardship in quiet faith?

- What is the author telling his readers?
- What is the message to us today?

Have group members find a symbol for the passage from the surrounding area. For example, the clouds in the sky to represent "a great cloud of witnesses" (verse 1).

4. Hike to the next spot. Ask a young person to read Hebrews 12:12-17. Ask:

- What is the author telling his readers?
- What is the message to us today?

How is Esau an example of no faith?
How did God respond to h[...]

Have group members find a symbol for the passage from the surrounding area. For example, the path they're hiking on to represent "make level paths for your feet" (verse 13).

How can I grow stronger in faith?

5. Hike to the third spot. Ask a young person to read Hebrews 12:18-29. Ask:

- What is the author telling his readers?
- What is the message to us today?

What kind of kingdom are we inheriting?
How do I show thank[s] for this?

Have young people find a symbol for the passage from the surrounding area. For example, a campfire to represent "God is a consuming fire" (verse 29).

6. Finish your hike. Reward the hikers' perseverance with fruit and juice.

ACTION

Plan a hike-athon or walk-athon. Participants secure pledges for each mile they hike or walk. Donate the money to the March of Dimes or other organization.

HEBREWS 13:1-25 • CONCLUDING THOUGHTS

FOCUS
Guidelines.

PREPARATION
Each person will need three 4-inch-by-4-inch pieces of construction paper. On separate slips of paper, write each guideline listed in the "Insight"

INSIGHT
The writer provides Christians with a list of moral guidelines:

- Continue to love believers.
- Be hospitable to strangers.
- Care for prisoners.
- Care for the abused.
- Honor marriage and chastity.
- Keep life free from the love of money.
- Be content with what you have.
- Remember your leaders.

section. You'll need one slip for each person. Place the slips in a bowl. Gather a Bible, paper and pencils.

- Don't follow strange teachings.
- Offer praise to God.
- Do good.
- Share what you have.
- Obey your leaders.

In this study, group members will tear construction paper symbols of the teachings from the passage.

BIBLE STUDY

1. Give each person a construction paper square. Have young people tear symbols of themselves. A person could tear a circle and say it represents his even temper. Let each person share.

2. Pass the bowl containing the slips of paper. Ask each person to take a slip and listen while you read Hebrews 13:1-25.

3. Give each person another construction paper square. Ask him or her to tear a shape to symbolize the guideline that's written on his or her slip of paper. For example, a heart to symbolize love, a dollar sign to symbolize money or a halo to symbolize good.

4. Describe the symbols. Ask:

- Which guideline is the easiest for you to follow? Why?
- Which guideline is the most difficult for you to follow? Why?

5. Give each group member one final construction paper square. Form pairs. Ask young people to tear a shape to symbolize a guideline their partner demonstrates in his or her life. A person could tear a smile and tell his partner she praises God by her happiness and upbeat attitude.

ACTION

Give students each a piece of paper and pencil. Have them write the guidelines, refer to them often and practice them in their lives.

INTRODUCTION TO JAMES

"An Epistle of straw!" The church father was being a bit too harsh on this important part of the New Testament. He wanted more of an emphasis on faith than works. However, the author presents behavioral guidelines the church needed then as well as now.

This challenging Epistle is not like other letters of the New Testament that are addressed to particular people and communities. James is a homily or sermon in the form of a letter. Contemporary Christians tend to overlook it since it focuses so much on works and little on Jesus.

James presents a clear statement about ethical matters of the Christian life. He provides specific answers to questions raised by Christians living in a particular setting. Tradition says that James was Jesus' brother, born to Mary and Joseph. Various scholars have speculated whether he was Jesus' brother or Joseph's son by another marriage, or whether he was Jesus' cousin.

Despite his relation, James is concerned for the poor. He sides with them against the affluent. He's also concerned with how people treat each other in the faith. The rich and powerful are not better than the poor. He gives readers guidelines on how to act toward each other in particular situations.

JAMES 1:1-8 • TOSSED BY THE WIND

FOCUS
Wisdom.

PREPARATION
Gather a Nerf ball, beach ball, penny, Bible, pencils, Doublemint gum, posterboard, markers and glue.

INSIGHT
James gives a general, bare greeting, different from greetings found in other New Testament Epistles. He urges readers to accept the challenge of external trials as a means for growth and joy. Testing produces perseverance. Perseverance helps Christians mature.

James says a person can ask God for wisdom—in faith, not doubting. A doubting person is like a wave tossed about in the sea. A doubting person is "double-minded." He or she is unstable. This person has two views for each situation. If you don't know whose you are, you don't know how to do God's will.

In this study, group members will hear a story and give guidelines to avoid being "double-minded."

BIBLE STUDY

1. Warm up the students by playing soccer variations. Play inside and use regular soccer rules. Play with a Nerf ball, beach ball or penny instead of a soccer ball.

2. Toss the ball or penny from person to person. Each person who holds it reads one verse of the passage.

3. Say: "James warns about being double-minded. Double-minded means to doubt, to be unstable, and to be tossed back and forth like the waves. He says we are to seek wisdom from God.

"Think of a time you had two choices. You were tossed back and forth with your emotions; you knew you should do one thing yet felt compelled to do the other. Once when I was young I was playing with my dad's tools and broke a hammer. I didn't know whether to tell him, make up a story or pretend I didn't know anything about it. I ended up telling the truth."

4. Let the students describe a time they were double-minded.

5. Read "The Salesman." Stop before you reach the conclusion.

THE SALESMAN

Herb was an interesting man. He owned a small florist's shop and had a huge beer belly. It looked like his pants would drop at any moment. Herb was also smart. He hired my best friend from high school, Allan. Allan was one of those rare people who's both intelligent and clever. He had a way with growing things. Flowers, plants, trees and people seemed to spring to life at his touch. Herb let Allan run the store. The owner would just walk around and grumble.

One Christmas the store and its adjacent lots were filled with trees. At that time the Christmas tree business was unstable. One season the retailer would make a fortune, but the next year the retailer wouldn't make any money. Herb wasn't sure which kind of year it was going to be. He had just purchased heavily.

I was in the middle of a disagreement with my boss at the shoe store. We had parted company for the Christmas season. I knew he would want me back in a couple of weeks. In the meantime I needed a job. Allan talked Herb into hiring me.

Herb's trees were hard to sell. He didn't mark prices on any of them. He quickly walked through the place pointing with both hands and shouting out prices. In this whirl of confusion, it seemed he changed the price each time he looked at a tree.

I was holding a tree upright for a married couple. I slowly spun the tree so they could see all sides. Herb came roaring by and asked what price I had quoted the customers. I told him $4.50. He screamed at me: "This is the finest tree on the lot. It's worth twice that price. Do you think I run a charity for loonies? It costs $6.50 and not a cent less."

The young husband looked at me as Herb stormed away. "I'll take it for $4.50 as you quoted me." I tried to explain that I had been wrong. He looked at me and said: "You told us $4.50. That's what you promised." I sold him the tree for $4.50, folded the bills and put the money into my money pouch.

I shuddered as Herb came rushing up to me. He watched the couple put the tree in the car trunk and drive away. He turned to me. His eyes narrowed. "How much did you charge them for the tree?"

The moment of decision. I knew there was no receipt and that he couldn't tell from the money pouch how much I had collected for the tree.

6. Stop the story. Ask:
- What would you do in this situation?
- What are the options?
- How do you think the story ends?

7. Read the conclusion.

"Four dollars and 50 cents!" Herb howled like a wounded animal. He pulled me by my coat sleeve into his office. He grabbed my money pouch. I was defrocked. "Do you know how much money I owe? Do you know what these trees will do to me?" He was shaking hands full of due bills at me.

I had no defense. I just stood and watched him. He finally stopped. "You're stupid, Benson, but you're honest." With that he shoved the leather pouch stuffed with money into my hands and stormed out of the office.

8. Ask:
- Did the salesman do what was right? Explain.
- Did the owner do what was right? Explain.
- Have you experienced a similar incident? If so, describe it.
- What other times are we tempted to be double-minded?
- How can we have the wisdom to know how to react in each situation?

9. Give each person a piece of Doublemint gum and a pencil. Have young people each write one guideline on their gum wrapper to remember when faced with "double decisions." For example, "Pray for God's wisdom" or "Do what you feel is the right thing to do."

10. Read the bits of wisdom as a closing.

ACTION

Make a poster that says "Double Your Wisdom—Ask God." Glue the bits of wisdom to the poster. Display it in an adult Bible study class or in the narthex. Ask group members to remember the bits of wisdom when they are faced with hard decisions.

JAMES 1:9-12 • PRIDE IN HIGH POSITIONS

FOCUS
Cliques.

PREPARATION
Gather one choir robe and Halloween mask for each person. You'll also need a Bible, construction paper, tape, markers and scissors.

INSIGHT
The poor can take pride in their high positions. The rich can take pride in their low positions. James compares rich people to flowers that wilt under the blazing sun. The rich person who seeks material wealth will perish. James assures his readers that a crown of life is promised to those who endure trials and love God.

In this study, group members will hide their true identities by wearing robes and masks.

BIBLE STUDY

1. As the students come into the room, give each one a choir robe and mask. Have them cover their hands and hair so that it's difficult to recognize one another.

2. Read James 1:9-11. Then say: "This is a difficult teaching for our consumer-oriented culture. Many young people and adults desire fancy clothes, perfect makeup, stunning hair styles and the latest car as foundation stones for their identity.

"We're going to play a game of questions. Mix and mingle and ask questions to discover one another's identity. Ask questions that probe for values and other important factors that go beyond clothes and makeup. For example: 'How do you feel about attending church?' or 'How do you feel about Christ's forgiveness?' "

3. After about 10 minutes of mingling, group members guess one another's identity. They remove their masks once their identity is guessed. Ask:

●How are poor people viewed today? rich people?

●What qualities characterize various cliques in your school?

●How did you interact with each other as equals? (Nobody knew or judged the others by the basis of clothes, makeup, jewelry or hair.)

●How was this interaction different from when you are in school?

4. Distribute construction paper, markers, scissors and tape. Let each person create a crown for himself or herself.

5. Read James 1:12: "Blessed is the man who perseveres under trial, because when he has stood the test, he will receive the crown of life that God has promised to those who love him."

6. Ask group members to put on their crowns. Say: "Let's remember that we're all equal. It doesn't matter who has the best clothes or latest hair style. Let's set our sights on better things. We'll all receive the crown of eternal life because of God's love for us."

ACTION

Ask students to remember we all are equal in God's eyes. Have them reach out to a person they normally don't interact with. A person who's extremely popular and involved in activities could reach out to a shy, lonely person. He could ask the loner to a game or other school function.

JAMES 1:13-27 • GOD TEMPTS NO ONE

FOCUS
Temptation.

PREPARATION
Gather a Bible, a towel, bubble gum, hangers, pieces of yarn, a bowl of warm soapy water, and

INSIGHT
James will not let his readers say, "I am tempted by God." God doesn't tempt a person to do evil. Each believer is actually tempted by his or her own evil desire. This desire permits the growth of sin, and sin leads to death. On the other hand, every good and perfect gift is from God. We have come into being solely through God's initiative.

bright-colored refreshments such as lemonade, oranges or watermelon. Prepare the situation slips listed in the study. Make enough so each student will have one.

James speaks about self-control. Christians must be quick to listen, slow to speak and slow to anger. Anger does not bring about the righteous life God desires. Filthiness must be put aside and meekness embraced. Religious people don't gossip or lie. True religion is focused on visiting orphans and widows in their time of need. Believers must keep themselves from being polluted by the world.

In this study, group members will view various tempting situations and realize God doesn't tempt us.

BIBLE STUDY

1. Introduce the theme of temptation—sticky situations—with "Bubble Gum Mobile" from *Quick Crowdbreakers and Games for Youth Groups* (Group Books). Give each student a piece of bubble gum. Supply various colors such as green, pink and purple. Give students hangers and several pieces of yarn. Ask them to create a mobile from their bubble gum. Hang it in a prominent place. Young people can add to it each week!

2. Distribute the situation slips. Say: "We've just experienced a sticky situation. These people have experienced sticky situations too. They're not taking the blame for sin; they're blaming someone else."

3. Ask each student to read his or her slip.

● "My son is a good boy. He'd never take drugs on his own. He was influenced by the other boys. They tempted and misled him."

● "It wasn't my fault my girlfriend got pregnant. She should've stopped me. Besides it's her responsibility to see that she doesn't get pregnant."

● "Sure I got into trouble. Sure I ran away. There was nothing I could do with a family like mine. They were always pressuring me. 'Clean your room. Do your homework. Practice the piano.' Who do they think I am? If I had been left alone, I would've been okay."

● "I wouldn't drink if it weren't for the heavy responsibility of supporting a family. I receive bills for everything. I have to keep two jobs to provide for six children. I can't find any peace and quiet; they're always around."

● "If it weren't for my husband, I would've been a dancer. My teachers said I had the potential to be a star. But along comes Joe and we get married. I spend the next 15 years raising children. I could've been a star if it weren't for my family responsibilities."

● "So I do some things people don't like. Big deal. If I was a goody-goody, I wouldn't have friends. I don't really like to drink. I'm just supporting my friends."

4. When students finish reading, read James 1:13-18. Emphasize verses 13-15. Ask:

●How did each of these people blame someone else for a temptation?

●What does James say about blaming God for temptation?

●Where does temptation come from?

●When have you blamed another for something you were tempted to do?

5. Bring out the towel and bowl of warm soapy water. Read James 1:19-27.

6. Pass the towel to each person. Ask group members to describe filth or sins that separate people from God. For example, selfishness, self-pity, failure to notice others' hurts or taking God's gifts for granted.

7. Go to each person and wash his or her hands to symbolize that God cleanses each person from sin.

8. Tell group members that every good gift comes from God. Serve bright-colored refreshments such as lemonade, oranges or watermelon to symbolize our thanks for these gifts and for the Son's warm love.

ACTION

James says that pure and faultless religion is to look after orphans and widows in their distress. Gather the names of widows in your congregation. Let group members take turns bringing them to church, calling them on the phone and sending them cards.

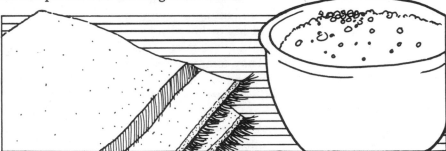

JAMES 2:1-26 • WORKS AND FAITH

FOCUS
The poor.

PREPARATION
Bring a Bible, gavel, marker and piece of poster-

INSIGHT
This passage focuses on the sinfulness of giving special treatment to the rich. All are equal before God. We are called to love our neighbor. Showing partiality to those with riches is to break the covenant and fall into sin. There will be no mercy for those who haven't shown

board. Ask two people to read the stories in the study. Ask a third volunteer to read the passage.

mercy to those who need it.

James presents one of the most compelling cases for the value of putting faith to work. Faith without the arms of work is nothing. Unfortunately, churches today tend to select either faith or works as the only pattern of life. The reality is that true believers must embrace both faith and works.

In this study, group members will create rules to change unjust situations.

BIBLE STUDY

1. Welcome the students by saying: "Welcome to the court chamber. Please enter quietly and be seated."

2. Proclaim that you are supreme judge of the world and your honored law is that everything in the world—all buildings, doorways, ceilings—is to be one foot shorter.

3. Ask students how this one rule would change their lives.

4. Invite the young person to read the first story. Ask students what law they'd make to change the situation. For example, "I'd rule that this church and all churches must offer the special Sunday school class."

●*Story 1:* First Church announced today that it will close its special Sunday school class for children with special needs. The minister said the class had been started two years before to help such children in their church. However, word got out about the special class and parents have been bringing their children from all over the city. "We don't want to be the dumping ground for everybody's troubled child. It's getting out of hand," remarked the minister. "This is a church for normal people. We're not here to babysit the world," said the church school superintendent.

5. Ask the other young person to read the second story. Ask students what law they'd make to change the situation. For example: "I'd rule that all churches must welcome outcasts to their worship services. I'd also order that usher to find the young man and bring him back."

●*Story 2:* I was invited to preach at a church in a poor section of the city. As I walked to the church I noticed a young man following me. When I stopped, he stopped. I was scared. I finally turned around and asked him what he wanted. He said, "I'm a stranger to the city and I'm hungry."

I had enough time to stop with him at a diner. We ate and talked. He had been in the city four weeks. His money was gone and he was desperate. I told him I was a minister. He said that church had always been important to him at home in the rural South. He asked if he could accompany me to church.

When we arrived, I sat him in a pew and asked the usher to look after him while I prepared to preach. After the service I didn't see the young man anywhere. I asked the usher about him. "Well, I kept my eye on him.

He didn't look like our kind of people. I told him he better move along, and he left.''

6. Ask the third person to read James 2:1-26. Ask how James' order to respect the poor could change the world.

7. Title the posterboard ''Rules to Live By.'' Ask students to list rules Christians should live by to make the world a better place to live. Rules could be: ''Help the poor. Welcome outcasts. Show God's love by your actions.'' Read the rules in unison. End by pounding the gavel and saying, ''So ruled.''

ACTION

In verse 15, James talks about people who lack food and clothing. Publicize in a local newspaper and in your church bulletin that your youth group will be hosting a food and clothing drive to help a charity. One Saturday, group members go door to door requesting old clothes or canned goods for the organization. The next day, congregation members bring clothing and canned goods to church. Organize the clothing and canned goods and give them to the organization.

JAMES 3:1-18 • THE TONGUE IS A FIRE

FOCUS
Gossip.

PREPARATION
Cut out leaf shapes from construction paper. Gather a Bible, markers, tape and yarn. You'll also need refreshments such as grape juice, grapes and grape bubble gum.

INSIGHT
In this passage, James offers a blistering discourse on the dangers of misusing the human tongue. All kinds of animals and sea creatures can be tamed, but humans are unable to tame their tongues. They're unable to keep mischief and serious grief from coming out of their mouths. Praises and curses come out of the same mouth. This shouldn't be. ''Can both fresh water and salt water flow from the same spring?''

James defines the important role of wisdom. This great tool for good can also be used to destroy others. Earthly wisdom is envious and selfish. Heavenly wisdom is pure, peace-loving, considerate, submissive, full of mercy and good fruit, impartial and sincere.

In this study, group members will construct a grapevine of gossip guidelines.

BIBLE STUDY

1. Play the childhood game "Gossip." Gather everyone in a circle. Whisper a few fact-filled sentences to the person on your right. For example: "Did you know Susan was out late last Friday night? She didn't tell her parents and they were frantic with worry. Susan went out with a boyfriend who her parents can't stand." The person whispers the message to the student on his or her right. The process continues until the person on your left receives the message. He or she reports what he or she heard.

2. Tell the group the original message. Ask:
- Why do people gossip?
- Why does gossip get distorted?
- What's the worst thing someone has said about you? How did you find out about it?
- What do we gossip about?

3. Say: "Sometimes gossip is referred to as the 'grapevine.' A message travels from mouth to mouth until everyone knows it (or some version of it)." Read James 3:1-18.

4. Distribute a construction paper leaf and marker to each person. Ask students each to write a gossip guideline on their leaf. Examples could be:
- Is the message exaggerated? Don't say it.
- Is the message hurtful? Don't say it.
- Don't repeat gossip.
- Would you want someone to say the same about you? If not, don't say it.
- Is the information considerate? pure? peace-loving? If not, don't say it.

5. Tape the leaves along a piece of yarn and make a grapevine of gossip guidelines. Read the tips.

6. Serve refreshments such as grape juice, grapes and grape bubble gum. Tell group members to have a "grape" day and avoid gossip.

ACTION

Ask young people to look out for gossip this next week. Tell them not to pass along juicy news second hand. If they feel like sharing hurtful news nobody else knows, don't initiate it. Stop gossip in its track.

JAMES 4:1-17 • WORLDLINESS

FOCUS
Desire for possessions.

PREPARATION
Gather a Bible, magazines, department store catalogs, construction paper, glue and scissors.

INSIGHT
James targets the dangers of misdirected lusts. People kill and covet but can't become satisfied. People don't have because they don't ask God. When they ask they don't receive because they ask with wrong motives. We are called to submit ourselves to God and to resist the evil one. If we will draw near to God, God will draw near to us.

James underscores the danger of the tongue waging war within the community. The self-confidence of the rich and independent is only an illusion. Who really knows about tomorrow?

In this study, group members will make two collages—one about earthly desires and one about God's will for our lives.

BIBLE STUDY

1. Invite students to thumb through the magazines and catalogs. Give each person a piece of construction paper, scissors and glue. Have participants search the magazines and catalogs, cut out pictures of anything they desire (cars, houses, jewelry) and glue the pictures to the sheets.

2. Explain the collages. Read James 4:1-17.

3. Distribute another piece of construction paper to each person. Say: "Keep in mind James' words about earthly possessions and gain. Make another collage of things you'd desire according to God's will." Students could cut out pictures to represent their desire to be healthy and have a happy family.

4. Explain the collages. Compare them with the previous ones. Ask:
- How are they similar? different?
- How do we know what God would like us to have?
- How do we know what to pray for?
- James says, "When you ask, you do not receive, because you ask with wrong motives, that you may spend what you get on your pleasures" (James 4:3). How can we ask with right motives?

5. Gather around both kinds of collages. Ask students to hold hands. Say in unison: "If the Lord wills, we will live and be blessed. Amen."

ACTION

Invite group members to take home both collages. For further devotions have them read about earthly possessions and desires: Matthew 19:16-22;

Luke 12:15-21, 33-34 and desiring God's will: Psalm 40:8; Matthew 6:9-13; 12:50; 1 Peter 3:17.

JAMES 5:1-20 • CONCLUDING WORDS OF ADVICE

FOCUS
Praise and worship.

PREPARATION
Gather songbooks, Bibles, paper, pencils, small slips of paper, matches and a metal trash can.

INSIGHT
The author warns the rich. They will weep and wail. The riches they have collected will rot and be destroyed. Fine clothing, gold and silver will corrode. The exploitation of workers will end in rebellion. All who seek to be rich will be slaughtered. Since they have killed the righteous, they themselves will be killed.

James urges patience in suffering. When people are in trouble they should pray. When people are happy they should sing songs of praise. When people are sick they should ask for others' prayers. All Christians should confess their sins and pray for one another.

In this study, group members will plan a portion of the study and base it on a portion of the passage.

BIBLE STUDY

1. Ask students with birthdays in the following groupings to form a small group: January-March, April-June, July-September and October-December. Have students line up within their small groups according to birthday. Make it difficult by ruling, "No talking."

2. Have them plan the following portion of the study:
- January-March = The lesson.
- April-June = Prayer for the suffering and sick.
- July-September = Songs of praise.
- October-December = Confession.

3. Give each group Bibles, paper and pencils. Tell group members they are going to design the Bible study. Have them read the passage, then create their portion of the study. Here are some ideas:
- *The Lesson:* Ask participants to read the passage responsively. Divide the group in two smaller groups. One group reads even-numbered verses; the other group reads odd-numbered ones. Discuss questions such as:
  ►What does this passage mean to us today?
  ►What one bit of advice do you want to remember?

●*Prayer for the suffering and sick:* Gather everyone in a circle of silence. Have participants think of friends, relatives or acquaintances who are suffering or sick. Pray, "God, hear our prayers for these people who are suffering and sick . . ." Let each student say the name of his or her friend, relative or acquaintance.

●*Songs of praise:* Lead songs of joy and praise such as "Sing Halleluiah" or "This Is the Day" from *Songs* (Songs and Creations). Have participants find "musical instruments" from around the church such as pots and pans, metal spoons or plastic containers. Accompany the tunes with your instruments.

●*Confession:* Distribute pencils and small slips of paper. Ask each person to write one sin on his or her slip. Place a metal trash can in the center of the room (or use the fireplace). Ask students to toss in their slips. Burn the slips. Say, "God forgives all your sins."

4. Participate in the study when all groups finish planning.

ACTION

Ask group members to follow this format for their daily devotions:

●*The Lesson:* Choose a favorite scripture. Think how it helps you today.

●*Prayer for the suffering and sick:* Read the newspaper. Pray for the suffering and sick mentioned in the news.

●*Songs of praise:* Thank God for five things that happened to you today.

●*Confession:* Think of a sin you've committed. Confess your sin. Receive God's forgiveness.

1 PETER

INTRODUCTION TO 1 PETER

The bully punched me with his fist. My vision rocked as I wiped the stream of blood from my lip. The world seemed to be spinning, and it was hard to stand. The jeers and laughter of the playground crowd came at me in waves. I couldn't lift my hands to ward off the next volley of blows. I didn't want to fight back. Yet the bully kept pounding my head and shoulders.

This childhood incident took place a long time ago. I was an innocent being battered by the cruelty of a playground bully and a laughing mob.

Peter is writing to persecuted Christians in the northern area of Asia Minor. He encourages them to stand firm in the face of difficulties. They should follow Christ's example as an innocent who was persecuted.

1 PETER 1:1-25 • *REJOICE THROUGH PERSECUTION*

FOCUS
Disabilities.

PREPARATION
Gather a Bible, a ball, blindfolds, earplugs, mittens, ropes, paper and crayons. On a separate slip of paper, write each conversation bit listed in the study. Ask three volunteers to read them.

INSIGHT
Peter recalls the readers' high calling. They are a chosen and holy people, purified by Jesus' blood. The author offers a prayer of thanksgiving for Jesus' saving work for those who believe.

Peter urges the Christians to be glad even though they suffer temporary trials during life. These challenges test the genuineness of their faith.

Peter encourages his readers to prepare their minds for action. God calls for obedience. They can't fall back into the negative influences of their former lives. They are holy because of their special relationship with God. The quotation from Isaiah 40:6-8 points out that all life is passing but God's Word is forever.

In this study, group members will experience handicaps and talk about suffering.

BIBLE STUDY
1. "Disable" each person as he or she enters the room. Use these ideas:
● Loss of vision: Blindfold a young person.
● Loss of hearing: Place earplugs in a young person's ears.
● Loss of dexterity or touch: Place mittens on a young person's hands.
● Loss of the use of a limb: Tie one arm to a young person's side.

2. Participate in simple activities. Toss a ball from person to person. Or distribute paper and crayons and have group members draw a symbol of their favorite hobby or sport. For example, a book to symbolize reading or a ball and bat to symbolize softball.

3. Let participants "remove" their disabilities. Ask:
● How were these simple tasks difficult because of your disabilities?
● How did the deaf people know what to do in the drawing exercise? How did everyone manage when we played catch?
● How did you feel during these activities?
● If you were really disabled in these ways, how could you remain joyful and thankful?

4. Say: "Peter encourages Christians enduring persecution. Christians should remain hopeful and continue to be happy. Trials are temporary. Life is short. God's Word is eternal." Read 1 Peter 1:1-25.

5. Ask three volunteers to read these conversation bits:

● "I'm 40 years old. I was one of the last people to contract polio. I was in an iron lung for months. They didn't think I'd live, but I did. I spent years in a wheelchair. I wouldn't give up. I earned a master's degree from the university in order to teach. But the school system wouldn't let me teach. I went to be interviewed for a job in an Arizona office. The cab carrying me pulled up in front of the office. The driver opened the door and I fell into the street. I broke both legs and had to spend six months in the hospital."

● "My daughter has Down's syndrome. She's special, yet people don't realize it. It's strange always having a child in the home. My husband and I worry about what will happen when we die. Who will care for her then?"

● "I mostly hang out. There aren't any jobs here. Just junkies, pimps and whores in our neighborhood. I've tried to find employment, but you need experience. What's a man to do?"

6. Ask:

● How are these people handicapped?

● What would Peter say to encourage them through their tough times?

● What are other trials we suffer? (For example, loneliness, guilt or fear of failure.)

● What would Peter say to encourage us through our trials?

7. Place all the handicap materials in a pile. Gather around the materials and pray for the ability to rejoice during suffering.

ACTION

Contact and comfort disabled people in your community. Ask students each to meet a person who suffers from the handicap they experienced in the study. Have them assist the person in some way. A young person who was blindfolded during the study could meet and visit with a blind person. A mittened young person could meet an older woman who suffers from arthritis. The young people could offer to write letters for these people.

1 PETER 2:1-25 • A ROYAL PRIESTHOOD

FOCUS

A chosen people.

PREPARATION

Collect two robes and two crowns from your

INSIGHT

Peter says the readers are to rid themselves of the pettiness of malice, deceit, hypocrisy, jealousy and slander. He calls them a royal priesthood, a chosen people, a holy nation. There was a time when they weren't God's people, but now—through grace—they are

church's supply of Christmas pageant costumes. Gather a Bible, piece of yellow posterboard and scissors. Each person will need a pencil and a copy of the handout.

God's people.

The author lists obligations, rules and guidelines for Christians to follow. Christians must submit to authority, show love, fear God and honor the king. Following these guidelines will silence those who seek to discredit the Christian community with charges of civil disobedience.

When Peter tells Christians to submit to authority and slaves to submit to their masters, he doesn't approve of the situation. He seems to be speaking from the perspective that the time is short before Christ's return, and Christians are to act accordingly. Peter recognizes the suffering these obligations entail. He points to the example of Christ's suffering. Christ was without sin, yet he suffered for the sin of others.

In this study, group members will experience royalty and rank a list of Christian obligations.

BIBLE STUDY

1. At one end of the room, place a robe and crown in one pile and a robe and crown in another pile. Divide group members in two teams by having them one at a time say, "Royal," "Priesthood," "Royal," "Priesthood." All "Royals" form one group; all "Priesthoods" form another.

2. Run a relay. The first person in each team runs to the pile, puts on the robe and crown, turns around five times, takes off the robe and crown, runs back to the line and tags the next person. First team done wins.

3. Say: "You each have been robed and crowned. You are a royal priesthood. You are God's chosen people. Listen to God's Word." Read 1 Peter 2:1-25.

4. Distribute the pencils and handouts. Tell students that a royal priesthood needs to follow some behavior guidelines. Have them rank the items from most to least important.

CHRISTIAN OBLIGATIONS

Instructions: Rank these obligations in order of importance (1 = most important; 10 = least important).

_____ Do what authority figures tell you to do.

_____ Show love to all believers.

_____ Fear and love God.

_____ Avoid sin.

_____ Live good lives.

_____ Don't hate.

_____ Don't be a hypocrite.

_____ Don't be jealous.

_____ Grow spiritually.

_____ Other: _____.

---

5. Discuss the rankings. Ask:

● How did you prioritize the obligations? Which one is most important? Why? Which one is least important? Why?

● What does it mean to be chosen by God?

● How does Christ's example help us live? What Christian-living guidelines has he demonstrated?

6. Cut a piece of yellow posterboard in the shape of a crown. Title it ''God's Chosen People.'' Ask group members to sign their names on it. Post the crown where everyone can see it. Leave it up for a few weeks as a reminder that we are God's chosen people.

ACTION

Ask students to practice one obligation from the handout. A person could obey authority by doing what his dad asks him to do. Another person could show love to all believers by giving each group member a Hershey's Kiss.

1 PETER 3:1—4:11 • *LIVING FOR GOD*

FOCUS

The Christian life.

PREPARATION

Gather a Bible, paper, pencils and pieces of wire.

INSIGHT

Peter offers practical advice for husbands and wives. He gives more advice for wives than for husbands. This is probably because wives with unbelieving husbands were in a more difficult and dangerous position than believing husbands with unbelieving wives. Peter says wives must be submissive to their husbands. This accommodating approach creates a bit of discomfort for most modern believers. We live in a time when many husbands and wives both work to keep their standard of living at a desired level. Women are no longer considered the "weaker sex." Yet the call for a mutual covenant of faithfulness and respect between husband and wife speaks powerfully to Christians today. The covenant between man and woman is blessed by God and calls for faithfulness.

Peter reminds the readers that the quality of Christian love is important. He says they should live in harmony with each other, be sympathetic, love one another, be compassionate and humble, and forgive instead of desiring revenge. He uses Psalm 34:12-16 to prove this point. God's eyes are on the righteous. Peter affirms that Christ is our model for righteousness and has won our salvation through his work.

Peter relates Christ's work to the persecution of Christians. The end is near. Peter urges the readers to be clear-minded and self-controlled. They are to love one another and offer hospitality without grumbling.

In this study, group members will form a wire sculpture of one of Peter's teachings on living a Christian life.

BIBLE STUDY

1. Play a game such as "Laughing Line" where girls compete with guys. Girls form a line. Guys make faces or tell jokes to make the girls laugh. (No tickling allowed!) Girls try to refrain from laughing. Then the girls try to make the guys laugh. See who succeeds in the shortest time.

2. Say: "Peter offers his readers guidelines for living as Christians. He first lists guidelines for husbands and wives." Read 1 Peter 3:1-7.

3. Divide the guys and girls into two groups. Have the guys meet in one room, the girls in another. Give each group a piece of paper and pencil. Each group's task is to list 10 qualities the students would look for in a marriage partner. For example, fun-loving, Christian and good with children.

4. Regroup and discuss the lists. Ask:
● How are the two lists similar? different?
● How are the two lists similar to Peter's message? different?
● If you could label one quality as most important, which would you choose? Why?

5. Say: "Peter stresses love for one another as an important quality of Christian living. He goes on to give other guidelines."

6. Give each person a piece of wire. Explain that you're going to read the rest of the passage and they're to form a symbol of one of Peter's Christian-living guidelines. Students could shape a heart to represent love, a cross to represent reverence to Christ or a smile to represent hospitality.

7. Read the passage and let the students form symbols. Discuss their creations.

8. Have students affirm each other by exchanging symbols. They each explain why their symbol reminds them of the person. For example: "You can have this heart. It reminds me of you, because you're the most caring person I know. You're always there when I need a friend."

ACTION

One guideline Peter gives his readers is to extend hospitality to others. Ask young people to invite their friends to the next youth group meeting or Bible study. Plan a time of devotions, fun games and good refreshments.

1 PETER 4:12-19 • THE PAINFUL TRIAL

FOCUS
Suffering.

PREPARATION
Gather two towels, a Bible, tape and glue. Each person will need a marker and a 1-inch-by-4-inch piece of construction paper.

Ask one young person to

INSIGHT
Peter summarizes a theme he discussed earlier. He calls his readers "dear friends." He tells them not to be surprised at the painful trials they are suffering. They will suffer abuse from pagans. They shouldn't be ashamed but should praise God. Suffering for the sake of the gospel is an honorable service.

In this study, group members will consider suffering and write words of advice or encouragement to help people survive tough times.

read the passage and another young person to read the following true story about Dr. Richard Stevens:

Dr. Richard Stevens is a minister for the Dutch Reformed Church in South Africa. He is black. Because of his color he's been arrested several times for gathering black students with white students for study and worship.

Several years ago the security police went to his house and arrested him in the presence of his children. Stevens recalls: "They put handcuffs on me and started to lead me to jail. I stopped in front of my young children and said: 'Remember this: These aren't chains of shame. It's an honor to be arrested for the cause of freedom and truth. Do not forget the moment your father was taken to jail because of the gospel of Christ.'"

BIBLE STUDY

1. Divide the group into two teams. Ask members to "chain" themselves together by linking arms. Place a towel in the pocket of the last person in each line. Each team tries to grab the other team's towel. Each team must remain linked throughout the game.

2. Say, "People suffer chains and punishment for being a Christian today as well as in Peter's time." Ask the volunteer to read the true story.

3. Ask the other volunteer to read 1 Peter 4:12-19.

4. Let students each share a moment from their own life when it cost them to be a Christian. For example, when they didn't go along with peer pressure. Ask:

● Why would anyone want to be a Christian if it means suffering?

● How does this message of suffering compare to the "easy" Christianity of radio and television that promises wealth, success and fame if a person has faith?

● How does Christ help us through our suffering?

5. Give each person a marker and strip of construction paper. Have students each write words of advice or encouragement to help Christians through suffering. For example, "Keep your eyes on Christ" or "Remember, God is with you and gives you strength."

6. Ask each person to share his or her advice or encouragement. As students share, have them glue their strips in a circle and link them in a paper chain.

7. Invite young people to hold on to the chain. Offer a prayer of thanksgiving for Christ's strength and support through times of suffering. Hang the chain on the meeting room wall.

ACTION

Encourage students to be aware of the suffering in the world. Ask them to listen to the news on the radio and television and read the newspaper. Have them pray each night that God will support and strengthen suffering people.

1 PETER 5:1-14 • *SHEPHERDS OF GOD'S FLOCK*

FOCUS
The Good Shepherd.

PREPARATION
Gather a Bible, paper, pencils, and books and pictures of shepherds.

INSIGHT
The author concludes his message to the church. Leaders are shepherds of God's flock. They have special responsibilities to their members. The whole community is facing persecution, pain and suffering. Peter says to stand firm because they know others are undergoing the same kind of sufferings.

Peter concludes this Epistle with personal notes in his own hand. He offers peace to all who are in Christ.

In this study, group members will look at pictures of shepherds, write a story about qualities of good shepherds and discuss Christ, the Good Shepherd.

BIBLE STUDY
1. Welcome students. Invite them to look at the books and pictures of shepherds.

2. Gather students and ask them to share the qualities needed by a shepherd. For example, a good sense of the environment and alertness.

3. Divide the group into pairs. Give each pair a piece of paper and pencil. Ask pairs each to write a short story about a shepherd who displayed all these good qualities. For example: "There once was a shepherd who had a flock of 100 sheep. The shepherd knew each sheep, knew his surroundings and was extremely alert. One day a lion crept up to the grazing flock. The shepherd saw the danger at once and pelted the lion with stones. The sheep were safe once more."

4. Read the stories. Then read 1 Peter 5:1-14. Ask:
● How is Jesus like a shepherd?
● How are we like sheep?
● How does our Good Shepherd guide us through life?
● How does our Good Shepherd protect us from evil?

5. Say: "Peter asks his readers to greet one another with a kiss of love. Instead, we're going to greet one another with handshakes." Invite group members to shake a person's hand who:
● Is caring.
● Is forgiving.
● Is a good leader.
● Loves God.

ACTION

Ask the Sunday school superintendent to let your group members present an opening for the preschool through elementary children. Or have students volunteer to teach a lesson during vacation Bible school. Let the students read their stories, show the pictures and explain how Christ is the Good Shepherd.

2 PETER

INTRODUCTION TO 2 PETER

"Let out the dog. Bring in the milk. Turn off the lights. Turn down the heat. Watch for snakes."

Such a checklist guides young people while their parents are out of town. The writer of this letter also tries to guide those he loves while he is away.

This letter identifies itself as being written by Peter; however, the early church was not sure. Only toward the end of the fourth century 2 Peter was added to the church's canon of scripture.

The author is writing to the Christian community at large about widespread heresy. He believes Christians must walk in the way of correct moral behavior in order to be ready for Christ.

2 PETER 1:1-21 • KNOWLEDGE OF CHRIST

FOCUS
Answers to tough questions.

PREPARATION
Gather a Bible, pencils, markers, newsprint, 3x5 cards, and newsmagazines such as Time and Newsweek.

INSIGHT
The passage focuses on how the knowledge of Jesus operates in believers. Christians should "make every effort to add to your faith, goodness; and to goodness, knowledge; and to knowledge, self-control; and to self-control, perseverance; and to perseverance, godliness; and to godliness, brotherly kindness; and to brotherly kindness, love" (2 Peter 1:5b-7).

The author refreshes the readers' memories of the early faith of the church. He is an eyewitness to Christ's glory. He tells of his firsthand experience of seeing Jesus' Transfiguration on the sacred mountain (Matthew 17:1-8). The readers must pay attention to God's Word. It is a light shining in darkness.

In this study, group members will find news stories on suffering people and discuss answers to tough questions.

BIBLE STUDY
1. Gather group members in a circle. Let each one complete the following sentences:
- One fun thing that happened to me last week in school was . . .
- One school activity I'm looking forward to is . . .
- The purpose of school is . . .

2. Say: "One purpose of school is to teach facts and pass on knowledge. Peter tells us we are given all things through the knowledge of Christ. How do we gain knowledge of Christ?"

3. Give students a few minutes to answer. Read 2 Peter 1:1-21.

4. Divide into small groups. Give each group a magazine, piece of newsprint and marker.

5. Ask students in each group to find a story of a person facing a crisis such as a farmer losing his farm, an innocent victim suffering from AIDS or a child suffering from abuse. Ask small groups to write 10 hard questions this person might ask. For example: "Why did this happen to me?" "Did God do this to me for a reason?" "How am I going to get the strength to survive this trial?"

6. Ask each small group to describe the person and read the 10 questions. Ask:
- How would you answer these questions?

● What knowledge would you pass on to the people in the news stories?

● How do you gain knowledge of God's will?

● What guidelines does Peter give to Christians? (For example, "Hold fast to the knowledge of Christ" or "During this life we suffer; we'll be rewarded in heaven.")

7. Close with a question-and-answer time. Give each person a 3x5 card and pencil. Have students write any questions they have concerning life or faith. For example: "Why do bad things happen to good people?" or "Why doesn't God answer my prayers?"

8. Collect the cards. Read the questions one at a time. Let young people share their knowledge by answering some of the tough questions.

ACTION

Save the questions you don't get to. Use them as discussion starters at your next retreat, lock-in or Bible study. Discuss the fact that many questions are unanswerable. We may not find out the "whys" of certain things until we arrive in heaven.

2 PETER 2:1-22 • FALSE PROPHETS

FOCUS
Truth and lies.

PREPARATION
Gather Bibles, paper, pencils, and gossip newspapers and magazines.

INSIGHT
Peter focuses on false prophets who work secretly among church members and mislead them. God's past judgments (Noah, Lot, and Sodom and Gomorrah) show how God will punish these false teachers. Peter warns believers not to slip back into sin. This is like a dog returning to his vomit or a pig returning to its mire after a bath.

In this study, group members will discern false statements from true ones.

BIBLE STUDY

1. Give students a few moments to think of three personal statements—one true and two false. For example: "I like anchovy pizza. My dog can do 15 tricks. My dad used to play professional baseball."

2. Let each person present his or her statements. Encourage students to guess which statement is true.

3. Say, "Christians in Peter's time were also bombarded with false teachings." Read 2 Peter 2:1-22.

4. Distribute gossip magazines and newspapers. Ask students to find a scandalous news item that deals with love affairs, drinking, drug abuse or illegitimate children. Invite them to report the information they find, then ask:

- How do we know what information is true?
- How do we know what information is false?
- How do we know what information is exaggerated?

5. Divide into small groups. Give each group a Bible, piece of paper and pencil. Ask groups to rewrite 2 Peter 2:1-22 as if they were writing a younger sister or brother. Have them address questions such as:

- Who are the false teachers of today?
- What false teachings do we need to avoid?

An example of a letter is: "Dear brother: Beware of the negative peer pressure that surrounds you. Beware of so-called 'friends' who try to get you to drink . . ."

6. Invite the small groups to read their letters.

7. Gather in pairs. Have group members discuss:

- A time they listened to wrong (false) advice.
- A time they listened to good (true) advice.
- A time they experienced God's forgiveness.

ACTION

Ask group members to pass on a "true fact" or piece of good advice to their younger brothers or sisters. They can use the ideas from the letters written during this session.

---

2 PETER 3:1-18 • CHRIST'S SECOND COMING

FOCUS
The final days.

PREPARATION
Plan to have this study around a campfire. If it's too cold outside, meet around a fireplace in the church or someone's home. Bring Bibles, paper,

INSIGHT
Peter reminds his readers that in the last days scoffers will come and urge believers to follow their passions. Scoffers deny Christ's second coming.

The author reminds the readers that the Lord's time is different from ours: "With the Lord a day is like a thousand years, and a thousand years are like a day. The Lord is not slow in keeping his promise, as some understand slowness. [The Lord] is patient with you, not

pencils, marshmallows, sticks and songbooks.

wanting anyone to perish, but everyone to come to repentance" (2 Peter 3:8b-9).

In this study, group members will meet around a campfire or fireplace and discuss Christ's second coming.

BIBLE STUDY

1. Gather around the campfire. Sing favorite songs such as "Give Me Oil in My Lamp" from *Songs* (Songs and Creations). Make up your own verses such as "Give me wood for my fire, keep me burning for the Lord" or "Give me heat for my feet, keep me running for the Lord."

2. Invite group members to take turns reading each verse of 2 Peter 3:1-18. Ask:

● What kind of people scoff at us today and lead us away from our faith?

● What does Peter mean when he says, "With the Lord a day is like a thousand years, and a thousand years are like a day"? How is this thought comforting?

● How do you feel knowing God doesn't want anyone to die; God wants everyone to repent?

● How does this fire represent the day of the Lord? (Reread verses 10-13.)

● What does it mean to trust God for salvation?

● What does it mean to grow in knowledge of Christ?

● Should we fear the fiery final days? Why or why not?

3. Let group members roast marshmallows and continue to talk about this passage. Say: "God's timing is different from ours. We think the end surely must be near, but we don't really know. It's all according to God's timing. We must keep these thoughts in mind and strive to live as Christ would have us live."

4. Close with songs such as "Seek Ye First," "Spirit of the Living God" or "Father, We Adore You" from *Songs*.

ACTION

Give each group member a pencil and piece of paper. Encourage students each to write three ways they are going to change their lives to walk closer with God. For example:

● Get up 15 minutes earlier each morning for devotions.

● Cheer up or encourage one person each day.

● Thank God for blessings each day.

INTRODUCTION TO 1 JOHN

"Now be good and don't hang out with those bad kids."

All of us experienced this kind of unsolicited advice from parents when we were children. We may have resented such direction, and we certainly hid it from our friends. Yet our parents were right to caution and advise us. As we grow older we find ourselves repeating our parents' examples of parenting.

This Epistle has the same parental tone to it. The author addresses his readers as if they were children. Are they just babes in the faith? The writer is worried about those who face the challenge of false teaching. Will peer pressure lead them from Christ?

The author of 1 John doesn't say his name, but in 2 and 3 John he refers to himself as "the Elder." Since the vocabulary is similar, some scholars think this author and the author of the Gospel of John are the same.

This brief letter gives us a rare glimpse of the life of the early church. We can feel a mentor's practical concerns as he writes to a community of faith. Many verses assure readers of Christ's love. Many favorite prayers for confession and pardon come from 1 John.

1 JOHN 1:1-10 • *LIGHT AND DARKNESS*

FOCUS
Forgiveness.

PREPARATION
Gather a Bible, candles and matches.

INSIGHT
John focuses his message on the truth that God is light, not darkness. If we walk in the light, we have communion with God and with one another. Jesus' blood washes away all our sins. A popular liturgical prayer of confession and pardon is based on verses 8-9.

In this study, group members will experience the darkness of sin and the light of forgiveness.

BIBLE STUDY

1. Invite group members into the room. Ask them to imagine they are Christians from the early days of the church. Read 1 John 1:1-6 as a letter to them from John. (Stand near the light switch so you can shut off the lights after you read these verses. Allow a few moments of confusion.)

2. Light a candle and read verses 7-10 by candlelight.

3. Pass the candle to each person and ask him or her to share how he or she has walked in Christ's light recently. For example, he or she can tell of a noble deed or a loving gesture.

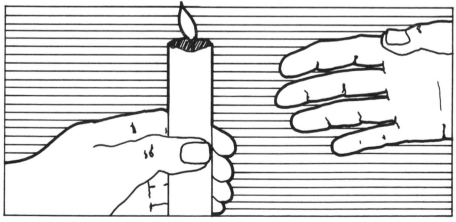

4. Pass the candle again and ask each person to compare Christ with the candlelight. For example: "Christ is the light. He overcomes darkness. One little flame destroys darkness."

5. Blow out the candle so the room is dark once again. Ask each person to silently confess a sin—something he or she did to let God down this past week.

6. Relight the candle. Give each person a candle. Pass the flame from your candle to the candle of the person on your right. Say: "God is light. God overcomes darkness and forgives your sins." Ask that person to pass the flame and repeat the message. Continue until everyone's candle is lighted.

7. Close with a prayer of confession and pardon. Read verse 8 and have students repeat it. Then read verse 9 and have them repeat it.

ACTION

Encourage students to memorize 1 John 1:8-9. Encourage them to say the verses many times a day. At the beginning of the next session, ask group members what happened to them during the time they walked in the light of God's forgiveness.

---

1 JOHN 2:1-29 • FAITH THROUGH THE AGES

FOCUS
Spiritual growth.

PREPARATION
During this study, you'll divide students into three groups: children, teenagers and senior adults. Supply children's chairs (from the Sunday school department), tennis rackets, shawls and golf clubs for the students to use as props for their roles. Gather Bibles and pencils. Each person will need two copies of the handout.

INSIGHT
The writer addresses his readers as "dear children." He also switches from "we" to "I" in reference to himself in this intimate and personal appeal to the church.

John doesn't want the readers to sin. If they do sin, however, they have an advocate in Christ, God's Son. John reminds the church to obey the commandments. He says if people claim to be walking in the light of truth yet hate their neighbor, they're still in darkness. When Christians actively love their brothers and sisters in the faith, they're bathed in the light.

John addresses children, older people and young people. They have been faithful and have overcome the forces of evil. He warns them of the danger of loving the world or anything the world produces. The world passes away, but the one who does the will of God lives forever. He tells the readers it is the last hour. False teachers have come. The readers must be confident in and loyal to the true faith.

In this study, group members will pretend they are in one of three age groups: children, teenagers and senior adults.

SYMBOLS THROUGH THE AGES

Instructions: Circle your assigned age group. Read each of the concepts listed from 1 John 2:1-29. How would someone in your age group view the concept? Draw a symbol to represent the views. For example, a Bible to represent true faith.

Child   Teenager   Senior Adult

Obedience:

Love:

Forgiveness:

Second coming:

True faith:

BIBLE STUDY

1. As young people enter, divide them into the three groups: children, teenagers and senior adults. Ask the participants to use the props to signify their roles. For example, children could sit in the small chairs, teenagers could hold tennis rackets, and senior adults could hold golf clubs or wear shawls.

2. Let the children each share a memory of church and Sunday school.

3. Let the teenagers describe experiences they're having now in church and Sunday school.

4. Let the senior adults each complete this sentence: "When I'm retired I hope my faith . . ." For example, "I hope my faith has spread to all of my family" or "I hope my faith has grown larger than a mustard seed."

5. Ask all age groups to listen as you read 1 John 2:1-29.

6. Say: "John was talking to children, young people and older adults. He told them many things, ranging from obedience to true faith." Distribute the handouts and pencils. Have group members circle their assigned age group. Ask: "How would a person from your age group view each concept John talks about? Draw a symbol for each one."

7. After several minutes, discuss the symbols. Ask:
● How are the symbols similar? different?

●Do our views change as we grow older? Explain.

●Is it possible for us to grow older and our faith to remain stagnant? Explain.

●How can we continue to grow spiritually as we grow older?

8. Close by praying: "God, help us continue to grow spiritually. Help us to be confident in our faith, no matter how old we are. Amen."

ACTION

Give the students each another handout and have them ask a younger brother or sister to define each concept. Then, have them ask a parent to define each concept. Finally, have them ask a grandparent or retired neighbor to define each concept. Compare the differences and similarities at the beginning of the next session.

1 JOHN 3:1-24 • GOD'S LOVE

FOCUS

Spreading God's love.

PREPARATION

Gather a Bible, mirrors, clown white and red makeup, black eyebrow pencils, baby powder and soft-bristled brushes. Ask group members to bring clownlike clothes from home: old band uniforms, baggy overalls, housecoats and old polka dot pajamas.

Ask a person who is familiar with clown ministry to lead your students through the steps of becoming a clown: symbolism, makeup, costumes and actions. A good resource for this study is *Clown Ministry*, by Floyd

INSIGHT

The author reminds his readers that God loves them so much; God calls them children. John says those who sin break God's law. A child of God does not continue to sin.

John reminds his readers of the message they've heard from the beginning: We must love one another. He uses the story of Cain and Abel to explain how we can fall under the control of the evil one.

We should not be surprised that the world hates us. We know that we have passed from death to life, because we love one another. Since Christ laid down his life for us, we must lay down our lives for one another. Love is not simply words or speech; it must be translated into action.

In this study, group members will spread God's love through clown ministry.

BIBLE STUDY

1. Instruct group members to grab a partner for a pantomime time. Ask them to

Shaffer and Penne Sewell (Group Books).

silently act out these scenes:
● Two young children catching a ball.
● Two senior adults catching a ball.
● Tossing and catching a beach ball.
● Tossing and catching a 20-pound bag of dog food.

2. Say: "You just experienced silent communication. You silently acted out messages. You used exaggeration. A clown uses these same skills. A clown is a symbol of Christ's love. Bright-colored costumes and bouncy personalities reflect the joy of being a Christian. A clown's white makeup symbolizes Christ's death; the other colors symbolize his Resurrection.

"We're going to transform ourselves into clowns. We're going to spread God's love with this unique ministry."

3. Introduce the clown minister. Have him or her lead the students in creating their clowns.

4. Apply makeup by following these basic steps:
● Use the black eyebrow pencil to create facial designs: outline the lips, and draw a circle around the tip of the nose and on each cheek.
● Spread clown white outside the black lines. Cover the entire face and neck. Leave the inside of the black lines clear so you can add color.
● Powder the makeup; let it set; brush off excess.
● Use the red makeup to color in the designs.
● Powder the makeup; let it set; brush off excess.
● Re-outline the black lines.
● Highlight the eyes by using the black eyebrow pencil to draw a triangle on the outside corner of each eye.

5. Let group members try on their clownlike clothes.

6. Ask the clowns to hold hands and form a heart—not a circle. Have them listen as you read 1 John 3:1-24.

7. Brainstorm ways the clowns can put love in action. For example: Go to a grocery store and give away flowers. Stand on a street corner and hand out cards that say "Smile, God loves you." Greet people with hugs and handshakes as they come out of church.

ACTION

Choose one of the ideas and put love in action. The clown is a wonderful symbol of Christ; clowning is a unique way to spread his love.

1 JOHN 4:1-21 • LOVE ONE ANOTHER

FOCUS
Love.

PREPARATION
Gather a chocolate heart, Bibles, paper, pencils, small boxes of candy hearts, red construction paper, scissors and crayons. Each person will need a copy of the "I Love . . ." handout.

INSIGHT
John warns the readers to test the spirits. Many false prophets have gone into the world. God's children are victorious because the Lord lives in them. God's children are to love one another. Those who know God live in love. God shows us love through the Son. God is love.

In this study, group members will play a sign-up mixer and give a little love away.

BIBLE STUDY
1. Distribute a pencil and handout to each person. Give group members five minutes to find autographs for each item. Award a chocolate heart to the first person done.

2. Say: "We love many things. John says if we love God, we also should love our brothers and sisters. We're going to find out other things he says about love."

3. Divide into two teams. Give each team paper and several Bibles. Have the groups read 1 John 4:1-21 and list as many facts about love as they can find. Say that the group with the most facts wins a prize.

4. Gather the groups and discuss the new-found facts. Facts could be: God is love. We're to love one another. If we love, we know God. We love because God first loved us.

5. Award the winning group a small box of candy hearts for each fact listed. (Say that a true sign of love is sharing!)

6. Distribute red construction paper, scissors and crayons. Have students each design a heart of love.

7. Gather in a circle. Have one group member describe a time someone in the group showed love. For example, "This person sent flowers to my mom when she was in the hospital." The group member then gives his heart to the person he described. That person repeats the process. Continue until each person has given and received a heart.

I LOVE . . .

Instructions: Find a person who loves one of the following items. Ask him or her to sign on the corresponding line. Try to get a different person to sign for each item.

I love . . .

1. Pepperoni pizza _____

2. Hot chocolate on cold nights _____

3. Scary movies _____

4. Youth group on Sunday nights _____

5. Romance novels _____

6. An early morning jog _____

7. Sleeping late on Saturdays _____

8. Winter _____

9. God _____

10. My brother or sister in Christ _____

ACTION

Invite group members to spread a little love around this week. Have them each give their red construction paper heart to a person and say why they appreciate that person. A group member could give her heart to a friend and say, "I appreciate your willingness to listen."

1 JOHN 5:1-21 • GOD HEARS PRAYERS

FOCUS
Prayers.

PREPARATION
Gather Bibles, paper and pencils.

INSIGHT
John tells his readers to love God and carry out the commands. God gives believers eternal life. If we believe in the Son, we have life. If we ask anything according to God's will, God hears us and grants our requests.

In this study, group members will experience various prayer positions and discuss their prayer lives.

BIBLE STUDY

1. Invite students to share memories of their first prayer times. For example, "I remember kneeling by my bed and praying, 'Now I lay me down to sleep' while my mom listened." Notice the variety of experiences.

2. Divide into three groups. Assign each group one prayer position: standing with head bowed and hands folded, standing with head and hands raised, and kneeling with head bowed and hands folded.

3. Give each group a Bible, piece of paper and pencil. Divide the passage into three parts and assign each part to a group. Use these groupings: 1-5; 6-12; 13-21.

4. Ask the groups each to write a prayer relating to their passage. A prayer from verses 13-21 could be: "God, help us be confident. Help us know you hear our prayers. Help us ask according to your will. Thank you for your Son, who gives us eternal life. Amen."

5. Let each group lead the others with their prayer. Have everybody participate in the three prayer positions. Ask:
- Which position was most comfortable for you? Why?
- In what position do you pray? Does position matter? Explain.
- How often do you pray?

6. Close with a prayer Christ used as an example—the Lord's Prayer (Matthew 6:9-13).

ACTION

Ask students to keep a prayer journal. On one side of a sheet of paper, have them write "Prayers Asked"; on the other side, have them write "Prayers Answered." Encourage students to keep track of their prayers and God's answers. Remind them to include adoration, confession and thanksgiving in each prayer.

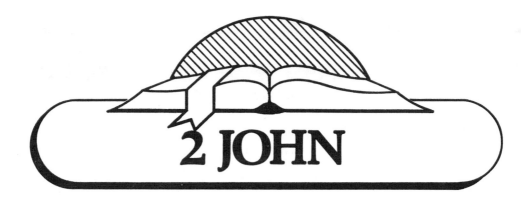

2 JOHN

INTRODUCTION TO 2 JOHN

"One rotten apple can spoil the whole barrel." My grandmother's wisdom-filled cliché proves to be true. Bad influences can damage a young person's development.

The author of 2 John is concerned about the danger of false prophets among his spiritual children. The letter is addressed to "the chosen lady and her children," probably referring to a church in Asia Minor. The author is informal and direct in this brief Epistle. Yet the warmth and respect of the greeting and farewell suggest a special relationship between him and this church.

2 JOHN 1-13 • WALK IN OBEDIENCE

FOCUS

A walk in faith.

PREPARATION

Gather a Bible, a Nerf ball or a football, socks, paper, pencils and a long strip of butcher paper. Make footprints out of posterboard. Write the following words, one on each footprint: "Walk in obedience to God's commands." Repeat the message several times. Tape the footprints to the floor leading into your meeting room.

INSIGHT

Three blessings are often found at the beginning and end of Christian letters. "Grace" describes God's freely given love toward us. "Mercy" conveys God's lovingkindness or compassion for us. "Peace" has many meanings in the Bible. In Christian letters it seems to express a sense of completeness and reconciliation between brothers and sisters.

The writer seems to summarize 1 John in this passage. He warns the chosen lady to be wary of deceivers who deny Christ's humanity. John warns against offering hospitality to these false teachers.

In this study, group members will play "feet" games, go on a follow-the-leader hike, trace their footprints and discuss walking in obedience to God's commands.

BIBLE STUDY

1. Play games that have to do with feet. Play football indoors using a Nerf ball or play outdoors if the weather is nice. Another game is "Grab a Sock." Ask all group members to take off their shoes. (Supply socks for those who aren't wearing any.) Divide the group into two teams. The goal is for students on one team to "de-sock" the other team. The game is played on hands and knees.

2. Take the students on a follow-the-leader hike. Walk them on a narrow ledge or line to test their balance. Have them walk on tiptoes, then walk while bending their knees and while stooping low. Take them to a high place (such as a balcony) and a low place (such as a basement).

3. Come back to the regular meeting place and have group members march in place. Say: "We're to walk in obedience to God's commands. We're to keep our eyes on God while we balance on a ledge of uncertainty, when we feel 'up,' when we feel 'down,' when we're blessed with happy hilltop experiences and when we experience down-in-the-valley blues."

4. Keep marching in place. Pass a Bible from person to person. Ask each student to read one verse from 2 John. Let everyone rest.

5. Distribute paper and pencils. Have each young person trace his or her foot on the paper. Ask students to draw symbols or write phrases from 2 John to help them remember to walk in obedience to God's commands.

6. Share the footprint drawings.

7. Ask young people to march in place one more time and repeat each line after you:

God.

Help us keep our eyes on you.

Keep us walking in your will.

Help us obey your commands.

Thank you for your Son, our Savior and example.

Amen.

ACTION

One Sunday, lay a long piece of butcher paper on the hallway floor. Invite congregation members each to trace one of their feet and sign their name within the footprint. Get as many "feetographs" as possible. Title it "(Name of Church) Members Walk in Obedience to God's Commands." Hang it on one wall of the concourse.

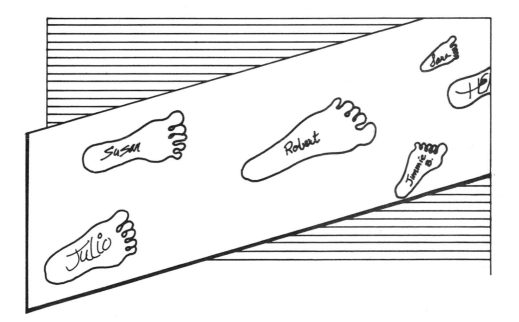

3 JOHN

INTRODUCTION TO 3 JOHN

"You mind your brother! He's older and he knows what's right." Well, Mom may have been wrong in discerning who was at fault in that particular dispute, but she was right in ordering both of us to stop arguing.

The Elder wrote a quick message to Gaius, a faithful church member. A person named Diotrephes put himself first and denied the Elder's authority The Elder must be listened to.

The author hopes to talk with Gaius face to face. The problems of leader ship can be resolved; a family squabble must come to an end.

3 JOHN 1-14 • DON'T IMITATE WHAT IS EVIL

FOCUS
"Verbicide"—crimes of the tongue.

PREPARATION
Tape a long piece of butcher paper to one wall. You'll also need markers and a Bible.

INSIGHT
The Elder informally greets Gaius. He commends Gaius for his hospitality. He then addresses an internal issue of a local church leader, Diotrephes, who is ambitious. Diotrephes puts himself first, doesn't offer hospitality and denies the Elder's authority.

The author thinks well of Demetrius, who perhaps delivered this letter. He apologizes for the shortness of his note and hopes they can talk face to face.

In this study, group members will write gossip on a graffiti wall, discuss verbicide—crimes of the tongue—and affirm each other.

BIBLE STUDY

1. As group members enter, give them each a marker and have them write juicy gossip on the butcher paper. Encourage them to "change the names to protect the innocent." For example, "Did you hear about Jean Marie? She's pregnant."

2. Read some of the gossip on the graffiti wall. Say: "Another name for gossip is verbicide—crimes of the tongue. Listen to a portion of a devotion from the *Student Plan-It Calendar* (Group Books). 'Committing verbicide feels good. We enjoy putting down someone in front of friends, sarcastically responding to parents and other family members, invoking the name of God to damn—the possibilities are endless. But verbicide doesn't feel so good when we are the victims. Verbicide devastates us, causing tears, heartaches and a poor self-image.'" Ask:
- When have you experienced verbicide?
- How did you feel?

3. Read 3 John 1-14. Ask students to listen to the account of verbicide this letter addresses. Ask:
- Who committed verbicide?
- What did he say and do?
- How did the Elder respond?
- Have similar situations occurred in your church? Explain.
- How should we respond to verbicide?

4. Ask students for ways verbicide can be detected and prevented. For example: "Run gossip through a series of questions: Is it true? fair? necessary? If not, forget it."

5. Pray: "God, help us use our tongues to compliment, comfort, encourage and support. Amen."

6. Say one young person's name and allow one minute for young people to offer compliments, comfort, encouragement or support. Continue this process until everyone has been affirmed.

ACTION

Encourage students to use the series of questions to test gossip they hear (or are tempted to repeat) during the next week. Is it true? fair? necessary? If not, forget it.

INTRODUCTION TO JUDE

"Hey Jude . . ." The old song by The Beatles made the name "Jude" popular years ago. Clearly, the early church knew this terse Epistle by the same name.

Authorship is attributed to Jude, the brother of James and of the Lord. As with other questions of authorship, scholars' opinions vary. Jude was accepted in the canon (or official book of the Christian faith) by the end of the fourth century.

Jude addresses heresy among the Christians. He urges his readers to stand firm against these irregular teachings.

JUDE 1-25 • THE SIN OF THE GODLESS

FOCUS
False teachings.

PREPARATION
Gather paper, pencils, Bibles, newsprint and markers. Bring an album or cassette tape of "Hey Jude" by The Beatles and bring a record player or cassette tape player. Ask five volunteers each to read one of these tips at the appointed time during the study:

● *Tip 1:* Build yourself up in your faith.

● *Tip 2:* Let the Spirit guide your prayers.

● *Tip 3:* Be merciful to doubters.

● *Tip 4:* Tell others about Christ; save them from the fire.

● *Tip 5:* Show mercy mixed with fear.

INSIGHT
The author prays for the gifts of God's mercy, peace and love. He urgently warns the Christians about the sin of godless men. Jude draws upon Old Testament stories of how God punishes sinners. The fall of Sodom and Gomorrah provides a graphic example of how unnatural lust leads to the punishment of eternal fire.

God will judge grumblers, faultfinders, those who follow their own evil desires, those who boast and those who flatter for their own advantage. Believers must build themselves up in their faith and pray in the Spirit. Christ's mercy will bring them to eternal life. Believers must be merciful to those who doubt, and they must snatch others from the fire and save them.

Jude concludes with a benediction. He glorifies God who is truly pure. God has glory, majesty, power and authority forever.

In this study, group members will list ways to find false teachers and hear tips on how to persevere through confusing times.

BIBLE STUDY
1. Play a quick crowdbreaker to begin this session. Give each person a piece of paper and pencil. While you play the song "Hey Jude," students try to list as many words as they can that rhyme with "Jude." For example, mood, dude, food and crude.

2. Say, "The winner gets to read aloud the letter of Jude." (Or the winner can choose someone else to read it.)

3. Divide into small groups. Give each group a Bible, a piece of newsprint and a marker. Have groups title their newsprint "False Teacher Finders." Ask each small group to look through Jude and list items that alert us to false teachers. For example, "They deny Christ," "They are immoral," "They seek to destroy" and "They are unreasoning."

4. Discuss the lists. Ask:

● What alerts us to false teachers?

● Who are false teachers today?

●How can the items on these lists help us when we're faced with false teaching?

5. Say: "In the last days there will be scoffers and false teachers. They will try to divide believers. Jude tells his readers ways to persevere." Ask the volunteers each to read their tip.

6. Ask students in the small groups to rewrite Jude's benediction (verses 24-25) in words that reflect their lives today. For example: "To God, who forgives our sins and makes us happy. All praise and power are God's forever."

7. Read the benedictions.

ACTION

Ask students each to choose one tip and act on it this next week. A person could choose Tip 1 and develop a plan for daily devotions. A person could choose Tip 4 and invite a friend to a youth group activity or Bible study.

REVELATION

INTRODUCTION TO REVELATION

For centuries Christians have been intrigued with the end of the world. "When will the end come?" "What will the end days be like?" People search Revelation for answers to these questions and for clues to the end times.

Revelation is an apocalypse—a writing that symbolically represents the triumph of good over evil. This literature deals with the end times. Revelation looks ahead to a time when the forces of good led by God will overcome evil.

Revelation is probably the most misused, abused and unused book in the Bible. Misused and abused, because people quote verses out of context and are widely divergent in their interpretations. Unused, because people tend to avoid things that are confusing and hard to understand.

The first readers of this book lived in a time of persecution. The political leaders were intentional enemies of the Christian faith. The author was exiled to the island of Patmos. He knew many of the readers would be martyred. Revelation uses codes, symbolism and poetic imagery to speak about the dangerous times and to comfort Christians with the knowledge that God is victorious.

Some Christians view the author's use of numbers as a clue to establishing an exact calendar of when the final battle will be fought and when Christ will return victoriously. Every age of history consists of people awaiting Christ's return on a particular day. People have gathered on housetops to await Christ's arrival. They've stored food in cellars to prepare for days of destruction.

There is a brilliant sense of the dramatic in this book. The literary landscape is filled with a colorful array of images as the good and bad battle for victory. Great composers have been inspired to set this majestic language to unforgettable music. The words have inspired poets, artists and other people throughout history.

John calls for the faithful to support and comfort each other. He encourages believers to gather around Christ during persecution and suffering.

REVELATION 1:1-20 • WRITE WHAT YOU SEE

FOCUS
Hidden meanings.

PREPARATION
Gather Bibles, news-print, markers and refreshments. Cut key shapes out of construction paper. Prepare clues for a treasure hunt (see the first step in the "Bible Study" section).

INSIGHT
The preface assures the readers that the book is God's Word and Christ's testimony. John blesses those who read, hear and take to heart what is written in this book.

He addresses the seven churches in Asia. He grants grace and peace from God (who is, who was and who is to come), from the seven spirits before the throne, and from Jesus Christ who is raised from the dead.

The author says he was on the island of Patmos, exiled for his testimony of Christ. On the Lord's Day (Sunday) he was in the Spirit (a trance) when a loud voice instructed him to write a book and send it to seven churches: Ephesus, Smyrna, Pergamum, Thyatira, Sardis, Philadelphia and Laodicea.

In this vision, John saw seven golden lampstands and someone "like a son of man" dressed in a robe and golden sash. His head and hair were white and his eyes blazed. He held seven stars in his right hand. John fell as dead at Christ's feet.

The risen Lord told him not to be afraid. He told him to write down everything. The lampstands are the seven churches, and the seven stars are the angels of the seven churches.

In this study, group members will decode clues and search for a treasure.

BIBLE STUDY
1. Plan a treasure hunt for the participants. Give the young people the first coded message; it leads to the next message. Participants follow the clues to the "treasure." (Don't tell them that the treasure is refreshments; let them be surprised.) Coded clues could be:

●*Clue 1:* Go to the room that warms your soul. (This is the furnace room. Hide the next clue here.)

●*Clue 2:* Proceed to the place where you hear God's Word. (This is the sanctuary. Hide the next clue here.)

●*Clue 3:* Onward to a children's wonderland. (This is the nursery. Hide the next clue here.)

●*Clue 4:* Onward to the place where food is prepared. Fill your stomachs with your treasure. (This is the kitchen. Place a note by the refreshments that says "You've made it. Here's your reward.")

2. While group members eat the refreshments, introduce Revelation by saying: "Revelation is called an apocalypse. It uses codes or symbolic messages to offer hope during persecution. It says good ultimately will win over evil. The apocalypse was written to persecuted Christians. The symbolism was probably understood by them, but it's difficult for us to define each symbol today. Throughout history, people have tried to guess when the end will come according to this book's meaning."

3. Read Revelation 1:1-20 one verse at a time. After each verse ask:
- What is the writer telling his readers?
- How does the message apply to us?

4. Form teams of threes. Give each team a Bible, piece of newsprint and marker. Assign each team a section of the passage.

5. Tell students they must pass on this message to a contemporary reader. Have them imagine they live in a time of persecution so it's important that non-believers can't understand what's being communicated. For codes, group members could use citizens band slang or regional terms, or they could develop their own. For example, they could assign a number to each letter of the alphabet and rewrite their passage using numbers.

6. Share the coded messages. Have participants guess the meanings. Ask:
- Why is Revelation's message vital to Christians today?
- What trials do we face?

7. Read Revelation 1:17b-18: "Do not be afraid. I am the First and the Last. I am the Living One; I was dead, and behold I am alive for ever and ever! And I hold the keys of death and Hades." Ask:
- Who is the First and Last?
- How do you feel knowing Christ has overcome death and evil?
- How does this knowledge help you through tough times?

8. Say: "Christ holds the keys of death and Hades. He is the key to eternal life. We'll live forever in heaven through him."

9. Give each person a marker and a construction paper key. Encourage students to write on the keys comforting thoughts about Christ. For example: "Christ is the way to eternal life." "Christ is the First and Last. He was at the beginning of time, and he'll be there at the end of time." "Christ is in control. He holds the key to death." "Christ is with us through all our trials."

10. Share the "key messages" as a closing prayer.

ACTION

Invite students to take home their keys as reminders not to be afraid. Christ is with us always. Divide the group into two teams. Have each team create a new coded-clue treasure hunt for the next session. Students try to find answers to the clues and find the treasure at the end of the search.

REVELATION 2:1—3:22 • LETTERS TO SEVEN CHURCHES

FOCUS
Warning and hope.

PREPARATION
Make seven signs out of posterboard. Write one of the following names and passages on each sign: Ephesus (2:1-7); Smyrna (2:8-11); Pergamum (2:12-17); Thyatira (2:18-29); Sardis (3:1-6); Philadelphia (3:7-13); Laodicea (3:14-22). Post the signs at various places around the room. Under each sign place a Bible, a magazine, scissors, paper and pencils. Copy the "A Letter to You" handout for each person.

INSIGHT
Seven letters are written to seven churches. Each church is assigned an angel. The first letter is addressed to Ephesus. Jesus knows their actions and how they stayed strong under persecution. However, they have abandoned their first love. They must repent. If they don't, God will remove their lampstand from its place. The Ephesians have this in their favor: They hate practices of false teachers (practices such as eating food offered to idols). The overcomers in Ephesus will have the right to eat from the tree of life.

The second letter is addressed to Smyrna. Jesus knows their afflictions and poverty. He counsels them not to fear future sufferings. If they are faithful even to the point of death, they'll receive the crown of life.

The third letter is addressed to Pergamum. "Satan's throne" may refer to the imperial seat in that town. When forced by the authorities, the faithful didn't deny Christ. One believer was even killed. They're commended, then Christ warns them about evil behavior. Some of them eat food sacrificed to idols and commit sexual immorality. He warns them to repent. Manna (like the food given to the Israelites in the wilderness) will be given to those who conquer these temptations. The white symbolizes joy.

The fourth letter is addressed to Thyatira. Jesus commends them for their love, faith, service and perseverance. They're doing more than they did earlier. However, they tolerate Jezebel, who calls herself a prophetess. She seduces believers into sexual immorality and to eat food sacrificed to idols. Jesus has given her time to repent, but she's unwilling. She'll be cast on a bed of suffering. Jesus will give authority to those who overcome and do his will.

The fifth letter is addressed to Sardis. These people have a reputation of being spiritually alive, but they're spiritually dead. Jesus urges them to repent. Some people, however, aren't falling from the faith. They haven't soiled their clothes. They'll walk with Christ, dressed in white, for they're worthy.

The sixth letter is addressed to Philadelphia. Jesus knows their works and holds an open door for them to inherit eternal life. He'll protect them from the hour of trial. The Philadelphians must hold to what they have so no one will take their crown.

The seventh letter is addressed to Laodicea. These people are neither cold nor hot in their faith. They're lukewarm—worse than either extreme. These mellow ones deceptively assume they're rich and need nothing. They don't realize they're wretched, pitiful, poor, blind and naked. They must repent. Jesus stands at the door and knocks. If a person hears his voice and opens the door, Jesus will come in and eat with him or her.

In this study, group members will learn about the seven churches addressed in this passage, then they'll each receive a letter of affirmation.

A LETTER TO YOU

Dear _____,
I appreciate these qualities in your life:

Signed,

Permission to photocopy this handout granted for local church use only. Copyright © 1988 by Dennis C. Benson. Published by Group Books, Inc., Box 481, Loveland, CO 80539.

BIBLE STUDY

1. Play "Heads Up Seven Churches." Choose seven people to stand at the front of the room. Ask all others to sit and close their eyes. Say: "No peeking. Some of you will feel a tap on your shoulder. Keep your eyes closed. Only open them when you hear 'Heads up seven churches.'"

Each of the seven people taps another youth group member then goes back to the front of the room. When all seven are back to the front say, "Heads up seven churches." The seven tapped people stand. Each one receives three chances to guess who tapped him or her. If the person guesses correctly, he or she changes places with the person at the front. Play several rounds.

2. Give each student a number from one to seven. Assign each group to one of the seven signs and say that each group has to do the following:
- Read the passage.
- Rewrite the message in today's terms.
- Find a magazine article on a similar incident.
- Find a symbol from around the room that represents the passage.

The group assigned to Pergamum could write: "Some of you people remember your faith, but some of you sin and worship idols. Stop it. Ask for forgiveness. You'll be forgiven." The members could cut out a magazine article about a lottery winner who carelessly spent his earnings. They could find a coin to symbolize idol worship.

3. Give the groups plenty of time to complete the tasks. Go to each one, offer assistance and answer questions.

4. Share the findings.

5. Distribute the handouts and pencils. Gather in a circle. Ask each person to write his or her name in the blank. Have young people each pass their paper to the person on their right. Then ask students to write an affirmation and sign their name. Pass the papers to the right and repeat the process. Continue until each person receives his or her letter of affirmation signed by all the group members.

ACTION

Revelation 3:15-16 tells about lukewarm faith. It is neither hot nor cold. Ask students to think of how their faith is lukewarm. Encourage them to think of one way to "heat it up." For example, they could read their Bible every night, or they could bring one new person to church or youth group each month. Discuss the ideas at the next session.

REVELATION 4:1—5:14 • WORSHIPING AT THE THRONE

FOCUS
Persecution.

PREPARATION
Arrange the chairs in your meeting room so they face different directions. Darken the room. Prepare another room: Place chairs

INSIGHT
John sees a heavenly door standing open. A trumpetlike voice invites him in. Someone is sitting on a throne. An emerald rainbow encircles the throne. There are 24 elders sitting on 24 other thrones. They're dressed in white and wearing gold crowns. Lightning flashes and thunder rumbles. Seven lamps are blazing. Before the throne is a sea of glass, like crystal.

Four creatures are around the throne.

249

in a circle and a small candle in the center. Bring matches, newsprint, paper, pencils, a marker and a Bible. Ask two volunteers to read the persecution cases.

They're covered with eyes. The first is like a lion, the second is like an ox, the third has the face of a man, and the fourth is like a flying eagle. They have six wings and praise God day and night. When the creatures praise God, the 24 elders fall down and worship. John sees images similar to those in Ezekiel 1:22-28.

John reports about heavenly worship around God's throne. The one who sits on the throne is holding a scroll. It has writing on both sides and is sealed with seven seals. It reminds us of Ezekiel 2:9-10: "Then I looked, and I saw a hand stretched out to me. In it was a scroll, which he unrolled before me. On both sides of it were written words of lament and mourning and woe."

John weeps because no one is worthy to open the seals and read the scroll. Then an elder tells him that the Messiah could open it. He next sees the slain Lamb take the scroll. The creatures and elders fall down before the Lamb. Each one has a harp and a bowl of incense. They sing and worship. Suddenly thousands and thousands of angels join in singing praise to the Lamb.

In this study, group members will hear persecution cases and plan a worship to praise God for helping them through tough times.

● *Maria—Central America:* It happened so quickly. The door was smashed down. It was like an explosion. The family thought it was a bomb. Men with machine guns and loud voices overwhelmed the house. They dragged her husband, Juan, from bed. Some of the intruders pointed their weapons at Maria and the children. Others beat Juan with the butts of their pistols. They were careful with their blows. They knew how to inflict pain while keeping the victim conscious.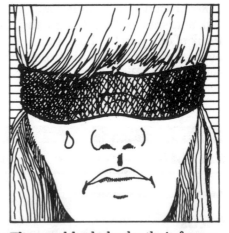

The intruders beat and raped Maria. They suddenly broke their frenzy of violence and dragged Juan's limp body through the doorway and into the darkness. Maria tried to comfort her hysterical children. She experienced a strange silence of disbelief. She was bruised and violated. Her husband was gone. They had done nothing wrong. They were not "political." They did have a weekly Bible study in their home. Although she would return again and again to the central police station, the answer to her plea always would be the same, "We know nothing about your husband.'' Maria would never see her husband again.

●*Ben—Beirut:* He could see light by peeking beneath the edges of his blindfold. Were his captors still in the room? He was hogtied. His body ached from the chains connecting his hands to his feet. If only he could move his body. He could feel the strain on his bladder. His captors hadn't let him use the bathroom since the night before, when he was chained into this uncomfortable position. They better come soon.

Why was he a hostage? He had done nothing wrong. His whole work had been one of service and care to the poor of this country. One just couldn't be a Christian American in this setting. Twelve months of captivity seemed impossible. How much longer could he take it? How he missed his family.

BIBLE STUDY

1. Lead each person to a chair in the darkened room. Ask for total silence. Invite the two volunteers to read their persecution cases. Ask students to reflect on the situations and imagine they face similar persecution.

2. After a few minutes, have young people close their eyes and join hands in a long line. Lead them through the building until they're disoriented.

3. Lead them to the other prepared room. Seat them in the circle of chairs. Light the candle, then have them open their eyes.

4. Ask each person to compare his or her feelings about the two rooms. Ask:

●How did you feel sitting alone in a darkened room, facing different directions? How is this like being persecuted?

●How do you feel sitting in a circle with a candle lighting the room? How is this like Christ's comfort during persecution?

●What dreams would you have if you faced persecutions similar to Maria's or Ben's?

●How would you want God to treat those who were mistreating you?

●What beliefs would you cling to so you could survive the persecution?

●Which of God's promises would be the most important to you? Why?

5. Read Revelation 4:1-11. Say: ''Christians were persecuted when Revelation was written. John was offering them hope.'' Ask:

●How are we persecuted today? What trials do we face? (For example, peer pressure, sexual temptation and drug abuse.)

●How does this passage give us hope to survive life's tough times? For example: ''It's comforting to know God is greater than all the earth. There is hope of eternal life with the Son.''

6. Turn on the lights and read Revelation 5:1-14. Tell the students that Revelation 4:1—5:14 reflects how worship can take place.

7. On newsprint list various worship aspects mentioned in the passage such as movement, music, praise, focusing on God and participation.

8. Divide in small groups and assign each an aspect of worship. Distribute paper and pencils, then have students create contemporary worship ideas. A group assigned to movement could develop an "action prayer":

Dear Lord, (Raise arms.)
Help us survive (Touch shoulders.)
Tough times. (Put back of hand to forehead.)
Help us know (Point finger to head.)
That you overcome all evil. (Point finger to heaven.)
Thanks be to God. Amen. (Bow head.)

9. Participate in a closing worship using the contemporary ideas.

ACTION

Secure permission from your minister to lead portions of worship one Sunday. Read Revelation 4:8b: "Holy, holy, holy is the Lord God Almighty, who was, and is, and is to come." Sing "Holy, Holy, Holy, Lord God Almighty" from your church hymnal.

REVELATION 6:1-17 • THE FOUR HORSEMEN

FOCUS
Catastrophes.

PREPARATION
Bring several newspapers to class. Unfold them and lay them end to end in a large circle. Go to the library and check out a sound-effects album with the sound of galloping horses. Bring a record player. You'll also need a Bible and an album of any music.

INSIGHT
John sees the Lamb open the first of the seven seals, and he hears one of the creatures say, "Come!" A white horse and its rider appear. The rider holds a bow and is given a crown. He goes out to conquer. This is the first of the four horsemen who accomplish God's purposes.

The process is repeated and the second seal is opened. A fiery red horse comes out with the power to take away peace from the Earth. He is given a great sword.

The opening of the third seal unleashes a black horse. Its rider holds a pair of scales in his hand. He makes an economical statement that probably relates to the conditions of that time.

The fourth seal reveals a pale horse. Its rider is named Death; Hades follows close behind. They're given the power to kill by sword, famine, plague and wild beasts.

The fifth seal exposes the souls of the martyrs. They are told they'll be avenged and are given white robes.

The sixth seal uncovers a variety of natural disasters. Every human being seeks to escape God's wrath.

In this study, group members will search newspapers for contemporary examples of war, famine, disease and death.

BIBLE STUDY

1. Gather students in a circle around the newspapers. Explain: "I'll play music while you walk in a circle around the newspapers. When I stop the music, you stop. Point your finger to a random spot on a newspaper and choose a word. Use that word to describe your past week. For example, if I choose the word 'offered,' I could say: 'Last week, I offered to help my mom cook dinner. Unfortunately the dinner turned out to be a disaster. Next time she'll turn down my offer.' " Let each person share. Repeat the entire process three or four times.

2. Ask students to walk around the circle of newspapers again. While they walk, play the sound-effects album and read Revelation 6:1-2. Stop the album and say: "Some scholars say the white horse and conqueror are probably references to Christ. Others believe they symbolize Rome's enemy at that time. Search the newspaper near you to find a contemporary example of a conqueror. An example of a good conqueror could be a missionary doctor who works in a poor nation fighting starvation." Share the examples.

3. Ask young people to walk around the circle of newspapers. Play the album and read Revelation 6:3-4. Say: "The red horse symbolizes war. Search the newspaper near you to find a contemporary example of war." Share the examples.

4. Ask young people to walk around the circle of newspapers. Play the album and read Revelation 6:5-6. Say: "The black horse symbolizes famine. Find a contemporary example of famine." Share the examples.

5. Ask young people to walk around the circle of newspapers. Play the album and read Revelation 6:7-8. Say: "The pale horse symbolizes pestilence, or fatal contagious disease. Search the newspaper near you to find a contemporary example such as a story about AIDS." Share the examples.

6. Ask students to walk around the circle. Play the album and read Revelation 6:9-11. Say: "These verses talk about martyrs—people who give their lives for the faith. Find a contemporary example of a martyr." Share the examples.

7. Repeat the process one final time and read Revelation 6:12-17. Say: "These verses describe catastrophes preceding the end. Look through the newspaper near you for a contemporary example of a catastrophe." Share the examples.

8. Say: "We face many of the trials of the early Christians. War, famine, disease and earthquakes have afflicted humanity throughout history. But God is our support and strength through these trials. God was there when the world began. God is with us throughout life and will be with us when the world—as we know it—ends. The Lord God will be with us forever.''

9. Have students each randomly choose one word from the newspapers and use it in a closing prayer. Let each person contribute.

ACTION

Encourage students to be aware of the suffering around them. In our society it's easy to forget that so many people are suffering. Encourage group members to pray each night for God to comfort those facing death, famine, war or disease.

REVELATION 7:1-17 • A HOST OF MARTYRS

FOCUS
God's comfort.

PREPARATION
Gather a blindfold for each person. You also will need a Bible and white robe. Set up chairs in a circle.

INSIGHT
There is a pause between the opening of the sixth and seventh seals. A great persecution will prepare the way for the end. A seal marks the foreheads of God's servants. The number 144,000 is a symbol of the completeness of God's people.

A host of martyrs in white robes stand around God's throne. These witnesses will never again hunger or thirst. They won't suffer from heat. The shepherd will lead them to streams of living water. God will wipe away every tear from their eyes.

In this study, group members will be blindfolded and will imagine the passage.

BIBLE STUDY

1. Blindfold each person as he or she enters the meeting room. Carefully guide the students to the circle of chairs.

2. Inform them that Revelation was written to those who suffered. John was bringing the gospel of hope to those who eventually would give their lives for Christ.

3. Read Revelation 7:1-17 slowly and dramatically. Encourage students to picture the words in their minds. Ask:

● What images do you see?

● How do these verses make you feel?

● How would these verses comfort early persecuted Christians?

4. Take off the blindfolds and pass around a robe. Say: "This robe symbolizes the white robes of the multitude of righteous people. Through life we suffer loneliness, grief and pain; later we'll be rewarded and eternally blessed by God." Ask:

● What price do you pay to be a Christian at school? work? home? (For example, being teased for a belief.)

● How does this passage help you risk being a Christian? (For example, God will wipe away all our tears; suffering now will be worth the comfort later.)

5. As a closing prayer, reread a variation of verses 16-17: "Never again will you be hungry. Never again will you be thirsty. Never again will you suffer scorching heat. Christ is your shepherd. He guides you to fresh, living water. God will wipe away all your tears."

ACTION

Give each person a blindfold and say: "Open your eyes to God's promise of comfort and eternal life. Risk living for Christ each day. Know that God will comfort us and heal our hurts." Have students keep the blindfolds as reminders to keep their eyes open to ways to serve God. A young person might notice an elderly person struggling to put groceries in her car. He could help her. Encourage group members to describe their experiences at the next session.

REVELATION 8:1—9:21 • THE SIX TRUMPETS AND THE PLAGUE

FOCUS
Time.

PREPARATION
You'll need a three-minute timer (with grains of sand in it), paper, pencils, tape and Bibles.

INSIGHT

The Lamb now opens the seventh seal; all heaven is silent for 30 minutes. John sees the seven angels with seven trumpets. Another angel offers much incense with the saints' prayers. The angel puts fire in the container holding the incense and throws it to Earth. Thunder rumbles, lightning flashes and an earthquake occurs.

The angels sound their instruments one after another. With each sound a terrible thing happens on Earth: hail and fire mixed with blood are hurled to the Earth; something like a mountain is thrown into the sea; a great blazing star (named Wormwood, which is a bitter drug that symbolizes God's punishment) falls to the Earth; and the sun, moon and stars darken.

A fifth angel blows his trumpet. A star falls from the sky (a fallen angel?), and he has the key to the bottomless pit. He releases smoke and locusts. They are sent to destroy the grain of those who don't have God's seal on their foreheads. The locusts look like horses prepared for battle. Their faces look like human faces, their hair is like women's hair and their teeth are like lions' teeth.

The sixth trumpet releases four angels from the river Euphrates. A third of humanity is killed. (The Euphrates was a border between Rome and her enemy the Parthians.)

Some idol worshipers are still alive and have not repented. This compares to Exodus 8:15, 19, where Pharoah's heart was hardened against the plagues.

In this study, group members will race against a three-minute timer to complete certain activities.

BIBLE STUDY

1. Divide into small groups. Tell the groups they are going to race against time to do various tasks. The team who accomplishes each task first wins a point. Use the timer to time the groups. Use these ideas:
- Build the tallest human pyramid.
- Attach a piece of tape to the meeting room ceiling.
- Take off and put on your shoes and socks, stamp three times and yell, "We want it now."

2. Pass around the timer. Ask each person to share a time he or she was waiting for something important such as Christmas or a visit from a relative. Ask:
- What was the time like?
- What makes waiting so hard?
- Do good times move faster than bad times? Explain.

3. Divide the passage into four or five parts and ask volunteers to read John's words. Say: "God's time is not like our time. A thousand years are like a day to the Lord. Christians in John's time were persecuted. They were waiting and waiting and waiting for relief. John assures them that evil will be destroyed."

4. Distribute paper and pencils. Read the description of the locusts (9:7-10). Ask students to draw the locusts.

5. Let students each show their creation and share the element of the story that most frightens them. Ask:
- Why are these thoughts scary for us?
- Is it right to "scare" people into believing? Why or why not?

- When do you think the end will come?
- Do we, as believers, have anything to fear? Explain. (Read 9:4.)
- Can we predict when the end will be? Why or why not?
- Rather than fearing the end, how can we use our lives—right now—to the fullest?

6. Start the timer again. While the grains of sand flow to the bottom of the timer, allow a few minutes for a silent prayer. Encourage students to ask God to help them use their time to the fullest. When the sand collects at the bottom of the timer say, ''Amen.''

ACTION

Help young people realize their lives are a gift from God. We should be thankful each moment. We should use our time to the fullest. Ask young people to take time to appreciate their lives. Ask them to notice at least one new thing each day and thank God for it.

REVELATION 10:1-11 • THE BITTERSWEET SCROLL

FOCUS
Bitterness.

PREPARATION
Go to a candy shop and purchase candies with a sweet exterior and sour interior. Buy nine candies for each person. You also could contrast sweet with sour using fruit (a sweet apple and a sour lemon). Bring a Bible.

INSIGHT
John sees a powerful, mighty angel coming down from heaven. The angel is robed in a cloud with a rainbow over his head. He is holding a tiny scroll. The angel places one foot on the sea and the other on land.

John is about to write, when a voice tells him to seal up what the seven thunders spoke and not write it down. The angel says there will be no more delay.

John is ordered to eat the small scroll. It's sweet in his mouth (because it's from God) but bitter in his stomach (because of the curse of judgment). He is told that he must now prophesy.

In this study, group members will taste sweet-and-sour candy and compare it to the passage.

BIBLE STUDY

1. As students enter, give them each a piece of candy. Encourage students to savor the candy.

2. Ask young people to share the good memories the sweet taste brings back to them. For example: "When I was 5 years old, my brothers and I would get a special treat every Saturday. My parents gave us some change and allowed us to buy whatever candy we wanted. I always bought taffy."

3. Invite students to experience the sweetness turning sour. Ask: "Have you ever anticipated something pleasant only to find it a bitter experience? Explain." For example, anticipating a fun party but having a rotten time.

4. Give group members another piece of candy and read the passage. Invite them to share one aspect of presenting the gospel that causes someone "emotional indigestion." For example, being embarrassed by those who publicly announce "messages" from God. "God told me you should repent or you'll be damned tonight."

5. Let students describe times they tried to share Christ with someone who didn't want the good news. Ask, "What negative reactions hurt the most?"

6. Say: "John was told to prophesy. He has the sweet Word of God but the sour message of judgment. We need to focus on the sweetness of Christ's saving grace through the bitterness of everyday trials and disappointments. We need to share the sweet Word of God no matter what bitter reactions we receive."

ACTION

Give each person seven candies. Ask group members each to give one of these candies to one person each day. If they feel comfortable they can say, "Have this candy and know that God loves you." Share the experiences at the next study.

REVELATION 11:1-19 • TWO WITNESSES

FOCUS

Christ's eternal reign.

INSIGHT

John is given a measuring rod and told to measure God's temple. The outer court can't be measured; it'll be destroyed by the world.

PREPARATION

Gather various colors of construction paper and colored chalk. You'll also need Bibles, tape, a record player and an album of "The Messiah" by G.F. Handel.

Two witnesses prophesy for 3½ years of Roman rule.

John uses Old Testament imagery in this passage. The two witnesses are unnamed, but resemble Moses and Elijah as the symbols of law and prophecy. Whoever harms them are severely punished. These witnesses have the power to control the sky and rain.

When they finish their testimony, the beast comes up from the bottomless pit and kills them. Their bodies lie in the street; people refuse to bury them. Some people are happy over the death of law and prophecy. However, after 3½ days God breathes life into the witnesses and takes them to heaven. (This is a word of hope to persecuted Christians.)

There is an earthquake and many are killed. The second woe has taken place. The third would come. The seventh angel blows a trumpet and loud voices say: "The kingdom of our Lord and of his Christ, and he will reign for ever and ever" (Revelation 11:15b).

In this study, group members will design chalk drawings of the passage.

BIBLE STUDY

1. Play "The Messiah" as students enter. Invite them to sit and listen to the music. Turn down the volume slightly. Read Revelation 11:1-19. Tell students that this passage has inspired many people through the ages. "The Messiah" is just one example.

2. Distribute various colors of construction paper and chalk. Ask students to draw their feelings—their inspirations—about this passage. For example, a person could draw bright-colored designs on a black piece of construction paper. The black could symbolize destruction, the colors Jesus' triumph.

3. Share the drawings and the feelings.

4. Play "Hallelujah" from the album. Close by reading together verse 15b.

5. Post the chalk drawings under a sign that says "He Will Reign for Ever and Ever."

ACTION

Ask students to think about this question: "If Christ reigns forever, what does that mean for my life?" Ask them to write down their thoughts and bring them to the next session. Thoughts could be: "It means that Christ is Lord of everything. He's in control. I shouldn't worry."

REVELATION 12:1-17 • *THE MOTHER OF US ALL*

FOCUS
The church.

PREPARATION
Gather paper, pencils, feathers, Bibles, blank cassette tapes, tape players and microphones.

INSIGHT
John describes a woman who appears in heaven and gives birth to a child. She cries out in pain as she is about to deliver a baby. The woman first represents Israel (verse 5), then the church persecuted by Satan (verse 13).

A great red dragon appears. He has seven heads, 10 horns and seven crowns. His tail sweeps a third of the stars and flings them to Earth. He wants to devour the child as he comes into the world. God snatches up the baby and takes him to heaven. A place in the desert has been prepared for the woman. She stays there 3½ years.

Michael—champion of Israel—and his angels fight the dragon. The beast is thrown out of heaven. When the dragon sees that he has been cast aside, he pursues the woman. She is given eagle's wings so she can go into the desert and be taken care of.

The dragon spews water out of his mouth to sweep away the woman. But the Earth helps the woman by opening its mouth and swallowing the water.

In this study, group members will record stories of the passage and discuss the church.

BIBLE STUDY

1. Divide into several small groups; give each group a Bible, cassette tape, tape player, microphone, paper and pencils. Tell young people their first task is to create and record a greeting for the class. For example: "Welcome. Welcome to our group. Listen well and hear the scoop. Jesus loves us, yes he does. He thinks we're special just because." Play the recorded greetings.

2. Have each small group read Revelation 12:1-17. Say that the woman first represents Israel (from whom Christ was born), then she represents the church. Ask groups each to write a story about the passage—a story the members could tell a little brother or sister. Then have the groups record the stories. For example: "Once upon a time a woman gave birth to a Son. His name was Jesus. Satan wanted him out of the way. God protected his Son. The church continued on Earth. Satan wants to persecute and hurt believers. God will punish Satan and bless God's children forever."

3. Play the recorded stories. Ask:
   • According to this passage, how does Satan feel about the church?

●How does evil hinder (or get in the way of) ministry?

●What is the church's goal? (For example, to tell others about Christ.)

●How should the church deal with evil? (For example, speak out against child abuse, sexual abuse and pornography.)

4. Reread verses 6 and 14 and say that the church is nourished and taken care of by God. God provides unexpected help in times of trouble.

5. Give everybody a feather to represent the eagle's wings in verse 14. Ask each person to complete this sentence: "I know God cares for me because . . ."

ACTION

Spread God's Word and affirm your church. Have young people work on a musical. Advertise it and invite people from the community. Step up the pace of witnessing with a lively, enjoyable performance. Show people that church can be fun and meaningful.

REVELATION 13:1-18 • IN QUEST OF THE BEASTS

FOCUS
Bad influences.

PREPARATION
Bring a Bible, balloons, tape, construction paper, streamers, scissors and markers.

INSIGHT
John describes a beast rising out of the sea. This one has 10 horns and seven heads. The horns have crowns and each head bears a blasphemous name. The beast is comprised of leopard, bear and lion attributes. The dragon passes on its power to this evil force. The beast represents the Roman empire and its claim on a divine line of rulers. The Roman empire is inspired by the dragon to persecute believers.

The beast speaks blasphemous words. He has authority to make war against believers. All the world seems to be following Rome (the beast) and only those whose names are written in the book of life can be saved. All the saints must be patient and faithful.

John sees another beast coming out of the Earth. It has two horns like a lamb but speaks like a dragon. He is called the false prophet. He provides great signs and wonders to trick the people into making an idol of the beast (worshiping the emperor).

The beast marks followers on the forehead or right hand. Nobody can buy or sell anything unless he or she has the mark. The chapter closes with the introduction of the beast's number 666. There is much scholarly debate over the number's meaning. Hebrew and Greek names have numerical equivalence. It would be dangerous for the author to name the beast, so he uses the numerical equivalent. Neron Caesar (or Nero Caesar) satisfies the numerical code.

In this study, group members will make balloon symbols and discuss bad influences.

BIBLE STUDY

1. Give each person a balloon and have him or her blow it up and tie it. On "Go," each person asks three others their name and favorite hobby. After young people have done this, they pop their balloons. First person to pop his or her balloon wins. Share the facts the group members learned.

2. Read Revelation 13:1-18. Supply balloons, tape, construction paper, streamers, scissors and markers. Ask participants to create two "balloon beasts" to symbolize the beasts in the passage.

3. Say: "Many scholars interpret Revelation differently. One interpretation is that the beast from the sea was Rome, who persecuted Christians. The beast from Earth was a prophet who encourages emperor-worship. Some people say the beast is Russia. We all face 'beasts' in our lives. We face troubling times and pressure to do bad things."

4. Let group members describe their balloon beasts. Then have them tell how the beasts are working today. Ask:

● Who are the beasts—or bad influences—in our time? What shape do they take? (For example, cult leaders or false teachers who sway people away from Christianity.)

● What bad influences do you face in school? (For example, peer pressure.)

● How do you deal with this pressure at school?

● Where do we receive our strength to remain focused on Christ?

5. Explain that the Christian writer C.S. Lewis said as soon as we think we have identified Satan, we better be careful. The most important skill of evil is the ability to mislead us. Ask, "How can we clearly view God and not be misled by bad influences?" (For example, read scripture, attend church, listen to parents and develop good friendships.)

6. Say: "We will face bad, evil influences at every point in life. But God will sustain us during these times." Have everyone pop their balloon beasts.

ACTION

Encourage group members to think of a good influence in their lives such as a good friend, family member or teacher. Have them take a step toward developing this relationship. They can set up a weekly time to talk or send regular notes of appreciation.

REVELATION 14:1-20 • REST FROM LABORS

FOCUS
Death.

PREPARATION
Gather candles, matches, paper, pencils, Bibles and somber music.

INSIGHT
John sees those worshiping the Lamb. The Lamb's followers (144,000 of the faithful) meet for the final time on Mount Zion. John hears heavenly voices singing. These worshipers are celibates; they follow the Lamb everywhere. An angel says to fear and glorify God, because the hour of judgment has come. A second angel announces Babylon's fall. The third angel announces doom for those who follow the beast and bear its mark.

John calls for patient endurance against Rome's great power and temptation. Next the writer sees one like a son of man with a crown of gold and sharp sickle. The Lamb will harvest the wicked upon the Earth with the sickle.

In this study, group members will write cinquain poetry about their feelings about death.

BIBLE STUDY

1. Darken the room, light a few candles and play the somber music. As students enter, give them each a piece of paper and pencil.

2. Say: "Although we're Christians, we fear death and its unknown quality. Think of these scary feelings—the negative, dark, scary feelings of death. Jot them down. They can be words or phrases."

3. Allow a few minutes of silence. Announce that each individual is going to write a cinquain poem about feelings of death. This form of poetry originated in France, and the name refers to the French word for the number five. Explain that there are five lines in the poem. The first line is one noun, which is also the title. The second line is two adjectives or a phrase to describe the noun. The third line is three action words or a phrase about the title. The fourth line is four words to describe a feeling or feelings about the title. The fifth line renames the title in one word. For example:

Death
Final breath
Last of life
Lonely, unknown, frightening, despair
Darkness

Encourage students to use the feelings they wrote on their papers.

4. Invite individuals to share their poems with the large group. Ask:
● What are some of these negative feelings of death?

● Why do we feel like this?

● What is the most common, fearful feeling of death?

5. Turn on the lights. Read Revelation 14:1-20. Repeat verse 13b: "Blessed are the dead who die in the Lord from now on." Ask another person to read the comforting words of Psalm 23. Point out that God is with us through life and death. Ask another person to read John 3:16. Point out that God gave us a great gift—forgiveness of sins through Christ, the Son. Ask:

● What feelings come from these verses? (For example, hope and comfort.)

● How should Christians view death?

6. Stop for a few minutes and have the young people think of the happy, hopeful feelings of death. Have them jot down their thoughts. Encourage everyone to write a second cinquain poem, this time with the happy, light feelings of death. For example:

Death

Peaceful rest

Onward to heaven

Hopeful, joyous, warm, content

Life

7. Share the poems with the large group. Notice the difference between the two sets of poems. Ask, "Why does hope replace fear?"

8. Close by asking God to comfort those who mourn so they may know the peace that is in store for them.

ACTION

Encourage young people to read and reflect on death and God's assurance of eternal life. Have them read Isaiah 25:8; Hosea 13:14; John 3:16, 18, 36; 10:27-30; 1 Corinthians 15:54-56; 2 Timothy 1:7-10; 1 Peter 5:7. Invite students to answer these questions:

● What does the Bible say about death?

● Do we need to fear death and the end times? Why or why not?

● What hope does Jesus offer?

REVELATION 15:1—16:21 • GOD'S WRATH

FOCUS

Punishment.

INSIGHT

John sees seven angels with seven plagues. Those victorious over the beast are standing beside a sea of glass and fire. They sing the

PREPARATION

Gather bowls, spoons, cotton balls, blindfolds, Bibles, paper, pencils and a loaf of bread. Make three stations with the following supplies in each station: one blindfold, one bowl filled with cotton balls, one empty bowl and one spoon.

song of Moses. Out of the temple come the seven angels with seven plagues. They are dressed in clean, shining linen and wear golden sashes.

One of the four creatures gives the angels seven golden bowls filled with God's wrath. The temple is filled with smoke from God's glory. No one can enter the temple until the seven plagues are over.

The first bowl causes ugly and painful sores (compare to Exodus 9:8-12). The second bowl turns the sea to blood and everything in the sea dies. The third bowl turns rivers and springs to blood. The accompanying song says this is a response to Christians' blood spilled by the beast's followers. The fourth bowl leads to the scorching of human sinners by fire. The fifth bowl plunges the beast's kingdom into darkness. The sixth bowl dries up the Euphrates. The seventh bowl causes flashes of lightning, rumblings, peals of thunder and a severe earthquake.

In this study, group members will discuss the seven bowls of wrath—God's punishment for evil.

BIBLE STUDY

1. Divide students into three groups and ask them to go to one of the three stations. Say: "Blindfold one person. This person's task is to spoon the cotton balls from one bowl to the other. Allow one minute. Then take off the blindfold and count the number of cotton balls he or she moved. Try it again with another person. See who can move the most cotton balls."

2. After several minutes, gather the young people in a circle. Place seven empty bowls in the center.

3. Read Revelation 15:1—16:21 and say: "The people who first read this book were seeking to be faithful to Christ when Christianity was illegal. People were forced to worship the Roman emperor. They faced extreme economic pressure. People had to be sealed with the emperor's seal or they couldn't buy or sell. It was a time of great suffering. John gave them hope. He said good would eventually win over evil and evil ones would be punished."

4. Divide into seven small groups. Give each group a bowl, Bible, piece of paper and pencil. Assign each group one of these sections of the passage: 16:2; 16:3; 16:4-7; 16:8-9; 16:10-11; 16:12-16; 16:17-21. Have the small groups describe in their own words the punishment listed in their passage.

5. Announce the first group by saying, "The first bowl of wrath . . ." Let the first group share its insight and place its bowl in the center of the circle. Then say, "The second bowl of wrath . . ." Let the second group share its insight. Continue this process until all seven groups have shared.

6. Pass the loaf of bread and ask students how Christ—the bread of life—supports them when they suffer.

7. Ask each person to take a piece of bread and eat it as you pray: "Thank you for hope during suffering. Thank you for support during trying times. Thank you for forgiveness. Thank you for eternal life. Amen."

ACTION

Ask young people to compare this passage to the plagues in Egypt during Moses' time. Have them read Exodus 7—12 and bring their insights to the next session.

REVELATION 17:1—18:24 • ROME'S FALL

FOCUS
Sin.

PREPARATION
Ask someone to role play a doctor. He or she will simulate an autopsy. The doctor will need plastic gloves, a surgeon's mask and gown, a bowl of

INSIGHT
John is taken to see the punishment of the great prostitute. This image reflects the church's view of Rome. This city was the source of persecution for the new faith. Rome is drunk on martyrs' blood. She is riding a red beast with seven heads. Each head is one of seven kings. The woman is sitting on seven hills. (Rome was thought to have been built on seven hills.) The beast (Emperor Nero) and his kings will conduct war against the Lamb, yet

water and a towel. Place the following items on a long table: a purple scarf, some jewelry, an empty wine bottle, some cinnamon or spice, a rock, and a sign that says "Mystery, Babylon the great, the mother of prostitutes and of the abominations of the Earth." Cover the items with a white sheet. You also will need a Bible.

the Lamb will overwhelm them. The harlot will be destroyed.

John sees an angel with great authority coming down from heaven. He shouts about the evil character of doomed Babylon (which is Rome). Another voice sings about the martyred saints. People who follow the beast weep and mourn. The merchants of greed mourn because their material lust has come to nothing. A powerful angel picks up a boulder and throws it into the sea as a forecast of Rome's future.

In this study, group members will view an "autopsy" of the fallen city.

BIBLE STUDY

1. Gather students around the operating table. Read Revelation 17:1—18:24. While you are reading have the "doctor" prepare for the autopsy. Have the doctor wash his or her hands and put on plastic gloves, a mask and a gown.

2. Let the doctor approach the table and perform an autopsy on the patient. Say: "Our attending physician will perform an autopsy on the patient 'Rome.' We'll see just what factors caused her death."

3. The doctor takes out a purple scarf and jewelry. Reread 17:3-4. Pass around the items and encourage students to share what the items symbolize today. (For example, greed or desire for possessions.)

4. The doctor removes the sign. Pass it around and ask students to draw some parallels between the sin of ancient Rome and our own culture. For example, "We take our eyes off God and worship worldly possessions."

5. Repeat the process by pulling out these items and reading these verses:
- An empty wine bottle—18:3.
- Cinnamon or spice—18:11-17a.
- A rock—18:21-24.

6. Say: "So ends our autopsy of Rome, the fallen city. The verdict is 'death by sin.' "

7. Have each person choose one item and think of how it symbolizes a sin of today's culture. For example, a piece of jewelry could symbolize desire for more possessions. Begin a prayer with these words: "God, forgive us for these sins . . ." Let group members each say the sin symbolized by their item. On "Amen," cover the items again with the sheet.

ACTION

Say, "The sins that tempted Rome still tempt us today." Encourage group members to be aware of this thought and make a conscious effort to act on it. A young person might feel tempted to buy a new outfit even though she doesn't need it. She could give the money to church. Share the efforts at the next session.

REVELATION 19:1-21 • HYMNS OF PRAISE

FOCUS
Praise.

PREPARATION
Gather hymnals, songbooks, kazoos, paper, pencils and Bibles.

INSIGHT

This chapter contains hymns of praise to God. John reports a great multitude shouting joyous songs. The first song summarizes the Lamb's victory over the wicked woman. The 24 elders and the four living creatures join in worshiping God—praising the Lamb's marriage to the church.

An angel tells John that those invited to this marriage supper are blessed. John falls down to worship the angel. The angel says to worship only God.

Heaven is standing open and John sees a white horse. The rider (Christ) is called Faithful and True. He judges and makes war. He is an awesome figure with blazing eyes, many crowns and a mysterious name. His robe is dipped in blood and his name is the Word of God. His armies are dressed in white linen and are riding on white horses. Out of his mouth comes a sharp sword that destroys the nations. He squeezes the wine of God's wrath on the enemies. On his robe and on his thigh is inscribed "King of kings and Lord of lords."

In this study, group members will plan a "Hymn-Sing."

BIBLE STUDY

1. Give each student a kazoo when he or she comes into the room. Practice playing the instruments to tunes such as "Psalm 100," "Onward Christian Soldiers" or "When the Saints Go Marching In" from *Songs* (Songs and Creations).

2. Let each person read a verse of the passage. After each verse is read, have young people blow their kazoos. Say: "Revelation 19 is full of praises to God. Hymns and songs throughout the ages offer praise to our Creator."

3. Divide in small groups. Give each group a hymnal, songbook, piece of paper and pencil. Tell group members their goal is to plan a Hymn-Sing—an hour of singing favorite hymns—for the congregation.

4. Ask each small group to choose two favorite hymns. Have students write a brief introduction to each hymn. For example: " 'When the Saints Go Marching In' is a traditional spiritual. It talks about the saints marching into heaven. The people who sing want to join in with the band of marching saints."

5. Gather as a large group. Introduce the favorite hymns. Decide an order to sing them in during the Hymn-Sing. Choose a time, date and place for the songfest.

6. Close by singing a few favorite hymns.

ACTION

Advertise the Hymn-Sing in your church and community. Arrange to have someone play the organ. You could jazz up the singing with guitars, drums and kazoos. Celebrate! Praise God! And make a joyful noise!

REVELATION 20:1-15 • THE BOOK OF LIFE

FOCUS
Eternal life.

PREPARATION
Gather a Bible, large sheets of construction paper, markers, tape, posterboard, scissors and clear Con-Tact paper. Ask students each to bring a children's book from home. If they don't have one at home, they can purchase one relatively inexpensively. Tell students the books will be donated to a children's home.

INSIGHT
John sees an angel come down from heaven with a key to the bottomless pit and a great chain in his hand. He binds the dragon and chains him for 1,000 years. He throws the monster into the pit and seals it over him. At the end of 1,000 years, the dragon is set free for a short time.

John sees the souls of those who had been beheaded for their faith—those who had not worshiped the beast or its image. They're alive again and they rule with Christ for 1,000 years. This is the first resurrection.

When 1,000 years have ended, Satan is released and continues his deceptive work. God uses fire to destroy him. The devil is thrown into the lake of fire.

John sees the white throne of God. He sees the dead standing before the throne and the books opened. The dead are judged by what has been recorded. If anyone's name isn't written in the book of life, he or she will be thrown into the lake of fire with death and Hades.

In this study, group members will read books, make book covers and bookmarks and discuss eternal life.

BIBLE STUDY

1. Gather in a circle and listen to a few of the children's stories. Ask:

●How many of you remember hearing these stories when you were children?

●What values do the stories teach children?

●How is evil presented?

●How is good presented?

2. Read Revelation 20:1-15. Say, "The book of life includes the names of people who are saved." Ask:

●How does God decide whose names to include in the book?

●How does God define evil? (For example, not doing God's will.)

●How does God define good? (For example, hearing God's Word and obeying the command to love others.)

3. Distribute construction paper, markers, scissors, tape, posterboard and Con-Tact paper. Tell group members to do one of two things:

●Design a book cover from the construction paper. Use a marker to write a message from the passage such as "Christ has written my name in his book. I'll inherit eternal life."

●Design a bookmark from posterboard. Decorate it with a message and cover it with Con-Tact paper.

4. Share the creations.

ACTION

Encourage students to cover their Bibles or devotional books with the book covers. Or encourage them to use their bookmarks while they read. Tell them to remember that we have eternal life. Donate the children's books to a children's hospital or children's home.

REVELATION 21:1-27 • *WIPE AWAY EVERY TEAR*

FOCUS
Sadness and joy.

INSIGHT
John sees a fresh, joyous, exciting and new heaven and earth. The first heaven and earth have passed away. The new Jerusalem has

PREPARATION

Gather a Bible, a trash bag, newspapers, liquid soap, water, food coloring and empty thread spools.

come from heaven. She comes as Christ's bride. A loud voice assures all that every tear will be wiped from believers' eyes. Death will come no more. All pain and mourning will be gone.

God promises to make all things new. The Lord proclaims: "It is done. I am the Alpha and the Omega, the Beginning and the End." The faithful will be with him forever while the faithless will be cast into the burning lake.

One of the angels (who brought the bowls of God's wrath) offers to show John the Lamb's bride. John is taken to a place where he can see the Holy City. The view is breathtaking; the Holy City sparkles like jewels. It has 12 foundations. On them are written the names of the apostles. The angel describes the city's measurements. It's built from 12 precious gems and metals. The new Jerusalem doesn't need a temple because God and the Lamb are its temple. It doesn't need the sun or moon because God gives it light and the Lamb is its lamp.

In this study, group members will crumple newspapers and replace sad experiences with happy hopes.

BIBLE STUDY

1. Give everybody several sheets of newspaper. Tell group members to listen to the following situations and crumple a piece of newspaper for each one they've experienced:
- If you've ever been lonely . . .
- If you've ever been angry . . .
- If you've ever been hurt . . .
- If you've ever been gossiped about . . .
- If you've ever been rejected by friends . . .

2. Give someone a trash bag and ask him or her to collect the crumpled wads of sad experiences. Have the person throw away the "sadness."

3. Read Revelation 21:1-27. Say: "Jesus promises to wipe away all our tears and sadness. Every sad experience we've had will not compare to the happiness and joy we're promised for eternity."

4. Let students make bubble soap by combining a half cup of liquid soap with a cup of water and a dash of food coloring. Distribute empty thread spools. Dip one end of the spool into the soapy liquid. Put your lips to the other end, then blow bubbles! Celebrate the joy to come.

ACTION

Invite group members to spread joy this week. Have them make the bubble mixture and give it to a younger neighbor or a little brother or sister. Have them blow bubbles, laugh and play together.

REVELATION 22:1-21 • *BACK IN THE GARDEN*

FOCUS
God's presence throughout life.

PREPARATION
Gather Popsicles, markers, yarn, prizes and a Bible.

INSIGHT
John sees the river of life. It sparkles, and it flows from the throne of God and the Lamb. On each side of the river stands the tree of life. The heavenly city takes on the likeness of the original Garden of Eden. No longer will there be any curse. Believers will see God's face. God's name will be on their foreheads. God is the source of light.

John is told that the words are true and that God is coming soon. John falls down and worships the angel. The angel tells him to get up and worship only God. The angel says the time is near. Christ says: "Behold, I am coming soon! My reward is with me, and I will give to everyone according to what he has done. I am the Alpha and the Omega, the First and the Last, the Beginning and the End" (Revelation 22:12-13). Revelation ends with the words: "Amen. Come, Lord Jesus. The grace of the Lord Jesus be with God's people. Amen."

In this study, group members will run relays and experience being first and last.

BIBLE STUDY

1. Run relays: Bounce a ball up to a line and back. Hop on one foot up to a line and back. Run backward up to a line and back. Emphasize the "first" and the "last" by awarding prizes to the first team done and the last team done.

2. Give everyone a Popsicle. Read Revelation 22:1-21 while students enjoy the snack. Emphasize that Jesus says he's the First and the Last. He was in the beginning and he'll be with us forever.

3. Award a prize to the first one done eating a Popsicle and to the last one done.

4. Say, "This passage assures us that God is with us throughout history, throughout our lives and throughout eternity." Ask:
- How do you feel knowing God is present and near you?
- How do you feel knowing God was there when you were born?
- How do you feel knowing God will be there when you die?

5. Wash off the Popsicle sticks and give each person a marker and piece of yarn. Have each person tie his or her two sticks into the shape of a cross. Encourage students to write a comforting message on the cross such as "I am with you always."

6. Share the messages. Close with a prayer of thanksgiving for God's presence throughout life.

ACTION

Prepare fliers that say "God is with you forever. See? God loves you." One Sunday have young people clean the worshipers' car windows and place the fliers under their windshield-wiper blades.

TOPICAL INDEX